Looking Back on the
Vietnam War

War Culture

Edited by Daniel Leonard Bernardi

Books in this new series address the myriad ways in which warfare informs diverse cultural practices, as well as the way cultural practices—from cinema to social media—inform the practice of warfare. They illuminate the insights and limitations of critical theories that describe, explain, and politicize the phenomena of war culture. Traversing both national and intellectual borders, authors from a wide range of fields and disciplines collectively examine the articulation of war, its everyday practices, and its impact on individuals and societies throughout modern history.

Looking Back on the Vietnam War

Twenty-first-Century Perspectives

EDITED BY

BRENDA M. BOYLE

JEEHYUN LIM

RUTGERS UNIVERSITY PRESS

NEW BRUNSWICK, NEW JERSEY, AND LONDON

LIBRARY OF CONGRESS CATALOGING-IN-PUBLICATION DATA

Names: Boyle, Brenda M., editor. 1957– | Lim, Jeehyun, 1976– editor.
 Title: Looking back on the Vietnam War : twenty-first century perspectives /
edited by Brenda M. Boyle and Jeehyun Lim. Other titles: War culture.
 Description: New Brunswick, New Jersey : Rutgers University Press, 2016. | 2016 |
Series: War culture | Includes bibliographical references and index.
 Identifiers: LCCN 2015041070| ISBN 9780813579948 (hardcover : alk. paper) |
ISBN 9780813579931 (pbk. : alk. paper)
 Subjects: LCSH: Vietnam War, 1961–1975 | Vietnam War, 1961–1975—Peace.
 Classification: LCC DS557.7 .L66   2016 | DDC 959.704/3—dc23

LC record available at http://lccn.loc.gov/2015041070

A British Cataloging-in-Publication record for this book is available
from the British Library.

Visit our website: http://rutgerspress.rutgers.edu

Manufactured in the United States of America

For those who continue to feel the effects of the Vietnam War

CONTENTS

CHRONOLOGY

1897	After decades of colonizing and warring, France makes itself the government of the Indochina Union.
1919	Nguyen Ai Quoc (aka Ho Chi Minh) petitions the World War I Versailles Peace Conference for Vietnamese independence from France.
1930	Still seeking independence from France, Ho Chi Minh founds the Indochinese Communist Party.
1940	Japan occupies Viet Nam, retaining the French Vichy administration.
1945	Japan expels French officials from Viet Nam and recognizes Emperor Bao Dai as the head of Viet Nam's government. Ho Chi Minh declares the independence of the "Democratic Republic of Viet Nam."
1946	The First Indochina War begins when France tries to reassert its control of Viet Nam. The Viet Minh, a nationalist organization, opposes France's efforts to recolonize.
1948	The United States begins indirectly supporting the French financially in their war with the Viet Minh.
1950	The Soviet Union and the People's Republic of China recognize the (northern) Democratic Republic of Vietnam as the legitimate state of Viet Nam; the United States and Great Britain recognize as legitimate the (southern) State of Vietnam. France declares Cambodia, Laos, and Viet Nam to be autonomous states but still within the French Indochina Union. Laotian prince Souphanouvong breaks with the royal family to form the Pathet Lao, a left-leaning nationalist group sympathetic to (northern) Viet Nam's war for independence from France. The United States directly provides economic and military aid to France in its war with the Viet Minh. U.S. military personnel: about 60.
1953	U.S. financial aid to the French war effort totals 80 percent of French war costs.

1954–1955 U.S. president Dwight D. Eisenhower formulates the "domino theory"; France surrenders to the Viet Minh at Dien Bien Phu, ending the First Indochina War. The Geneva Peace Agreement temporarily partitions Viet Nam into north and south, guarantees elections in 1956, and facilitates moving hundreds of thousands of (mostly Catholic) refugees from north to south. Laos acquires independence from France; Cambodia's Prince Norodom Sihanouk declares Cambodian neutrality in international relations. The Second Indochina War begins with this partitioning.

1958–1961 Laos experiences conflict between a CIA-sponsored group and the country's popular prime minister; consequently, the Pathet Lao and North Vietnamese gain control of the Plain of Jars.

1960 The National Liberation Front (NLF) is formed in southern Viet Nam by the Communist Party of northern Viet Nam. The NLF's military arm is referred to derogatorily as "Viet Cong."
U.S. military personnel: about 900.

1961 U.S. president John F. Kennedy refuses to send U.S. combat units to Viet Nam but continues to send advisers to counsel the new South Vietnamese military. The United States begins to spray the defoliant Agent Orange in Viet Nam and stops in 1972.
U.S. military personnel: about 3,200.

1962 U.S. Military Assistance Command (MACV) is established in South Vietnam. Australian military advisers join the American ones already there. Laos is recognized as neutral by the United States and the Soviet Union, which drives CIA operations underground.
U.S. military personnel: 11,300.

1963 In June, protesting South Vietnam's president Ngo Dinh Diem's oppression of Buddhists, Buddhist monk Thich Quang Duc immolates himself on a Saigon street. In early November, the United States supports a coup against Diem that ends in the deaths of Diem and his brother, Ngo Dinh Nhu. Three weeks after the coup and deaths, U.S. president John F. Kennedy is assassinated and Vice President Lyndon Baines Johnson becomes president.
U.S. military personnel: 16,300.

1964 North Vietnamese allegedly attack U.S. Navy destroyers in the Gulf of Tonkin. With the Gulf of Tonkin Resolution the U.S. Congress authorizes President Johnson to use armed force in Viet Nam. The United States also covertly begins bombing Cambodia and the CIA begins building a secret army of ethnic Hmong people to fight the Pathet Lao in Laos.

U.S. military personnel: 23,300.

1965   In March Johnson authorizes Operation Rolling Thunder, the bombing of North Vietnam that persists for three and a half years. Johnson also authorizes secret bombing in Laos and, for the first time, the use of entire U.S. combat units—as opposed to advisers—in South Vietnam. Military forces from South Korea and Australia join their U.S. ally in Viet Nam. Antiwar activities begin at the University of Michigan and at a Washington, D.C., protest organized by Students for a Democratic Society (SDS). In November, the first meeting of U.S. and North Vietnamese military forces occurs in the Battle of Ia Drang.

U.S. military personnel: 184,300.

1966   Buddhists lead antigovernment demonstrations in cities all over South Vietnam.

U.S. military personnel: 385,300.

1967   In early April, Martin Luther King Jr. speaks out against the war in "A Time to Break Silence." Weeks later U.S.-wide antiwar demonstrations are held, including a rally of 300,000 in New York City.

U.S. military personnel: 485,600.

1968   In January and February, the Tet Offensive occurs. Afterward, renowned journalist Walter Cronkite opines that the United States should negotiate an end to the war. The massacre at My Lai occurs in March but is kept from the U.S. public until November 1969. The CIA's covert war in Laos is brought to light in closed-door hearings of the U.S. Senate Foreign Relations Committee. In April, Martin Luther King Jr. is assassinated, and in November, Robert F. Kennedy is assassinated. Just before the elections that make Richard M. Nixon president, Johnson ends Operation Rolling Thunder, three and a half years after it began.

U.S. military personnel: 536,100.

1969   Secret U.S. bombing of Cambodia continues and "Vietnamization" of the war in Viet Nam begins. Ho Chi Minh dies, massive antiwar demonstrations occur across the United States, the My Lai massacre is publicly revealed, and the U.S. Selective Service begins a draft lottery.

U.S. military personnel: 475,200.

1970   U.S. military actions in Cambodia, including the ouster of Prince Sihanouk by pro-American Lon Nol and the invasion of Cambodia by U.S and South Vietnamese forces, spur widespread protests in the United States. Protesting students at Kent State and Jackson State are killed by National Guardsmen and police.

U.S. military personnel: 334,600.

1971   Lt. William Calley is found guilty of murder in the My Lai massacre. Vietnam Veterans Against the War (VVAW) stage the Winter Soldier Investigations in Detroit and, in "Dewey Canyon III," throw their medals on the steps of the U.S. Capitol building. Daniel Ellsberg leaks the Pentagon Papers to the *New York Times*.

U.S. military personnel: 156,800.

1972   Nixon meets separately with leaders of the Soviet Union and the People's Republic of China for peace talks, but the talks break down and the United States bombs the North Vietnamese cities of Hanoi and Haiphong. Australian military forces are withdrawn from Viet Nam.

U.S. military personnel: 24,200.

1973   Peace talks resume, resulting in the Paris Peace Accords of January 27, 1973. The U.S. draft lottery ends, American prisoners of war are released, U.S. and South Korean military personnel leave Viet Nam by the end of March, and Congress terminates the president's unilateral authority to send U.S. forces into combat. CIA operatives are evacuated from Laos. The Vietnam War is over.

U.S. military personnel: 240.

1974   The South Vietnamese military continues to war against the (northern) People's Army of Viet Nam (PAVN), but without U.S. military aid. In August, U.S. president Nixon resigns as a result of the Watergate scandal and Vice President Gerald Ford becomes president.

1975   In early March, the PAVN begins its spring offensive in the South, and, with the Viet Cong, enter Saigon at the month's end. The remaining Americans and some Vietnamese allies evacuate the city by helicopter. Saigon is renamed Ho Chi Minh City, the country is reunified as the Socialist Republic of Vietnam, and the Second Indochina War ends. The United States severs all connections to Viet Nam. Hmong army leaders in Laos, previously under the guidance of the CIA, request evacuation but are denied. The communist government of the Lao People's Democratic Republic assumes power in Laos, as does the Khmer Rouge in Cambodia. The Socialist Republic of Vietnam begins sending Vietnamese citizens to reeducation camps. Approximately 3 million Vietnamese people died during the war.

1976   Jimmy Carter is elected president of the United States; he extends amnesty to Vietnam War draft resisters.

1977   The Socialist Republic of Vietnam is admitted to the United Nations.

1978   Dire conditions and oppression force many Vietnamese to flee Viet Nam secretly by boat. Their hazardous departures and squalid conditions in refugee camps across Southeast Asia call attention to the plight of the "boat people." The People's Republic of China discontinues aid to Viet Nam because of its discrimination against ethnic Chinese people in Viet Nam. The Socialist Republic of Vietnam and the Union of Soviet Socialist Republics (USSR) form an alliance. Viet Nam invades Cambodia and does not withdraw until 1989.

1979   The United States and the People's Republic of China establish diplomatic relations. China invades Viet Nam, remaining there for a month.

1980   Ronald Reagan is elected president of the United States. During the campaign he coins the term "Vietnam syndrome" and argues that the war was "a noble cause." In response to symptoms displayed by U.S. veterans of the war, post-traumatic stress disorder is added to the *Diagnostic and Statistical Manual of Mental Disorders.*

1982   The Vietnam Veterans Memorial in Washington, D.C., is dedicated.

1984   Vietnam War veterans win a settlement against Dow Chemical for its manufacture of Agent Orange.

1986   Economic reforms, known as the Doi Moi policy, are instituted in the Socialist Republic of Vietnam.

1988   Duong Thu Huong publishes her novel *Paradise of the Blind* in Vietnamese; its English translation is published in 1993.

1989   The Socialist Republic of Vietnam withdraws its military from Cambodia after eleven years. Le Ly Hayslip publishes her memoir, *When Heaven and Earth Changed Places.*

1990   Bao Ninh publishes his novel *The Sorrow of War* in Vietnamese; its English translation is published in 1994. Duong Thu Huong publishes *Novel without a Name* in Vietnamese; its French translation is published in 1994 and its English translation in 1995.

1991   Before launching the Persian Gulf War, President George H. W. Bush pledges "it will not be another Vietnam." At the five-week-long war's conclusion, Bush exalts "By God, we've kicked the Vietnam syndrome once and for all!"

1994   U.S. president Bill Clinton ends the decades-long U.S. embargo against the Socialist Republic of Vietnam.

1995   The United States normalizes diplomatic relations with the Socialist Republic of Vietnam.

1997   Lan Cao publishes *Monkey Bridge*, the first "Vietnamese American" novel.

2001   In an attack by Al-Qaeda operatives on September 11, two passenger planes crash into the World Trade Center towers in New York City, one crashes into the Pentagon, and a fourth crashes into a Pennsylvania field. In retaliation, the United States invades Afghanistan in October; plans to invade Iraq begin in November. Critics worry that war in Iraq will be another Vietnam War.

2003–2015   In March 2003 U.S. and allied forces invade Iraq. In November 2004, a plaque is added to the Vietnam Veteran's Memorial, commemorating Vietnam veterans who die after the war. An education center is authorized for the memorial site, and plans exist for those Americans who died in the Afghanistan and Iraq wars following 9/11/2001 also to be memorialized there. Massive numbers of allied forces remain in Iraq until 2011; U.S. forces leave Afghanistan by 2015. Estimates for costs of the three wars (including Pakistan, which the United States funds) run up to US$4.4 trillion and the deaths of 330,000 people directly from war violence.

NOTE ON THE TEXT

Over the years several different spellings of the country in Southeast Asia that was the site of Cold War conflict following World War II have appeared in western contexts: Vietnam, Viet Nam, Viet-Nam. Sometimes the spelling is indicative of a political position, and sometimes the spelling adheres to a prevalent form; often "Vietnam" is used as shorthand in the United States for the war, not the country. To distinguish between references to the conflict and the country where it occurred, the introduction has adopted two spellings: Vietnam for the war and Viet Nam for the country. Some of the volume's authors do not adopt the same distinction, however. Furthermore, some authors have included Vietnamese language in their essays, to a lesser and greater extent. In both cases, we editors have chosen not to alter their spellings or language choices.

Looking Back on the
Vietnam War

Introduction

Looking Back on the Vietnam War

BRENDA M. BOYLE AND JEEHYUN LIM

The American War in Viet Nam radically impacted the United States, its allies, and the Southeast Asia region during the Cold War, and its effects have continued to be felt in the United States and Southeast Asia for decades following. Even after the U.S. withdrawal from Viet Nam in 1973, the war continued to influence, via the "Vietnam syndrome," U.S. foreign policy and the constitution of U.S. military forces; the nation's conduct of war expanded, and the war had significant bearing on U.S. cultural narratives, memorialization practices, and attitudes toward authority. It likewise continued to impact Southeast Asian countries. Not only were landmines, disabled South Vietnamese veterans, Amerasian children, and Agent Orange left behind, but also millions of Vietnamese people were forced to flee the Socialist Republic of Viet Nam beginning with the fall of Saigon in 1975 and heightening in the 1978–1979 "boat people" crisis.

Although scholars continued to engage with the war and its effects in the United States following the war, with the Soviet Union's 1990 demise and the end of the Cold War, critical attention to the Vietnam War and its outcomes dwindled in the 1990s. In the United States at least, the war seemed to be a settled or an inconsequential matter of the past. That Bill Clinton could be elected president of the United States in 1993 with no U.S. military service on his record, let alone in the Vietnam War, exemplifies this seeming inconsequentiality. However, with the normalizing of relations between the United States and the Socialist Republic of Viet Nam in 1995, the opening of archives in the United States and Southeast Asian and former Soviet Bloc countries, and the U.S. initiation of similarly long-term wars comparable to Vietnam in Iraq and Afghanistan, this scholarship has rebounded. Much of that scholarship is based on discovery of new archival materials, often resulting in reconsiderations of the historical record of the war era.[1] Much of it, too, has been founded in the firsthand war experiences of its chroniclers.

Looking Back on the Vietnam War not only joins the scholarly rebound by tracing specifically social and cultural impacts of the Vietnam War, it also reconsiders what we think we know about the war. It questions who determines when war begins and ends, how war-incurred disability can determine a life, and why local cultures of death and commemoration are influenced both by battlefield clashes and later interpretations of those clashes. Crucially, the collection manifests the centrality of diasporic narratives to understandings of war. Consequently, this volume revisits received ideas, includes voices and circumstances from the war era that previously might have been regarded as insignificant, and reveals and reflects on twenty-first-century outcomes of the Vietnam War. In looking back from the vantage point of the twenty-first century, the collection looks anew at the war and its outcomes, bringing fresh insights to understanding war generally and the Vietnam War specifically.

Like the scholarly ones, cultural representations of the war also fluctuated in number after the mid-1990s, with those by Vietnamese Americans and other Southeast Asian people increasing as mainstream U.S. representations dwindled. By 2015, still in a time of war in the Middle East, the fortieth anniversary of the fall of Saigon generated many remembrances of the war. The documentary *In Country* (2014) may be the cultural product marking the March 30, 1975, fall—the ostensible end of the Vietnam War—that was the most widely discussed in mainstream media.[2] Made by two documentary filmmakers, Mike Attie and Meghan O'Hara, who followed a group of Vietnam War reenactors in Salem, Oregon, over the course of a single cycle of their reenactment, *In Country* suggests the Vietnam War may have joined the list of historical wars in modern reenactment.[3] While the documentary suggests that the Vietnam War maintains an important place in popular culture, after decades of movies, TV shows, films, and fiction on one or another aspect of the war, *In Country* also suggests that the place of the Vietnam War in the popular imagination may be in flux. The reenactors who have gathered to play out scenes of conflict in the imaginary jungle of Southeast Asia are a variegated group of men whose relationships to the Vietnam War as well as what they want from the reenactment vastly differ. A few are veterans of the Vietnam War; a few are current or ex-military men who have toured or are touring in the wars in Iraq and Afghanistan; a few are men who either have enlisted in the armed forces or who want to experience combat without enlisting. Their different identities are reflected in their different needs, and the reenactment at once serves as entertainment, therapy, and fantasy in letting these men vicariously (re)experience the Vietnam War. In fact, the world of the reenactors in the documentary may well be a microcosm of the multiple functions, narratives, and desires of the Vietnam War in contemporary society.

The multiplication and fragmentation of the meaning of the Vietnam War as illustrated in the documentary calls to mind Fredric Jameson's well-known characterization of the Vietnam War as "the first terrible postmodernist war."[4] Referring to the fusion of "a whole range of contemporary collective idiolects" in the language of Michael Herr's *Dispatches*, Jameson suggests the Vietnam War initiated the search for a new language of representation.[5] Of course the multiplicity one finds in *In Country* is quite different from what Jameson saw in Herr's communiqués from the Vietnam War. The sense of urgency and immediacy that leads to "the breakdown of all previous narrative paradigms of the war novel or movie," so palpable in Herr's 1977 book, is absent in the documentary's portrayal of the Vietnam War.[6] To put it slightly differently, Herr's *Dispatches* and the 2014 documentary inhabit different temporalities in the cultural work of mediating the Vietnam War to an American audience. The postmodernist sensibilities of the documentary, then, should be understood primarily in the historical context of today, not that of the war era. When this current context prevails, what stands out in the documentary's attempt to grasp at the meaning of the Vietnam War is the corroding of the majority view that the Vietnam War was "fundamentally wrong and immoral."[7] According to Fred Turner, national surveys on American attitudes toward the Vietnam War from 1975 to the early 1990s "have consistently noted that more than half of all Americans (and often as many as 70 percent)" had misgivings about the morality of the war.[8] If anyone finds the idea of Vietnam War reenactment shocking, this response is due to the moral taboo generated by the enduring public opinion in the couple of decades after the war.

Admittedly, there are still quite a few differences between more popular historical reenactments like the Civil War reenactment and the Vietnam War reenactment in *In Country*. While most Civil War reenactments are now public and often include a tourist industry, the Vietnam War reenactment in the documentary is private.[9] For scholars who study historical reenactment, the question of whether an audience is allowed or not is an important measure of the authenticity the reenactors seek. "To the extent that reenactors seek an authentic experience of 'time-travel' with their devotion to proper period attire, equipment, behavior, and battle conditions," says the historian James Farmer, "every audience is a hindrance."[10] In contrast to Civil War reenactors who "mak[e] a public statement about the honor of the men, and the cause, they are replicating" by having an audience, the Vietnam War reenactors seem focused on the performance of authenticity.[11] Yet, if the Vietnam War reenactment seems to be on the fringe in the world of historical reenactments by virtue of its closed quality, it does suggest a fraying of the moral taboo regarding the war.

For all the reenactors' quest for authenticity, the war in the world of reenactment depicted in the documentary is unmistakably a simulacrum and the
authenticity that is pursued an imagined one. As one reviewer put it,
"*In Country* after all is a documentary not about war, but about war games."[12]

What the rules of the game for reenacting the Vietnam War are, however,
may be worth a close look. For while historical reenactments are far from historiography, they reveal the felt connections between the past and the present.
Examining the prehistory of modern historical reenactments in the eighteenth
century, Simon During suggests that "it is the historicization of everyday life
that stimulates the view that the past requires forms of empathy to be understood."[13] While the reenactors in *In Country* do not give lectures to public audiences at "the traditional, pedagogical arenas of educational institutions" like
Civil War reenactors do, there is a vernacular history lesson embedded in the
game of reenactment.[14] This can best be seen in an early part of the documentary when one of the reenactors, a collector of Vietnam War memorabilia, lectures the reenactors on the lexicon of infantry soldiers in the Vietnam War. This
is the lexicon they will likely adopt for the reenactment, summed up in such
words as "antiestablishment" and "hippy" and the disturbing resurrection of
the racial slur "dink," used by U.S. soldiers to refer to the Vietnamese during the
war. That this slur should resurface in the transformation of war into play desta-
bilizes the "end of history" discourse, the often triumphalist touting of liberal
capitalism's victory with the demise of the Cold War's East–West geopolitics.[15]
The incorporation of the Vietnam War reenactment into what James W. Gibson
calls a masculinist paramilitary culture that sprang into existence after the
Vietnam War period may be a sign of capitalism's capacity to absorb past conflicts into present entertainment industries. Yet the specters of the "dink" also
obstruct a wholesale absorption of the Vietnam War into the culture and industry of entertainment, demanding instead a renewed attention to the vicissi-
tudes of historical knowledge and the past's relationship to life in the present.[16]
"The historicization of the everyday life" that undergirds the Vietnam War
reenactors' forays into the past points to a contemporary culture of militarism
that seemingly corresponds to what scholars variously term the "new American
empire" or "new American militarism."[17]

In Country refrains from overt editorializing on the part of the filmmakers
and instead focuses on communicating the varied perspectives of the reenactors. This technique has prompted at least one reviewer to complain that it
lacks an angle.[18] What story about the Vietnam War reenactment does the
documentary want to tell? The multiple threads in approaching the meaning of
the war, however, may be the point of the documentary as it provokes the viewers to imagine what their own relationship is to this war, easily the most con-
tentious war of the twentieth century. This volume is also a provocation to the

readers to rethink the meaning and significance of the Vietnam War for today, although it is clearer about what story it wants to tell. What are the specters of the "dink" that complicate an easy consumption of the Vietnam War as an event of the past?

The documentary incorporates several examples of what we call the specters of the "dink." The sole Vietnamese reenactor, Vinh Nguyen, who served in the Army of the Republic of Vietnam (ARVN), speaks of his unaccounted-for grief at the loss of his comrades and the Republic of Vietnam. Lucien "Doc" Darensburg, a young African American veteran who spent two tours in Iraq as a medic, speaks of enlisting to pay for college and the brutalities of combat he witnessed. Charles "Tuna" Ford, a white American man, married with three young boys, is troubled by the alienation from his wife caused by his deployment to Iraq and Afghanistan but asks what other job would provide his family with health care and put food on the table. The specters of the "dink" can be seen in elements of the Vietnam War that have inadequately been reckoned with yet continue to influence not only the lives of those directly affected by the war but also the culture of militarism that pervades contemporary society. For instance, the Vietnam syndrome tainted the American image of itself as a rescuer of the Third World and made it difficult for the South Vietnamese who resettled in the United States to narrate their experiences other than through scripts such as the narrative of the grateful refugee. Although the social anxieties caused by the draft during the Vietnam War are a thing of the past as the U.S. military now fills its ranks with volunteer soldiers, still the burden of enlistment and combat is unequally distributed across society in what the economist Christian Marazzi calls the "war economy."[19]

This volume participates in the renewed academic conversations on the legacies of the Vietnam War that have emerged with the opening of previously inaccessible archives and the comparisons drawn between the Vietnam and Iraq wars. Though the volume shares with the documentary *In Country* the idea that the meaning of the Vietnam War today involves multiple perspectives and narratives, it departs from the centrality of the (para)military experience in recollecting or revisiting the Vietnam War. It does this by focusing on how the war affected and continues to affect the lives of ordinary people. These people have created new lives from the war's rubble, sometimes being suppressed by the laws, policies, and dominant stories of their host society and sometimes affecting change in those laws, policies, and stories. While the histories of the Vietnam War have produced numerous studies on military policy, diplomacy, legislative, and executive decision making, less attention has been paid to the war's effects on ordinary people. To borrow from Heonik Kwon's conceptual framing in *The Other Cold War* (2010), this volume reorients the legacies of the Vietnam War from those of the Cold War superpowers interested in keeping the balance of power to those of the people who experienced the Cold War as a balance of terror. As Kwon notes, the "realist paradigm in international relations and history" has centered understandings of the Cold War on the West's experiences and ignored the "hot wars" experience of the postcolonial world.[20] According to Kwon, "an alternative mode of narration, one that incorporates but does not exclusively privilege the state's perspective and agency," is required to examine the wounds to communities that suffered directly from the geopolitics of the Cold War, wounds that gradually are becoming more visible.[21]

Notable for the reorientation proposed here is the recent surge of scholarly interest in the Southeast Asian diaspora.[22] Behind this academic direction is a host of conditions, not a few of which relate to a post–Cold War reordering of the global economy. Since the Socialist Republic of Viet Nam normalized relations with the United States and joined the Association of Southeast Asian Nations in 1995, travel to and trade with the republic for those Vietnamese who left the country since 1975 have become comparably easier. Vietnamese American communities have also grown and become politically active since 1975. As Jonathan H. X. Lee claims, since the 1990s Vietnamese American and Chinese-Vietnamese American communities are in their fourth stage of development, with American-born Vietnamese influencing the makeup of Vietnamese identity in America.[23] As Southeast Asian Americans assume an active role in the narratives of war, refugee, and resettlement experiences, aspects of the Vietnam War previously ignored are being brought to light.

Of the topics emerging in Southeast Asian diaspora studies, the topic of refugees has been productive across a number of fields. In her call for "critical refuge(e) studies," Yến Lê Espiritu offers the concept and term of "militarized refuge(es)" to bring together the fields of war and refugee studies that she says do not converge or cross in U.S. academe and its regimes of knowledge.[24] "This decoupling," she argues, "obscures the formative role that U.S. wars play in structuring the displacements, dispersions, and migrations of refugees to the United States and elsewhere."[25] Espiritu opens an epistemological space in the interstices of disciplinary conventions and norms through the figure of the militarized refuge(e). While most U.S. studies of Southeast Asian refugees have focused on the resettlement and assimilation of the displaced population, Espiritu's conceptualization of the refuge(e) as militarized reverses this scholarship's future-forward trajectory to investigate the impact of past militarism in the present, illuminating the continuum—rather than the break—between war and peace.[26] The literary and cultural critic Mimi Thi Nguyen's sustained deconstructionist study of "the gift of freedom" for refugees similarly examines the conditions and limits of liberalism as the ultimate answer to the violence of war.[27] In a vein similar to both Espiritu and Nguyen, historian

Jana K. Lipman explains how the refugee camps on U.S. territories and in its incorporated territories, such as Guam, were places where complex agencies and perspectives that exceed the Cold War binarism of communism and anti-communism could be seen.[28] The turn to refugees in studies of the Southeast Asian diaspora brings into high relief the fissures in liberalism as the end point of the Cold War. This volume is interested in these fissures—the brief intervals and openings that appear in hegemonic narratives of the Vietnam War—as the point of departure for reexamining received ideas about the Vietnam War and reflecting on the present conditions of remembering what the war has left behind.

A commensurate interest in refugees can be seen outside the U.S. academy as well. In a collection of essays that focuses on Hong Kong's role as both a temporary stopping place and a resettlement locale for Vietnamese refugees, *The Chinese/Vietnamese Diaspora: Revisiting the Boat People* (2011), the Hong Kong–based scholar Yuk Wah Chan argues that despite the sense among some academics that the topic of the "boat people" is a matter of the past, as the once-refugees have either been repatriated to Viet Nam or resettled in First World countries and the camps closed, the full social and cultural impact of the Vietnamese refugee crisis is yet to be assessed.[29] While initially it may seem to be just a bureaucratic attempt at expediency in processing refugee applications, the categorical distinction between "refugees" and "economic migrants" employed by the Hong Kong government in 1988 to limit the number of successful applications actually reveals the challenge of containing the effects of the war.[30] Noting migration through marriage as one of the most pervasive methods of outmigration from Viet Nam today, Chan identifies the "marriage migration" model as the successor to the refugee model of migration for the Vietnamese diaspora.[31] While it is not fully explored by Chan, the connection between the two models of outmigration suggests that the legacies of the American War may also inhere in contemporary biopolitics of the Vietnamese diaspora.

Viewed in light of this recent scholarship on refugees, the temporary military encampment in *In Country* cannot escape comparison to the carceral space of the refugee camps. Since both are current iterations of the Vietnam War's legacies, placing one next to the other disturbs the complacent consumption of the Vietnam War in mass media and demands critical scrutiny of popular culture appropriations of the Vietnam War. If the documentary *In Country* indexes the desire to reengage with the Vietnam War, we think that such desire could be productively channeled through dialogues with new academic knowledge on what has been previously ignored in studies of the Vietnam War, especially the stories and perspectives of the Vietnamese who previously have been called the "enemy."

The legacies of the Vietnam War are international and transnational. While U.S. scholarship has illuminated many aspects of how the war came to be, why it matters, and what its effects are for the United States, what the war meant and means for Viet Nam and for other countries that participated either by sending troops, by hosting Vietnamese refugees, or by both is less known. Recent studies address the unbalanced concentration on the American side of the story. For instance, Heonik Kwon's *Ghosts of War in Vietnam* (2008) or Christina Schwenkel's *The American War in Contemporary Vietnam* (2009) pay overdue attention to the fabric of Vietnamese lives after the American War by illustrating the mourning and memorialization practices that appeared in the Socialist Republic of Viet Nam and developed in tandem with postwar social changes.[32] Accounting for the lasting influences of the American War in a fast-changing society such as contemporary Viet Nam surely is a formidable task. Contemporary Viet Nam is, as the anthropologist Li Zhang puts it, "a country where colonial history, socialist legacies, and global capitalism traverse and give rise to multiple yet unstable postsocialist assemblages that defy any teleological thinking of history and social change framed by the ultimate antagonism between capitalism and socialism."[33] Expanding the knowledge about the Vietnam War's legacies in U.S. academe, however, needs to be accompanied by an expansion of knowledge about how the legacies of the American War are articulated and reconstructed in Viet Nam as the global economy brings the countries closer.

Recent edited volumes in history such as *America, the Vietnam War, and the World: Comparative and International Perspectives* (2003) and *Four Decades On: Vietnam, the United States, and the Legacies of the Second Indochina War* (2013) are welcome reminders that the Vietnam War involved multiple international actors in various capacities.[34] They demonstrate that assessments of the war at this point in time require careful attention to the different political and social contexts in which countries decided to stake a claim in the Vietnam War, either under the banner of the free world or under communism, and that the transnational circuits undergirding the war and marking its afterlives are still being mapped.

While the effects of the Vietnam War on a third country other than the United States and Viet Nam are varied, discussions of South Korean participation in the Vietnam War that have emerged in the last fifteen years or so may be one example of the ongoing international recovery of the meaning and effects of the war.[35] In 1999 a progressive newspaper in South Korea ran a series of articles on the atrocities of the South Korean military in Vietnam, spurring national interest in the topic.[36] Since then dialogues between South Korean and Vietnamese governments and civic organizations have spawned a number of memorials and peace projects that reflect competing ideological viewpoints and group interests. Progressive intellectuals' and civic groups' calls that South Korea acknowledge its role as an aggressor in the Vietnam War and try to atone for the atrocities committed by the South Korean military are met with conservative groups' concerns that criticisms of the military's actions during the Vietnam War are detrimental to national security and U.S.–South Korean relations.[37] The South Korean case does not only demonstrate that memories do not occur in a historical and social vacuum. As the historian Charles K. Armstrong suggests in the title of his article on the meaning of the Vietnam War for South Korea, "America's Korea, Korea's Vietnam," South Korean memories of the war link the two countries of Korea and Viet Nam in the geopolitics and economy of the Cold War.[38] While both countries inhabited the margins in Cold War geopolitics, the role South Korea played as an aggressor in the Vietnam War also exemplifies the fluidity and shifting nature of such geopolitics, something to be kept in mind in examining third participants in the Vietnam War. Guilt, which attests to the growth of a democratic civil society in South Korea, and grief based on the accumulated grievances from Japanese colonialism and U.S. military occupation are the two psychological conditions that contemporary South Korea struggles with in its relationship to the Vietnam War.

Moving away from the U.S.–Viet Nam dyadic focus typical of U.S.-based scholarship on the Vietnam War and toward triangulating with a third participant country such as South Korea concludes that the evolution of Cold War politics regarding the Vietnam War is still a fertile field of inquiry. South Korean struggles with reconciliation and reparations in regard to the Vietnam War can be the basis from which one examines the historical, social, and psychological conditions for reconciliation. Arguably, the idea of reconciliation has been an undercurrent in U.S. scholarship on the Vietnam War for decades. At a time when popular culture engagements with the Vietnam War in the United States replace the interest in reconciliation with an interest in reenactment, it is crucial to ask what is required for reconciliation, not just in foreign policies but also in terms of cultural understandings. Viet Thanh Nguyen, one of the contributors to this volume, elsewhere offers compassion and cosmopolitanism as crucial components for going beyond the violence of the Vietnam War and probes the social conditions for such feelings and sentiments. His observation that the paucity of "options for empathy besides the stories featuring Americans" for American audiences and the subsequent "compulsory empathy," which orients American responses to representations of the Vietnam War along national lines and along the divisive lines of us-versus-them and allies-versus-enemies is a message that should be heeded in the present time of wars.[39]

The question of what the Vietnam War has left us with today invites reflections on contemporary U.S. military interventions in Iraq and Afghanistan.

Much has been said about the parallel between the current wars in Iraq and Afghanistan and the Vietnam War. The Vietnam analogy saturates military and journalistic references to the Iraq War especially. Shortly after the U.S. invasion of Iraq, Gen. Anthony Zinni, using a familiar Vietnam War trope, said about Iraq: "I have seen this movie. It was called Vietnam."[40] The infamous photo from the 2004 Abu Ghraib scandal also indicts the war of the past. The hooded man, standing on a box, arms outstretched, electrical wires connected to various parts of his body, is a pose practiced by torturers around the world and is known by Brazilian torturers as "the Vietnam."[41] For many scholars and critics, Vietnam is a "lesson" not so well learned. In a recent edited volume pointedly titled *Iraq and the Lessons of Vietnam*, historians Lloyd Gardner and Marilyn Young contend that "the United States finds itself bogged down once again in a war against an enemy whose low-grade weapons defy the technological superiority of the world's greatest military power" and "the real lessons of Vietnam have been ignored."[42] At the same time there is also considerable concern about the proliferation of the Vietnam analogy in discussing U.S. policies and tactics in Iraq and Afghanistan. Historian of U.S. foreign policy Trevor B. McCrisken says, "The Vietnam analogy is being used . . . by different political actors in different contexts and with different objectives in mind."[43]

While it is important to be mindful that tenuous analogies can too easily conflate vast differences in the circumstances of the Vietnam War and contemporary wars in the Middle East, it is equally important to heed how contemporary engagements with the memories and legacies of the Vietnam War are influenced and shaped by the culture of militarism promoted by seemingly endless war. *In Country* is one telling example of how the culture of militarism becomes the matrix for new kinds of forgetting and remembering. In the documentary, Darensburg, the young African American veteran of the Iraq War, speaks of how his experiences in Iraq blunted his emotions, his ability to feel anything deeply. The psychological and emotional prison that Darensburg confesses to informs his need to reenact the Vietnam War. It also prevents him from engaging with other aspects of the war such as the losses of human lives in the much-disputed war, the complexities of military and foreign policies, the history of Viet Nam's anticolonial struggles, or the ethics of the whole affair. Against the dictates of a national commemoration of the Vietnam War that often remembers the war to shore up support for current military policies, the essays assembled in this volume intervene in contemporary conversations on the Vietnam War through their attunement to the very issues that go unacknowledged and unspoken in popular culture commemorations of the Vietnam War today.

To this aim, the collection adopts an interdisciplinary approach with an emphasis on the disciplines that attend to everyday life and explicate its importance, notably anthropology, cultural studies, and literary and film criticism. While their disciplinary orientations may vary, the essays in this volume coherently illustrate the afterlives of the Vietnam War that continue into the twenty-first century and that require us, once again, to confront and reflect on what this much-studied war has left behind. Rather than comprehensiveness, the volume pinpoints topics, issues, and questions that are foundational to approaching the cultural effects of the Vietnam War today. In this sense, the collection's essays can be viewed as a constellation—each essay at once standing alone yet illuminating the others—in contemporary examinations of the Vietnam War's legacies.

A number of essays focus on the ways in which the Vietnamese diaspora engage with and affect the legacies of the Vietnam War. Yến Lê Espiritu and Quan Tue Tran reveal the Vietnamese diaspora as a vibrant site for memorializing the legacies of the war that have been omitted or overlooked in national memories of the Vietnam War. While the Republic of Vietnam, or South Vietnam, is no longer an officially recognized state, Espiritu and Tran argue that a sentiment akin to nationalism—what could be called nationalism-without-a-nation—brings together people in the Vietnamese diaspora to collectively remember the war and engage in acts of mutual aid and solidarity. Espiritu's essay, which is an adaptation of a chapter from her recent book *Body Counts*, examines how the Internet becomes a productive site for memorializations of the Vietnam War that exceeds nation-state boundaries for the Vietnamese diaspora. Based on ethnographic research on the California-based Disabled Veterans and Widows Relief Association, which from its inception in 1992 has become one of the most exemplary organizations of Vietnamese mutual assistance today, Tran illuminates the potential of the Vietnamese diaspora to chart an afterlife of the war that resists both American and Vietnamese hegemonic memories.

Although their emphases and texts differ, Viet Thanh Nguyen, Lan Duong, and Jeehyun Lim indicate how Vietnamese American writers and artists chart new terrain in the literary production and cultural politics surrounding the Vietnam War, often traversing historical times and bridging geographical distance. Nguyen makes a strong case for the cultural work of Vietnamese American literature, whose multiplicity he acknowledges yet whose origins he traces to the Vietnam War, in creating understanding of the Vietnam War that reflects "the way history ideology, and nationalism has formed in at least two countries." Through her analysis of *Land of Sorrows* (1971) and *Journey from the Fall* (2007), two films produced in very different circumstances, the former directed by Ha Thuc Can of South Vietnam during wartime and based on an antiwar Vietnamese memoir by Nha Ca and the latter by the Vietnamese American director Ham Tran, Duong asks probing questions about memory,

archiving, and networks of dissemination. Lim revisits the works of Le Ly
Hayslip, both her work as a memoirist of *When Heaven and Earth Changed Places*
(1989) and *Child of War, Woman of Peace* (1993) and as a humanitarian nongovernmental organization worker who founded East Meets West Foundation, to
elucidate the construction of a diasporic Vietnamese woman's agency in the
interstices of political and economic liberalism.

Vinh Nguyen and coauthors Robert Mason and Leonie Jones contend with
the conditions of the Vietnamese diaspora outside of the United States. Nguyen
revisits Hong Kong's boat people crisis, rereading a Hong Kong film on the
Vietnamese boat people with an eye to the Vietnamese diaspora. While Ann
Hui's *Boat People* (1982) was largely received as an allegory of Hong Kong's
uncertain future, Nguyen shifts this frame of interpretation to consider the film
as a text about the Vietnamese diaspora. Mason and Jones bring together two
populations in Australia that have both been affected by the Vietnam War but
are seldom discussed in tandem: Australian veterans of the war and Vietnamese
resettlers. As the authors show, the recent policy of multiculturalism in
Australia is what enables this bridging. Yet the historically specific character of
Australian multiculturalism is also a reminder that diasporas often exist in
tension with and are informed by national policies.

Alongside the essays that illuminate the role of the Vietnamese diaspora in
contemporary examinations of the Vietnam War, the collection assembles a
number of essays that excavate underexamined stories of the Vietnam War in
the Socialist Republic of Viet Nam and in the United States. Heonik Kwon turns
to the mourning rites that have developed in postwar Viet Nam in light of
the ideological divisions created within families during the war and in the
new Vietnamese state's repression of former affiliations with the Republic of
Vietnam. Diane Niblack Fox discloses the lasting impact of the war for the
Vietnamese with her interview of a former North Vietnamese soldier who is
also a survivor of Agent Orange. Kwon's and Fox's discussions bring into high
relief the ongoing accounting of the Vietnam War for the Vietnamese who
suffered immeasurable losses of lives and damages to their land.

Revisiting a Marvel comic of the post-Vietnam era, *The 'Nam*, Cathy J.
Schlund-Vials traces the moments of narrative and visual complications where
Cambodia, referred to as a "sideshow" in the Vietnam War, emerges as a crucial
site for exposing the confusion and chaos of the war. Against the dominance of
the military sublime in contemporary visual representations of wars, Schlund-
Vials argues for a "vertiginous critique" that disturbs conventional ideas and
understandings about wars. The final essay, and one returning to questions
raised by the documentary *In Country*, Brenda Boyle's "Naturalizing War: The
Stories We Tell about Vietnam," addresses the power of the American literary
and film canons to naturalize the war by erasing evidence of the French war

preceding it. The ahistorical "friendly fire" trope they employ—that war is human nature, not a human condition, and thus is unavoidable—Boyle contends, is a legacy of the war and is problematically replicated not only in recent Vietnam War novels and films but also in those of the wars in Iraq and Afghanistan.

Together these essays illuminate the state of critical conversations on the Vietnam War from the perspective of everyday life. It is to be expected that in the years to come there will be increasing scholarly interest in the Vietnam War's lasting impact on Southeast Asia, the Vietnamese diaspora, and the international dimensions of the Second Indochina conflict. What stories are told about the Vietnam War at this point is of critical significance if *In Country* is any measure of the state of forgetting and remembering in popular engagements with the Vietnam War today. The world of the Vietnam War reenactment in *In Country* discloses the war as at once familiar and foreign. Deeply troubling is that what becomes familiar is the lack of critical perspectives in revisiting the violence of war and that what becomes unfamiliar is the vexed histories and experiences of those who most suffered from the war. This volume is a step toward questioning what is familiar and foreign in contemporary recollections of the Vietnam War.

NOTES

1. See appendices A and B.

2. The *New York Times*'s selection of a part of the documentary on the fortieth anniversary of the fall of Saigon is perhaps the most telling sign of *In Country*'s significance as a cultural document of how the culture of today engages with the Vietnam War. Another widely discussed documentary was Rory Kennedy's film *Last Days in Vietnam* (2014).

3. Vanessa Agnew, a scholar of historical reenactment, says that in current academic usage the term "include[s] everything from living history museums, technical reconstructions, and 'nostalgia' toys (e.g. tin figures, dioramas and architectural models) to literature, film, photography, video games, television shows, pageants, parades and reenactment's most ubiquitous instantiation, social and cyber groups devoted to historical performance." "History's Affective Turn: Historical Reenactment and Its Work in the Present," *Rethinking History* 11, no. 3 (2007): 300. In the United States, Civil War reenactment is one of the most popular types of historical reenactment. Scholars who have studied Civil War reenactment have noted various populist manifestations of investments in southern heritage. See James O. Farmer, "Playing Rebels: Reenactment as Nostalgia and Defense of the Confederacy in the Battle of Aiken," *Southern Cultures* 11, no. 1 (2005) and chapter 6 of Jim Cullen, *The Civil War in Popular Culture: A Reusable Past* (Washington, D.C.: Smithsonian Institution Press, 1995). In his study of Civil War reenactment in Aiken, South Carolina, Farmer notes that white American interest in reenactment far exceeds African American interest. Ibid., 63. Patricia Davis, however, shows that there are African American Civil War

reenactments that involve a cultural politics of memory quite different from Confederate reenactments. See Patricia G. Davis, "The *Other* Southern Belles: Civil War Reenactment, African American Women, and the Performance of Idealized Femininity," *Text and Performance Quarterly* 32, no. 4 (2012).

4. Fredric Jameson, *Postmodernism, or the Cultural Logic of Late Capitalism* (Durham, N.C.: Duke University Press, 1991), 44.

5. Ibid.

6. Ibid.

7. Qtd. in Fred Turner, *Echoes of Combat: Trauma, Memory, and the Vietnam War* (Minneapolis: University of Minnesota Press, 1996), 130.

8. Ibid.

9. Farmer says that while Civil War reenactments are mostly open to the public now, they were not always so. "Playing Rebels," 50. The filmmakers Attie and O'Hara also note the absence of an audience as an important difference between the Vietnam War reenactment and other war reenactments. "Unlike most war re-enactments," they say, "the pretend battles [Vietnam War reenactors] stage are private, free of spectators and created for the experience of the participants alone." Mike Attie and Meghan O'Hara, "Re-Enacting the Vietnam War," *New York Times*, November 10, 2014, accessed August 25, 2015, http://www.nytimes.com/2014/11/11/opinion/re-enacting-the-vietnam-war.html.

10. Farmer, "Playing Rebels," 50.

11. Ibid.

12. Noah Berlatsky, "Reenacting War to Make Sense of It," *Atlantic,* April 8, 2015, accessed August 25, 2015, http://www.theatlantic.com/entertainment/archive/2015/04/real-soldiers-with-fake-guns/388691/.

13. Simon During, "Mimic Toil: Eighteenth-Century Preconditions for the Modern Historical Reenactment," *Rethinking History* 11, no. 3 (2007): 315.

14. Davis, "The *Other* Southern Belles," 309.

15. For discussions of the end of the history debate in Vietnam War scholarship, see William V. Spanos, *American Exceptionalism in the Age of Globalization: The Specter of Vietnam* (Albany: State University of New York Press, 2008); and Lloyd C. Gardner, "The Final Chapter? The Iraq War and the End of History," in *Vietnam in Iraq: Tactics, Lessons, Legacies, and Ghosts,* ed. John Dumbrell and David Ryan, 8–30 (New York: Routledge, 2007).

16. James W. Gibson, *Warrior Dreams: Paramilitary Culture in Post-Vietnam America* (New York: Hill & Wang, 1994). For other discussions of masculinity and the Vietnam War, see Susan Jeffords, *The Remasculinization of America: Gender and the Vietnam War* (Bloomington: Indiana University Press, 1989); Brenda M. Boyle, *Masculinity in Vietnam War Narratives: A Critical Study of Fiction, Films, and Nonfiction Writings* (Jefferson, N.C.: McFarland, 2009); and Sylvia Shin Huey Chong, *The Oriental Obscene: Violence and Racial Fantasies in the Vietnam Era* (Durham, NC: Duke University Press, 2012).

17. Lloyd Gardner and Marilyn Young, eds., *The New American Empire: A 21st Century Teach-in on U.S. Foreign Policy* (New York: New Press, 2005); and Andrew Bacevich, *The New American Militarism: How Americans Are Seduced by War* (New York: Oxford University Press, 2005).

18. Gerald D. Swick, "'In Country'—An Unusual Documentary Looks at Vietnam War Reenactments," HistoryNet.com, April 8, 2015, accessed August 25, 2015, http:// www.historynet.com/in-country-an-unusual-documentary-looks-at-vietnam-war-reenactments.htm.

19. According to Marazzi, war comes to play certain roles in the New Economy—the term he uses to designate the changes to the post-Fordist economy since the mid-1990s—that it did not before. He says that war "absorb[s] a part of the *surplus* of informational goods" in the New Economy and that a global strategy, like the War on Terror, becomes necessary to create the need for defense against threats with the end of the Cold War. *Capital and Language: From the New Economy to the War Economy*, trans. Gregory Conti (Los Angeles: Semiotext(e), 2008), 151.

20. Heonik Kwon, *The Other Cold War* (New York: Columbia University Press, 2010), 18–20.

21. Ibid., 19.

22. Some examples include Sucheng Chan's *The Vietnamese American 1.5 Generation: Stories of War, Revolution, Fight, and New Beginnings* (Philadelphia: Temple University Press, 2006); Cathy J. Schlund-Vials's *War, Genocide, Justice: Cambodian American Memory Work* (Minneapolis: University of Minnesota Press, 2012); the journal *Positions: Asia Critique* 2012 special issue on Southeast Asian American Studies (guest editors Finoa I. B. Ngo, Mimi Thi Nguyen, and Mariam B. Lam), and the essay collection, *Southeast Asian Diaspora in the United States: Memories and Visions, Yesterday, Today, and Tomorrow*, ed. Jonathan H. X. Lee (Newcastle upon Tyne: Cambridge Scholars Publishing, 2015).

23. Jonathan H. X. Lee, "Sojourn in Hong Kong, Settlement in America: Experiences of Chinese-Vietnamese Refugees," in *The Chinese/Vietnamese Diaspora: Revisiting the Boat People* (New York: Routledge, 2011), 140–141.

24. Yến Lê Espiritu, *Body Counts: The Vietnam War and Militarized Refuge(es)* (Berkeley: University of California Press, 2014), 18, 17.

25. Ibid., 17.

26. Jana K. Lipman, "A Refugee Camp in America: Fort Chaffee and Vietnamese and Cuban Refugees, 1975–1982," *Journal of American Ethnic History* 33, no. 2 (2014): 58.

27. Mimi Thi Nguyen, *The Gift of Freedom: War, Debt, and Other Refugee Passages* (Durham, N.C.: Duke University Press, 2012).

28. Jana K. Lipman, "'Give Us a Ship': The Vietnamese Repatriate Movement on Guam, 1975," *American Quarterly* 64, no. 1 (2012); and Lipman, "A Refugee Camp in America."

29. Yuk Wah Chan, "Revisiting the Vietnamese Refugee Era: an Asian Perspective from Hong Kong," in *The Chinese/Vietnamese Diaspora: Revisiting the Boat People*, ed. Jonathan H. X. Lee (New York: Routledge, 2011), 3.

30. Sophia Suk-mun Law, "Vietnamese Boat People in Hong Kong: Visual Images and Stories," in *The Chinese/Vietnamese Diaspora: Revisiting the Boat People*, ed. Jonathan H. X. Lee (New York: Routledge, 2011), 124–125. Law cites a cartoon published in a local Hong Kong newspaper satirizing the idea that creating a categorical distinction between refugee and economic migrant could alleviate the problem of the precarious legal status of those placed in the camps. It "shows a female officer holding a refugee baby" and "ask[ing]: 'His father is a political refugee but his mother is an economic migrant. What should I do about his status?'" Ibid., 125.

31. Yuk Wah Chan, "The Repatriated: From Refugee Migration to Marriage Migration," in *The Chinese/Vietnamese Diaspora: Revisiting the Boat People*, ed. Jonathan H. X. Lee (New York: Routledge, 2011), 174.

32. Jayne S. Werner and Luu Doan Huyuh, eds. *The Vietnam War: Vietnamese and American Perspectives* (London: M. E. Sharpe, 1993); and Renny Christopher, *The Viet Nam War / The American War: Images and Representations in Euro-American and Vietnamese Exile Narratives* (Amherst: University of Massachusetts Press, 1995) are early academic attempts to approach the Vietnam War from the sides of both the United States and Viet Nam.

33. Li Zhang, "Afterword: Flexible Postsocialist Assemblages from the Margin," *Positions: East Asia Cultures Critique* 20, no. 2 (2012): 660. A note on how Zhang uses the term "postsocialist" may be in order here. Zhang makes it clear that her use of the term is not meant "to imply that socialist ideas and practices are fading away or are no longer relevant, nor . . . a rigid periodization." Her usage of the term, a sensitive one as she acknowledges, is geared to releasing the examination of "socialist and nonsocialist practices and logics" in contemporary China and Viet Nam from the grip of a state-oriented perspective. Ibid., 661.

34. Andreas W. Daum, Lloyd C. Gardner, and Wilfried Mausbach, eds. *America, the Vietnam War, and the World: Comparative and International Perspectives* (Cambridge: Cambridge University Press, 2003); and Scott Laderman and Edwin A. Martini, eds. *Four Decades On: Vietnam, the United States and the Legacies of the Second Indochina War* (Durham, N.C.: Duke University Press, 2013).

35. Australia's participation in the Vietnam War is perhaps the most widely studied example. Jeff Doyle, Jeffrey Grey, and Peter Pierce, eds. *Australia's Vietnam War* (College Station: Texas A&M University Press, 2002); John Murphy, *Harvest of Fear: A History of Australia's Vietnam War* (St. Leonards: Allen & Unwin, 1993); Gregory Pemerton, *All the Way: Australia's Road to Vietnam* (Sydney: Allen & Unwin, 1987); and Peter King, ed. *Australia's Vietnam: Australia in the Second Indo-China War* (Sydney: Allen & Unwin, 1983).

36. Charles K. Armstrong offers a more detailed account of the exposés published in the newspaper. *Hankyoreh*. "America's Korea, Korea's Vietnam," *Critical Asian Studies* 33, no. 4 (2001): 529.

37. For a discussion of three memorials initiated after the Korean military's atrocities in the Vietnam War came to light—the Korea-Vietnam Peace Park in Phu Yen, the Ha My hamlet memorial donated by the Korean Association of Vietnam War Veterans, and the Meeting Place for Vietnam War Veterans created in Kangwon province of South Korea at the site of Korean military training before deployment to Viet Nam—see Chung Ro Yoon, "Politics of Memory and Commemoration of the Vietnam War in Korea" *Korean Social Sciences Review* 3, no. 1 (2013): 1–32. South Korean civic organizations that participate in reparations for the Korean military's war atrocities during the Vietnam War and strive for reconciliation include Nawauri=I&WE, Medics for Vietnam and Peace, the Choongbook and Jeju branches of the Korean People's Artists Federation, and the Association of Young Writers for Viet Nam. Nawauri=I&WE, for example, has been engaged in various exchange programs in Viet Nam between 2002 and 2010, including providing monthly financial support for a small number of Vietnamese civilian victims of Korean military's war atrocities and aligning with the Vietnamese nongovernmental organization Goodwill to hold peace camps for Korean

and Vietnamese youths to remember the Vietnam War. This information has been provided by Jinseok Jo, chief of staff at Nawauri=I&WE.

38. Armstrong, "America's Korea, Korea's Vietnam," 528–529; and Yoon, "Politics of Memory and Commemoration," 5–6.

39. Viet Thanh Nguyen, "Remembering War, Dreaming Peace: On Cosmopolitanism, Compassion, and Literature," in *Four Decades On: Vietnam, the United States and the Legacies of the Second Indochina War*, ed. Scott Laderman and Edwin A. Martini (Durham, N.C.: Duke University Press, 2013), 147, 146.

40. Qtd. in David Elliott, "Parallel Wars? Can Lessons of Vietnam be Applied to Iraq?" in *Iraq and the Lessons of Vietnam: Or How **Not** to Learn from the Past*, ed. Lloyd C. Gardner and Marilyn B. Young (New York: The New Press, 2007), 21–22.

41. Darius Rejali. "A Long-Standing Trick of the Torturer's Art." *Seattle Times*, May 14, 2004, accessed February 11, 2014. http://old.seattletimes.com/html/opinion/2001928172_torture14.html.

42. Lloyd C. Gardner and Marilyn B. Young, eds., *Iraq and the Lessons of Vietnam: Or How Not to Learn from the Past* (New York: New Press, 2007), 2, 3.

43. Trevor B. McCrisken, "No More Vietnams: Iraq and the Analogy Conundrum," in *Vietnam in Iraq: Tactics, Lessons, Legacies, and Ghosts*, ed. John Dumbrell and David Ryan (New York: Routledge, 2007), 160. See also John Dumbrell, "The Iraq and Vietnam Wars: Some Parallels and Connections" in the same volume.

1

Vietnamese Refugees and Internet Memorials

When Does War End and Who Gets to Decide?

YẾN LÊ ESPIRITU

> It should not surprise anyone that Vietnamese Americans would want to remember amidst all that forgetting. One does not become recognizably human until one acts in one's history. And for that, one needs to have history.
>
> –Nguyên-Vo Thu Huong, *"Forking Paths"*

When wars begin and end are not indisputable historical facts but contested rhetorical positions. In U.S. public commemorations of the Vietnam War, the fall of Saigon in April 1975 marks the official end of the war, as U.S. media and officials extolled and sensationalized the last-ditch efforts to evacuate the shell-shocked refugees and encamp them at U.S. military bases throughout the Pacific archipelago. Ayako Sahara has argued that the "end" of the Vietnam War and its aftermath were the moments that the Gerald Ford and Jimmy Carter administrations represented Southeast Asian refugees as the white man's burden, and the United States as the magnanimous rescuers, in order to facilitate national rehabilitation for the loss of the Vietnam War.[1] U.S. efforts to reposition itself as savior of Vietnam's "runaways" suggest that humanitarian interventions are not merely about resolving a problem; they are also practices that "work principally to recuperate state sovereignty in the face of specific historical challenges."[2] In this chapter, I challenge dominant U.S. representations of the war as being contained within a specific timeframe, particularly as being "over and done with." As Stephen Whitfield notes, war has a geopolitical and a social temporality: even when war has ended in the geopolitical dimension, it has not necessarily done so in the social dimension.[3] Against the U.S. dominant remembering of the fall of Saigon in April 1975 as the war's unambiguous conclusion, I ask: when does war end and who gets to decide? Highlighting the ongoingness of the Vietnam War, I examine the Internet "memorials" that Vietnamese Americans have created and circulated online in order to remember their dead and to pass on their war memories to the next generation. These online memorials offer an alternative temporality: that the costs borne by the Vietnamese war witnesses, survivors, and their families linger long after the supposed ending of the war.

"Ghost Soldiers": The "Disappeared" of South Vietnam

As scholars, public historians, and the media have repeatedly documented, Americans have been obsessed with the "Vietnam War" as an *American* tragedy. Despite the voluminous literatures on the Vietnam War and Vietnamese Americans, few scholarly works have critically engaged the war as an important historical and discursive site of Vietnamese subject formation. Addressing this gap, this chapter is concerned with the ways that the Army of the Republic of Vietnam (ARVN) dead—and their families' grief—has gone officially unacknowledged in the United States.[4] Following Judith Butler, I conceptualize grief not as a private or depoliticized sentiment but as a resource for enacting a politics that confronts the conditions under which "certain human lives are more grievable than others."[5] Commemorating the South's war dead is not the same as valorizing them; rather, it is acknowledging that they are worthy of remembrance. As Hue-Tam Ho Tai exhorts, any study of the Vietnam War would need to include the dead of South Vietnam, lest we risk "turning them into the scholarly equivalents of the wandering ghosts of those who, dying unmourned, constantly haunt the living in an attempt to force their way into the consciousness of the community, to be acknowledged as worthy of being remembered if only because they once walked the earth."[6]

I conceptualize the organized forgetting of the more than two hundred thousand ARVN dead as a form of forced *disappearance*.[7] As scholars have documented, the state is eager to control the cultural production of war memories.[8] In the United States, the ARVN soldier has been disappeared from almost all historical accounts of the war. According to Philip Beidler, a Vietnam veteran–turned–English professor, "the ARVN soldier remains at best a creature of scattered references, hand-me-down scholarship, supplementary statistics squirreled away in the odd military history archive or document collection."[9] Invoking the ARVN in the United States would amount to recalling American war failure: "They died for a nation called the Republic of Vietnam. And in so doing, they became the image of [American] failure."[10] Beidler argues that the American vilification of the ARVN as corrupt, cowardly, and incompetent—and the (mis)treatment of them as nonexistent "ghost soldiers"—became necessary because "it reinforced our eventual mythologizing of our own army of Vietnam as betrayed, sacrificed, used up, hung out to dry."[11] In other words, the ARVN became the scapegoat for America's defeat in Vietnam.[12] At the same time, those on the American Left have reduced South Vietnamese fighters into mere puppets of U.S. imperialism, thereby erasing any legitimate position or human agency for South Vietnamese acting in contradictory ways in extremely complex realities of what was also a civil war in Vietnam.[13]

The forced disappearance of South Vietnam's soldiers is also evident in the steep opposition directed against Vietnamese American attempts to monumentalize their status as America's allies and collaborators. In 2009 Vietnamese Americans in Wichita, Kansas, fundraised to erect a monument in the Veterans Memorial Park of Wichita. They had envisioned a modest-sized bronze statue depicting an American service member with his arm "protectively" around the shoulder of a South Vietnamese comrade, with a plaque expressing their gratitude to their American allies and friends. To their surprise, American veterans objected to the proposed placement of the monument, insisting that the Memorial Park is reserved for "America's veterans who fought America's wars for America's armed forces." A compromise was struck: the monument would be placed on city-owned land adjacent to but separated from the Memorial Park by an earthen wall, referred to by one offended Vietnamese American as "the Berlin Wall."[14] In another case the original design of the Texas Capitol Vietnam War Monument, approved in 2005, featured four American servicemen representing different ethnic groups and a soldier of the Republic of Vietnam being treated by a U.S. medic. However, in July 2012 the executive committee unilaterally changed the name of the monument to the Texas Capitol Vietnam Veterans Monument and replaced the South Vietnamese soldier with an Asian Texan soldier—a belated and insulting attempt at "completing the ethnic diversity by adding the Asian American."[15] Although the figure of the South Vietnamese soldier was depicted as an object of U.S. rescuing mission, and its inclusion would have solidified the narrative of the "grateful refugee," its removal angered the local Vietnamese American community, for whom the ARVN figure represented "an important symbolic element concerning the suffering of the Vietnamese."[16] An online petition requesting that Gov. Rick Perry restore the original design, published by Vietnamese veteran Michael Do on October 6, 2012, characterizes the decision as "an insult to many Vietnamese American veterans and people in the Vietnamese American community."[17] These protests notwithstanding, the revised version of the monument, with the South Vietnamese soldier omitted, celebrated its groundbreaking in March 2013. In an effort to appease the Vietnamese American community, the committee points to a panel on the monument's pedestal that features three South Vietnamese soldiers: a wounded soldier being cared for by his two comrades. Not surprisingly, for Vietnamese Americans, the placement of the panel on the monument's pedestal undercuts the message of South Vietnamese soldiers serving as allies alongside U.S. troops.[18]

The only successful attempt thus far to erect a monument commemorating South Vietnamese soldiers took place in 2003 in Westminster, California—home of the largest Vietnamese community outside Vietnam. However, it is instructive to review the staunch opposition that the community faced along the way.[19] Unable to secure public funding, the $1 million statue was financed almost entirely with donations from the Vietnamese community. Even once the money was raised, most city officials and about 70 percent of non-Vietnamese residents in Westminster continued to oppose the project.[20] As in the Wichita case, the Westminster city officials and residents wrangled over the location of the memorial, with some balking at the initial proposal to place it at the Civic Center, complaining that it would be "too visible" there and that a *private memorial*" was inappropriate for city property.[21] Angering the Vietnamese community, council members ultimately relocated the project away from City Hall to a vacant lot on the far side of the Westminster Civic Center—a decision that required the community to raise an extra $500,000 to improve the site, which was "full of potholes and in need of leveling," for the statue installation.[22] The term "private memorial" is telling, as city officials and news reporters consistently referred to the memorial as a mourning place for only the Westminster Vietnamese community and Little Saigon visitors.[23] In other words, the Westminster Vietnam War Memorial, even when explicitly designed to honor the bond between South Vietnamese and American soldiers, could neither be designated nor perceived as deserving a place within America.[24]

The memorial design—a pair of fifteen-foot, three-ton, somber-looking bronze soldiers, one white American and one South Vietnamese, standing side by side and flanked by flags of the United States and the former Republic of Vietnam—also provoked resident ire. In an interview published in the *Los Angeles Times*, then-Westminster mayor Frank Fry intimated that "his council colleagues and other civic leaders always had a problem with the notion that the statue would show the Vietnamese and American together."[25] While some residents wanted to remove the South Vietnamese soldier altogether, others suggested that it might be more appropriate to replace the soldier with a refugee family "to convey the message that America freed them . . . and they are here now"—an attempt to assimilate the refugee experiences into the benign narrative of immigration and multiculturalism.[26] In 2003, after seven years of bitter struggle and twenty-eight years after the fall of Saigon, the Vietnamese community in Little Saigon was finally able to unveil the Vietnam War Memorial, the first and, at the time of this writing, only memorial in the world to commemorate South Vietnamese soldiers.[27] While the memorial can be read as a Vietnamese

American attempt to feature the intertwined histories of the United States and the Republic of Vietnam, artist Tuan Nguyen reveals that he has designed the memorial, which features the American GI with his helmet off and carrying an M-16 rifle and the South Vietnamese soldier carrying a similar rifle but with his helmet on, "to show that for the American the war is ending and he's ready to go, but for the South Vietnamese the war is still going on. We lost our country."[28]

Internet Memorials

In recent years, scholars have noted the increasing importance of new electronic media in shaping our contemporary remembrance practices, particularly the Web memorials that have begun to appear in cyberspace. In the United States, Internet memorials have been set up, oftentimes spontaneously, to commemorate such nationwide tragedies as the 1999 Columbine High School massacre and the September 11, 2001, attacks.[29] Entrepreneurs have also launched online memorial websites for private individuals to allow families and friends to mourn and celebrate the life of a lost loved one by penning life biographies, sharing stories and photos, and leaving tributes and videos in their memory.[30] Internet memorials, hosted either by private individuals or by for-profit groups, have become popular virtual gravesites—"'resting places' for the dead that can be visited with ease by the bodyless and faceless bereaved."[31] Highly interactive, online memorials entice because of their capacity to collect, preserve, sort, and display a theoretically infinite amount of "texts, drawings, photography, video, and audio recordings" and to hyperlink to different sources, producing an evolving and ephemeral patchwork of private and collective memories.[32]

The Internet has changed the power dynamics of representation for traditionally marginalized groups. Because digital technology allows users to "route around" the traditional gatekeepers and express themselves in ways that previous generations could not, it has enabled the instant circulation of sensitive or even censored materials to potentially millions of viewers.[33] As Mike Featherstone contends, with the Internet, "informational control and formation ceases to be in the form of the panopticon with its bureaucratic forms of control and surveillance" and the "knowledge becomes freer to flow through decentered networks."[34] Bereft of onsite memorials to honor the now-defunct ARVN, the Vietnamese diasporic community has taken to cyberspace to create what Evyn Lê Espiritu has termed a "subaltern digital archive" to preserve in perpetuity the stories of ARVN heroes in blogs, on websites, and in YouTube videos.[35] Although these Internet sites that commemorate South Vietnam's war dead are not technically online memorials, I argue that collectively they constitute a repertoire of countermemorials, part of an uncoordinated online movement to puncture the silence about South Vietnam's war dead and, by extension, its haunting history. Their virtual existence indicates that the dead—in this case, the ARVN soldiers—can never be completely managed and disappeared.

The Requiem

The website www.vnafmamn.com was established in 2005 by Timothy Pham, a former ARVN officer who came to the United States soon after the fall of Saigon in April 1975, "to pay tribute to all U.S. and Vietnamese airmen who flew the wings of freedom over the sky of Vietnam and never returned." As I scrolled down a page entitled "April 30th, 1975: Betrayed and Abandoned," under the heading "Requiem," I came across the photographs of the six celebrated ARVN high-ranking officers—Maj. Dang Si Vinh; Brig. Gen. Le Van Hung; Brig. Gen. Le Nguyen Vy; Maj. Gen. Nguyen Khoa Nam; Brig. Gen. Tran Van Hai; and Gen. Pham Van Phu—all of whom famously committed suicide on April 30, 1975, rather than surrender to the encroaching Communist forces.[36] The seventh photograph was a grainy, black-and-white photograph of my oldest maternal uncle, Col. Ho Ngoc Can: hands bound, surrounded by uniformed gunmen, laconically propped on a chair with a banner behind him that announces his captors' "resolve to punish" those like him who served the defeated Republic of South Vietnam. This photo was apparently taken at a public denunciation session, or what the vnafmamn website calls "the Communist Kangaroo martial court"; my uncle was apparently "publicly executed by the Communist firing squad" soon after this photograph was taken. In the Requiem, each photograph becomes a memorial: the South Vietnam flag adorning the photo corner, the military insignia signifying the deceased's achievements, and the tributes highlighting the heartrending circumstances of death. Celebrating heroism, martyrdom, and sacrifice, these memorials express a *belated* collective grief over the demised ARVN officers and soldiers, both those named and unnamed, whose deaths coincided with the death of South Vietnam and thus had gone largely unmourned. In an interview over e-mail, Timothy Pham, the vnafmamn webmaster, explains his reasons for constructing this online tribute:

> The deaths of other generals and Colonel Ho Ngoc Can were very much well known among the former members of ARVN after April 30, 1975. I decided to feature their sacrifices on my webpage because they are the symbols of Patriotism, Honor, and Duty that all ARVN soldiers had been taught and kept for their conducts during the time they were trained at any ARVN military school in South Vietnam. They also mirrored the images of uncounted numbers of lower ranking ARVN Officers and soldiers who had given their lives in the same circumstance on April 30, 1975, or on the days after.[37]

The tribute that accompanies each man's photograph serves as an epitaph that might have been inscribed on their tombs had the circumstances been different. While epitaphs are generally inscribed to honor the deceased, providing a brief record of their personal and professional accomplishments, these online epitaphs double as history lessons not only about the Republic of Vietnam but also about the evils of communism. Although the date of the collective suicides—April 30, 1975—speaks volumes about the officers' antipathy toward communism, the epitaphs still include explicit anticommunist references. As an example, the tribute for Maj. Dang Si Vinh includes excerpts from his suicide note in which he exclaims, "Because our family would not live under the Communist regime, we have to end our lives this way." For Brig. Gen. Le Van Hung, his decision to kill himself stemmed from his refusal to surrender to the ruthless Communist forces who "would spare nobody in Can Tho in order to win [and who] would not hesitate to shell Can Tho into rubble." In my uncle's case, his death has become a cause célèbre in the Vietnamese diasporic community not only because of his great courage in the face of death but also because his public execution provides a potent symbol and proof of Communist atrocities. His epitaph thus reads:

> On April 30, 1975, [Can] refused to surrender to the enemy. Along with His troops, Can was fighting with all his might, holding the provincial headquarters until 11:00 PM on May 1, when his forces were out of ammunition. In the last minutes, he ordered the soldiers to leave the headquarters for safety while he and a faithful Popular Force militiaman covered them with a machine gun. He fell into the hands of the Communist force after he failed an attempt to kill himself. He told the enemy that he wouldn't surrender, and asked them to let him salute the ARVN colors with his uniform on before the execution.

As soldiers' bodies are often used for the consolidation of the nation, the Requiem page, in commemorating the lives and deaths of the ARVN officers, simultaneously mourns another death: that of the nation of the Republic of Vietnam, which ceased to be when the South surrendered to the North on April 30, 1975.[38] The photos of the ARVN dead, adorned with the yellow-and-three-red-stripe South Vietnam flag, affirm the continuance of the Republic of Vietnam in the diaspora, and extol its status as a beloved nation worthy of being fought for and grieved over by its people.

In many ways, the hagiographic Requiem page, which exalts flags, soldiers' bodies, and militarism, is a nationalist project, one that singles out male war heroes to represent the defunct Republic of Vietnam to the exclusion of "the women, the children, and the men without ranks or guns."[39] As Cynthia Enloe reminds us, "nationalism typically has sprung from masculinized memory, masculinized humiliation, and masculinized hope."[40] And yet, even as we remain critical of nationalism, particularly its masculinist glorification of the defunct nation-state and its insistence on a homogeneous national culture and history, it is important not to minimize the meanings, symbols, emotions, and memories that these online memorials evoke for many Vietnamese in the diaspora. As I perused the "Guest Book" pages of the vnafmamn website, which logs close to two hundred messages as of March 2013, I was struck by the heartfelt and at times anguished posts, thanking Pham for creating this website—for providing a virtual space for diasporic Vietnamese to mourn their dead and, in turn, their country and former way of life:

> Thank-you for creating this website. What these men had done for their country and for their people should never be forgotten. I, myself thankful daily for them. And I hope that I am worthy of their sacrifices.
> Nguyen Thi Loan, USA, August 16, 2010

> Republic of Vietnam, ARVN and VNAF forever. Hope your website will have one new section in the near future: Fall of Hanoi.
> Vu Dinh, USA, May 25, 2006

> Thank you for creating this website, for the benefit of those who served our country under the flag of VNAF, their families, for perpetuating the ideals of patriotism, liberty, democracy among the younger generation, and to offer tribute to our fallen heroes.
> Nguyen Tan-Hong (VNAF Medical Service), December 5, 2005

In a touching gesture, Trong D. Nguyen of Houston, Texas, asks the webmaster to add his father's photo, "the only photo I have of him while in uniform," to the online memorial so that he too may be celebrated and memorialized. In short, the Requiem page enables Vietnamese in the diaspora to narrate a heroic story of war and flight from Vietnam and to write themselves into national memory and history.

The Requiem's prominent display of South Vietnam's war dead provides a virtual and visual critique of the Socialist Republic of Vietnam's erasure of the violence inflicted on South Vietnamese by northern troops and their allied forces in the South during the war and by the government in the form of postwar policies.[41] In promoting an anticommunist nationalist version of South Vietnam's history, the Requiem risks being assimilated into the U.S. narrative of "rescue and liberation." However, the Requiem does more than mourn the demise of the Republic of Vietnam and castigate the current Vietnamese government; it also pointedly critiques the American abandonment of Vietnamese allies. As mentioned earlier, the Requiem is part of a larger page entitled "April 30, 1975: Betrayal and Abandoned," whose stated purpose is to make visible the U.S.

"sellout of South Vietnam." The page begins with this strongly worded and italicized preamble about the perceived U.S. "betrayal and abandonment" of its South Vietnamese allies:

> Whenever talking about Vietnam War, most of the US politicians, offi-
> cials, journalists, or political pundits would mention it in a way the war
> is their own, the South Vietnamese at that moment seem to be invisible
> or just the bystanders, bearing no brunt of the war effort. But there was
> one day, only one single day in which all of them would shy away from
> that claim. The day they have nothing to do with that war. The day they
> return the outcome back to the South Vietnamese: The APRIL 30th 1975.
>
>   For that reason, one has heard some very familiar words like "The Fall
> of Saigon," "Evacuation," "Frequent Wind Operation," etc. Those techni-
> cal terms and euphemism are conveniently served just like the toilet
> papers to cover somebody's own mistakes and to wipe out his embar-
> rassing accident. So let's tell straight out what it is on that day:
> Cut-and-run.
>
>   April 30th, 1975: The day South Vietnam is delivered to Evil due to
> betrayal and abandonment.

The page then proceeds to display a series of photos of the atrocities committed against the South Vietnamese on "that fatal day," pointedly insinuating
that Americans were responsible for the fate of "the innocent civilians, the
abandoned plain soldiers, and the deads!" Importantly, at about the midway
point, the page features about a dozen of the now-iconic photos of U.S. last-
ditch efforts by helicopters and navy ships to evacuate fleeing Vietnamese out
of the country but headlines them with these unexpected words: "When the
Ally Cuts and Runs." In so doing, it refuses to celebrate U.S. rescuing efforts,
which have been key to the U.S. ability to renarrate national glory in the aftermath of the Vietnam War, insisting instead that we critically evaluate the role
that U.S. military and government policies played in bringing about the
demise of South Vietnam and the subsequent refugee outpouring. To underscore that point, right below the U.S. rescuing photos is an excerpt from
Quang X. Pham's *A Sense of Duty: My Father, My American Journey*, which likens
U.S. abandonment of South Vietnam to their family's desertion of their dog as
they fled Saigon: "We lost him in the dust cloud kicked up by the scooter. We
abandoned him, the same way the United States left South Vietnam, like a dog
that just didn't fit into its plans." This Requiem thus encapsulates the complex
political subjectivity of Vietnamese refugees in the diaspora: a tangle of nostalgia for the former Republic of Vietnam, antipathy for the current government of Vietnam, and resentment of America's "abandonment" of its South
Vietnamese allies.

Around the Web: "Moving" Memorials

In the mid-1980s Vietnam veteran John Devitt of Stockton, California, created a transportable half-size replica of the Vietnam Veterans Memorial, named the Moving Wall, and toured it across the country so that people who were unable to travel to Washington, D.C., might be able to access the wall and honor the American fallen men and women of the Vietnam War. First displayed to the public in Tyler, Texas, in 1984, the Moving Wall has visited more than a thousand towns and cities and been viewed by millions of people. As it moves across the country, the Moving Wall reaches a cross section of Americans, creating a temporary site of memory for diverse groups of people—from grieving family members to proud veterans to sympathetic bystanders—to either hold silent vigil or come together to pay homage to the dead.[42] In this section, I examine how Vietnamese online memorials also move, in this case around the Web, as users and webmasters circulate and repost photos, images, and tributes, and as they provide hyperlinks to redirect traffic to various memorials. Like the Moving Wall, these moving memorials travel around the Web, reaching a cross section of Vietnamese in the diaspora. However, unlike the Moving Wall, the online encounters are not scheduled months in advance through an application process; rather, they are commonly chance meetings with the disappeared of the Republic of Vietnam.

An Internet search of my uncle's story, using primarily Google but also other popular search engines, yielded thirty-two websites that feature articles or videos that commemorate his life and death.[43] In many ways my uncle's life is significant precisely because of its end—his refusal to surrender and his public execution at the hands of his North Vietnamese captors. I discovered that these different sites reference and borrow from each other, circulating roughly, sometimes exactly, the same biography of my uncle's military accomplishments and public execution. According to Timothy Pham, the webmaster of the vnaf-mamn website where I first sighted the requiem that showcased my uncle's picture, the biographies of the ARVN officers had been retrieved from the English-language website hosted by a group of Việt Quốc members. Short for Việt Nam Quốc Dân Đảng (VNQDD),[44] the Vietnamese Nationalist Party, Việt Quốc exists today only outside Vietnam and is recognized among some sections of the overseas Vietnamese community as Vietnam's leading anticommunist organization.[45] On the Việt Quốc site, the page devoted to the April 30 suicides contains neither photographs of the men nor the yellow-with-red-striped flag of the Republic of Vietnam, just facts about their military lives and the known circumstances of their deaths.[46] Thus unadorned, the page appears more as a somber history lesson than a hagiographic requiem, as presented on the vnaf-mamn website. In turn, the spruced-up content and photos of the requiem, replete with the South Vietnam flag, are reposted on other Vietnamese websites such as Michael Do's website, under the heading: "In Honor of the Memory of Our National Heroes." A former VNAF combat infantryman who spent "10 years of hard labor, starvation and torture in Communist concentration camps (1975–1985)," Do maintains an active bilingual English-Vietnamese website since 2002 whose objective is to "contribute positively to the struggle of our Vietnamese people to overthrow Communist regime for a free and democratic Vietnam."[47]

As the moving memorials travel around the Web, and land on various websites, they assume the form and purpose of that website, thus reaching a wide swath of people. Twenty-nine of the thirty-two websites are exclusively in Vietnamese, almost all of which have been established by ARVN veteran organizations to pay tribute to the military heroes of the Republic of Vietnam. The three other websites—vnafmamn, Việt Quốc, and Michael Do—deliberately use English in order to attract young English-speaking Vietnamese in the diaspora. As vnafmamn webmaster Timothy Pham explains:

> My website is aiming at the young Vietnamese Americans who could read English only (there are tons of websites on Vietnam war subject, or ARVN military associations' website, etc. but most in Vietnamese). As a Vietnamese vet, I used to hear so many war stories from former com- rades or friends at the coffee shops' table whenever we had a chance to get together. The stories we (the Vets) already knew, but after the coffee was over, we went home. No one else would know the stories, but us, the old Vets only! To young Vietnamese-Americans, I would like them to know the true history of Vietnam War that they wouldn't be able to find in U.S. media common sources. The good deeds and sacrifices of their fathers, uncles, grandfathers and countless unknown ARVN private sol- diers (most finished only elementary school, or due to poverty never had a chance to go to school), who are the stepstones for their existence in America.[48]

Judging from the guest book posts, it seems that the vnafmamn website is reaching its intended audience not only in the United States but also in Australia and Canada. Here is a sample of posts from young Vietnamese:

> Thank you for creating such a resourceful and unique website. For the first generations of Vietnamese born overseas, it sheds light on our parent's [sic] untold stories and repressed memories. Please keep up your website so we can continue to learn more.
>   P. Nguyen, Sydney, Australia, May 30, 2010

Thanks again for maintaining such an incredible website! I'm so inspired
and touched by all the sacrifices of your generation for our country.

                    T. Pham, Northern California, March 1, 2009

You have made an excellent website about the Vietnam War. It's a great
change from reading biased websites that mock the South Vietnamese.
Thanks to you, I'm able to do a year long school project which consists of
a sci-fi miniature army inspired from the ARVN.

                    Huynh Kinh-Luyên, Laval Quebec, March 13, 2010

The website also reaches young people in Vietnam, as indicated in this
poignant post:

Hi! I'm a 21 year old born and growing up in Da Lat. I came to this site
hours ago through some old pictures of Da Lat on the Internet. When
I saw the whole collection it almost brought tears to my eyes. You have
no idea how much this means to me. Thank you for creating this site.
Please keep it alive forever. And long live VNAF!

                    An Duy, Da Lat, September 16, 2011

An Duy's comments suggests that the online requiem, whose primary purpose
is to pay tribute to South Vietnamese war heroes, also has the potential to
disrupt the self-legitimation of the postwar nation of Vietnam.[49] Parents also
write in to thank Pham for creating the website for the younger generations,
writing, for example: "I'm very happy that the younger generation will have
the opportunity to learn about the sacrifices that the older generation of the
South Vietnamese Air Force has made to preserve our homeland."[50]

    In the same way, the primary objective of the Việt Quốc website is to pro-
vide English-speaking "young Vietnamese outside Vietnam" with "profound
insights into the true situation in Vietnam and the conflict between the communists and the non-communists" in the hope that they would "establish
strong bases for the democracy movement outside Vietnam against any kind
of dictatorship today or in the future in their Fatherland."[51] And Michael Do
posts this on his home page: "All 'the Right Stuff' soon will be passed to the
Vietnamese younger generations so that all the priceless lessons of Vietnam
War won't be lost in vain."

    However incompletely, these websites offer a panoramic view of the defunct
Republic of Vietnam through their stories, images, and political views, publicly
displaying and virtually circulating a record not only of national loss and death
but also of the *presence* of the disappeared but beloved Republic of Vietnam and
its people. For example, blogger Nam Ròm's website, which includes a prominent tribute to ARVN war heroes, showcases past as well as contemporary
images of Vietnam, pictures of POWs, and in-depth biographies of important

historical figures in the old Republic of Vietnam.[52] In short, these online memorials do more than honor the dead; they represent the Vietnamese refugees' desire to retrieve unspeakable absences and create presences in their place.[53]

Conclusion: "An Act of Sedition"

Against their mandated invisibility in the United States, first-generation Vietnamese have created alternative memories and memorials that both confirm and unsettle U.S. representations of the Vietnam War. Although this global digital exposure does not rectify the organized erasure of Vietnamese experiences in the United States, the always-in-progress character of Internet memorials, its life quality and its live quality, embodies the promises of and possibilities for forging a different version of history.[54] Because these online memorials exist outside the sites of hegemonic official memory, because these dead are not expected to *appear*, and because they appear nonetheless, an encounter with them is a disturbing confrontation. As in the case of the Mothers of Argentina who defiantly displayed photographs of their disappeared children in the Plaza de Mayo, the very center of state authority in Argentina, the public display of South Vietnam's war dead on the Internet is itself "an instance of an oppositional political imaginary at work, an act of sedition."[55] Created by, about, and for South Vietnamese refugees, online memorials constitute an alternative meeting place for the Vietnamese diaspora from which to transmit traumatic memory, forge cultural identity, and renarrate national history—all of which have the potential to challenge the U.S. historical amnesias that treat the Vietnamese wandering ghosts, both the dead and the living dead, as natural products of exile and migration rather than by-products of war and forced disappearance.

Acknowledgments

Portions of this chapter previously appeared in my book *Body Counts*, and are reprinted here with the permission of the University of California Press. YẾn Lê Espiritu, *Body Counts: The Vietnam War and Militarized Refugees.* © 2014 by the Regents of the University of California. Published by the University of California Press.

NOTES

In the Vietnamese language, diacritical marks are used to indicate tones and meaning. In this chapter, I use diacritical marks inconsistently. As a general rule, I have spelled names and words the way they are spelled in the original source, with or without the diacritical marks.

1. Ayako Sahara, "Globalized Humanitarianism: US Imperial Formation in Asia and the Pacific through the Indochinese Refugee Problem" (PhD diss., University of California, San Diego, 2012).

2. Nevzat Soguk, *States and Strangers: Refugees and Displacements of Statecraft* (Minneapolis: University of Minnesota Press, 1999), 189.

3. Stephen Whitfield, *The Culture of the Cold War* (Baltimore: Johns Hopkins University Press, 1991).

4. Nguyên-Vo Thu Huong, "Forking Paths: How Shall We Mourn the Dead?" *Amerasia Journal* 31 (2005).

5. Judith Butler, *Precarious Life: The Power of Mourning and Violence* (New York: Verso, 2004), 30.

6. Hue-Tam Ho Tai, "Commemoration and Community," in *The Country of Memory: Remaking the Past in Late Socialist Vietnam*, ed. Hue-Tam Ho Tai (Berkeley: University of California Press, 2001), 228.

7. The figure of the two hundred thousand ARVN dead is from Philip Beidler, "The Invisible ARVN: The South Vietnamese Soldiers in American Representations of the Vietnam War," *War, Literature, & the Arts: An International Journal of the Humanities* 19 (2007): 306.

8. Hue-Tam Ho Tai, "Faces of Remembrance and Forgetting," in *The Country of Memory: Remaking the Past in Late Socialist Vietnam*, ed. Hue-Tam Ho Tai (Berkeley: University of California Press, 2001), 177.

9. Beidler, "The Invisible ARVN," 306.

10. Ibid., 315.

11. Ibid.

12. Robert K. Brigham, *ARVN: Life and Death in the South Vietnamese Army* (Lawrence: University of Kansas Press, 2007).

13. Nguyên-Vo, "Forking Paths," 161. As Nguyên-Vo recalls: "I remember South Vietnam as a place where political dissent was very alive against first Diem, then Thieu, and the Americans, and also many independent views against the North's war-making in the South. And Vietnamese suffered or prospered at the hands of the US and the governments of the two Vietnams in myriad ways" (171).

14. Monica Davey, "In Kansas, Proposed Monument to a Wartime Friendship Tests Bond," *New York Times*, August 3, 2009, A12.

15. Ken Herman, "Vietnamese Soldier to Be Omitted from Veterans' Memorial," *Austin American-Statesmen*, October 2, 2012, http://www.statesman.com/news/news/local/herman-vietnamese-soldier-to-be-omitted-from-veter/nSRzt/#__federated=1.

16. Ibid.

17. On March 14, 2013, the petition had generated 314 signatures. However, the committee decided to proceed with the revised version of the monument, with the South Vietnamese soldier omitted, and celebrated its groundbreaking that same month. GoPetition, published by Michael Do, October 6, 2012, http://www.gopetition.com/petitions/please-return-to-the-initial-texas-capitol-vietnam-mon.html.

18. Herman, "Vietnamese Soldier."

19. Khuyen Vu Nguyen, "Memorializing Vietnam: Transfiguring the Living Pasts," in *What's Going On? California and the Vietnam Era*, ed. Marica A. Eymann and

Charles Wollengberg (Berkeley: Oakland Museum of California and University of California Press, 2004), 157.

20. Nguyen, "Memorializing Vietnam," 159.

21. Jerry Hicks, "War Memorial Prevails after Lengthy Battle," *Los Angeles Times*, October 19, 2001, emphasis added, http://articles.latimes.com/2001/oct/19/local/me-59066; and Vivian LeTran, "Vietnam War Memorial Gives Alliance Its Due," *Los Angeles Times*, September 21, 2002, http://articles.latimes.com/2002/sep/21/local/me-memorial21.

22. Nguyen, "Memorializing Vietnam," 159.

23. Le Tran, "War Memorial."

24. Nguyen, "Memorializing Vietnam," 157.

25. Mai Tran, "Statue Donors Asked to Give Again: Why Is Still More Needed for the Westminster Memorial Featuring American and South Vietnamese Soldiers Together, They Wonder," *Los Angeles Times*, March 8, 2003, B1.

26. Nguyen, "Memorializing Vietnam," 159.

27. Ibid., 153.

28. Qtd. in David Reyes, "Vietnam War Memorial Stirs Memory," *Los Angeles Times*, April 28, 2003, http://articles.latimes.com/2003/apr/28/local/me-statue28.

29. Maya Socolovsky, "Cyber-Spaces of Grief: Online Memorials and the Columbine High School Shootings," *JAC* 24 (2004): 467–489.

30. See, e.g., Legacy Multimedia, "Our Top Six Online Memorial Websites," accessed March 25, 2013, http://legacymultimedia.com/2012/03/05/our-top-six-online-memorial-websites/.

31. Socolovsky, "Cyber-Spaces," 469.

32. Ekaterina Haskins, "Between Archive and Participation: Public Memory in a Digital Age," *Rhetoric Society Quarterly* 37 (2007): 405.

33. John Palfry and Urs Gasser, *Born Digital: Understanding the First Generation of Internet Natives* (New York: Basic Books, 2008).

34. Mike Featherstone, "Archive," *Theory Culture Society* 23 (2006): 595.

35. Evyn Lê Espiritu, "'Who Was Colonel Hồ Ngọc Cẩn?' Theorizing the Relationship between History and Cultural Memory" (Senior thesis, Department of History, Pomona College, 2013), chap. 2.

36. See http://vnafmamn.com/black_april.html.

37. Timothy Pham, e-mail interview with author, March 24, 2013.

38. David W. Blight, *Race and Reunion: The Civil War in American Memory* (Cambridge, Mass.: Harvard University Press, 2001).

39. Nguyen-Vo, "Forking Paths," 157.

40. Cynthia Enloe, *Bananas, Beaches, Bases: Making Feminist Sense of International Politics* (Berkeley: University of California Press, 1990), 44.

41. Nguyen-Vo, "Forking Paths"; and Tai, "Faces of Remembrance."

42. "The Moving Wall." http://www.themovingwall.org, accessed February 13, 2013.

43. These search engines include Yahoo, Bing!, Ask, AOL, MyWebSearch, Blekko, Lycos, Dogpile, Webcrawler, Info, Infospace, Search, Excite, and Goodsearch. I thank my research assistant, Sally Le, for her help in compiling this database.

44. VNQDD has its own webpage, which is much more extensive and is exclusively in Vietnamese.

45. Spencer Tucker, *Encyclopedia of the Vietnam War: A Political, Social, and Military History* (Santa Barbara, Calif.: ABC-CLIO, 2000).

46. Although my uncle did not commit suicide on April 30, 1975, his widely publicized death at the hands of the communists is repeatedly lumped with the deaths of these high-ranking officers.

47. Michael Do, e-mail interview with author, March 23, 2013. In 2009 the michaelpdo website ranked in the top 15 percent of the more than 10 million web pages based on the number of readers.

48. Timothy Pham, e-mail interview with author, March 24, 2013.

49. I thank Nguyên-Vo Thu Huong for this insight.

50. Nguyen van Nga, Canada, March 23, 2008, translated from Vietnamese.

51. Viet Quoc, "Introduction," accessed March 24, 2013, http://www.vietquoc.com/INTRODUC.HTM.

52. "Nam Ròm." http://namrom64.blogspot.com/2012/08/nhung-vi-tuong-vnch-tu-sat-30041975.htm, accessed March 23, 2013.

53. Pierre Nora, "Between Memory and History: Les Lieux de Mémoire," *Representations* 26 (1989).

54. Walter Benjamin, "Theses on the Philosophy of History," in *Illuminations*, ed. Hannah Arendt (Fontana/Collins, 1973).

55. Avery Gordon, *Ghostly Matters: Haunting and the Sociological Imagination* (Minneapolis: University of Minnesota Press, 1997), 110.

2

Broken, but Not Forsaken

Disabled South Vietnamese Veterans in Vietnam and the Vietnamese Diaspora

QUAN TUE TRAN

After the Republic of Vietnam (RVN) collapsed on April 30, 1975, those who had served in the RVN military forces (RVNMF) during the Second Indochina War became second-class citizens in the newly formed Socialist Republic of Vietnam (SRV). Associated with the side that had lost the war, South Vietnamese veterans have endured a spectrum of hardship under the new regime.[1] While many subsequently fled abroad as political refugees, others, including over half a million disabled RVNMF veterans, remain in communist-controlled Vietnam.[2] Often living in abject poverty, these veterans carry with them the physical, psychological, and emotional scars of the battlefields. Moreover, they must also face the stigma of having served in the defeated "puppet army."[3] Unlike disabled Vietnam's People Army and Vietnam-era American veterans, whose services and welfare have been officially recognized and attended to by their respective governments, disabled South Vietnamese veterans are left to fend for themselves since the nation-state under which they had served no longer exists.

Four decades since the Second Indochina War ended, RVNMF veterans continue to be ignored in dominant narratives concerning that war and its legacies in Vietnam, in the United States, and in other international contexts. Several scholars have rightly noted that state-sanctioned and popular forms of organized forgetting have played key roles in mainstream disavowal of South Vietnamese perspectives of the war.[4] Yến Lê Espiritu, for example, asserts in this volume that the organized forgetting of more than two hundred thousand dead South Vietnamese soldiers in both Vietnam and the United States constitutes a form of "forced disappearance," which erases "any legitimate position or human agency for South Vietnamese acting in contradictory ways in extremely complex realities of what was also a civil war in Vietnam."

In the face of such erasures, the Vietnamese diaspora has emerged as a counterhegemonic site of remembrance that resists dominant war memories of both the Vietnamese and American states.[5] As some scholars have noted, Vietnamese Americans—most of whom had lived in and are sympathetic to the defunct RVN—have actively confronted such forgetting by constructing physical and virtual memorials as well as organizing annual public events to commemorate their involvements in the war and to mourn South Vietnamese war dead.[6] The Internet memorials to deceased South Vietnamese generals and soldiers that Espiritu examines in this volume exemplify some of those efforts. These "countermemorials," as Espiritu argues in this volume, "puncture the silence about South Vietnam's war dead and, by extension, its haunting history." They also offer insights into the transnational sociocultural politics that animate diasporic Vietnamese commemorative practices. As Nguyễn-võ Thu-hương reminds us, for diasporic Vietnamese in the United States "remembering in mourning, in commemoration, in symbolic local politics, is not a symptom of an incessant, pathological return to be cured with assimilationist remedies, but a way in which we can recover our histories which intersect, rather than coincide, with American nationalist history."[7] One could add that the mourning and remembering of South Vietnamese dead in diasporic space also counters the national liberation narrative espoused by the Vietnamese communist government to justify its embattled ascendance to power in Vietnam.

For diasporic Vietnamese worldwide, publicly mourning and commemorating the fall of the RVN and those who had died defending it is not only about the dead. It is also about the living as well as about extending the lifespan of South Vietnam, its citizenship, and its branch of nationalism beyond the RVN's premature geopolitical death in April 1975. Such extension vibrantly shapes a form of exile nationalism that animates diasporic Vietnamese sociocultural politics. Similar to what Phương Nguyễn has coined "refugee nationalism," which views refugees from South Vietnam as the central figure in modern Vietnamese history, South Vietnamese exile nationalism articulates an alternative version of modern Vietnamese history through the literal and symbolic expressions of South Vietnamese nationalist values in diasporic space.[8] Specifically tied to the anticommunist ethos that constituted the backbone of the RVN's geopolitics, the exile nationalism embraced by diasporic Vietnamese confronts the national narrative of the Vietnamese communist state while at the same time seeking recognition and inclusion in the national narratives of their host countries.[9]

In this essay I examine the contemporary mobilization of diasporic Vietnamese for the aid of disabled veterans and widows of deceased veterans of the RVNMF in Vietnam to offer a complex picture of South Vietnamese veterans, citizenship, and nationalism in diaspora. Drawing from oral histories,

correspondences, and public records of the California-based Disabled Veterans
and Widows Relief Association, I argue that diasporic Vietnamese supports for
RVNMF disabled veterans and deceased veterans' widows in Vietnam embody
both resistive and redemptive acts that constitute South Vietnamese exile
nationalism. On one level, in making visible the struggles of the former in postwar Vietnam, diasporic Vietnamese (particularly those who have resettled in
the United States) resist both postwar Vietnamese and American deliberate
forgetting of the RVN and the South Vietnamese who had defended it. On
another level, as they rally to support RVNMF disabled veterans and deceased
veterans' widows, diasporic Vietnamese actively express camaraderie, mutual
assistance, and gratitude to reinstate legitimacy and honor to South Vietnamese
military service personnel and, by extension, to South Vietnamese citizenship
and nationalism.

RVNMF Veterans in the Post–Vietnam War Era

Before the Republic of Vietnam collapsed, South Vietnamese veterans and their
dependents received a wide range of services and benefits administered
through the RVN Veterans Ministry. Examples included government-funded
institutions such as military hospitals, disabled veteran villages, and special
schools for children of veterans who died in combat. After the communist
victory ended the war, the South Vietnamese Veterans Ministry along with
other polities that made up the RVN dissolved, as did their auxiliary institutions. As members of the defeated military, RVNMF veterans immediately lost
whatever status, services, and benefits they had been receiving from their
government up to that point.

RVNMF veterans further encountered various forms of reprisal from the
communist victor in the postwar years. Denounced as puppets, traitors, and
U.S. imperialist collaborators by the new regime, many were detained in hard
labor camps scattered across the country. The length of their imprisonment
depended on their ranking and the nature of their military involvements. Once
released from those euphemistically called "reeducation camps" these veterans
and their dependents further faced housing, employment, and educational
discrimination. Among RVNMF veterans, disabled individuals are the least for-
tunate. Immediately after the war, the new government forcefully removed
wounded South Vietnamese soldiers from RVN-established military hospitals
despite their grave conditions and urgent needs for medical treatments.[10]
Moreover, through measures such as housing confiscation and forceful new
economic zone relocation orders, the new regime also evicted disabled RVNMF
veterans from special villages that the South Vietnamese government had
established for them.[11]

A glimpse of the challenges that disabled South Vietnamese veterans have faced is found in *Tattered Lives*, a collection of sixteen narratives compiled and edited by two Vietnamese philanthropists in France in 1999 to raise awareness among diasporic Vietnamese and an international audience about the misfortunes of those who had once defended the RVN and their dependents.[12] In one chapter a veteran who had lost both of his legs in combat conveys:

> After the war ended, disabled RVNMF veterans feel abandoned, uncertain about survival. We feel like children handicapped and orphaned at birth. . . . In places outside Saigon, the communists have confiscated houses once built by the South Vietnamese government to compensate disabled veterans. In My Thoi village, disabled veterans had 24 hours to vacate their homes. With nowhere to go, many went to Saigon, where they live on the streets, sleep in train stations, at bus stops, in market stalls, and in abandoned cemeteries. . . . We organize ourselves into small groups and obtain incense sticks from the local temples to resell them on street corners and in alleys. . . . There are many gravely disabled veterans who could not even sell incense. They have to beg on the streets.[13]

Invoking sympathy and empathy, this self-infantilized narrative bemoans the mistreatment of disabled RVNMF veterans after the war. The "handicapped children orphaned at birth" metaphor also indirectly criticizes the abandonment of disabled South Vietnamese veterans by both the failed RVN state and its American ally. Like others featured in *Tattered Lives*, this narrative also reminds the intended audience of the vulnerability and the continual struggles of disabled RVNMF veterans and dependents of deceased veterans as well as their impoverished conditions in postwar Vietnam.[14]

Such reminders found receptive ears among diasporic Vietnamese. In fact, by 1999, in the wake of the SRV's Đổi Mới economic reforms, which opened the door for diasporic Vietnamese philanthropic activities in Vietnam since the late 1980s, several nonprofit and charitable organizations have already emerged across the Vietnamese diaspora with similar missions to help disabled RVNMF veterans in Vietnam.[15] Given the absence of state support for disabled RVNMF veterans in Vietnam, these transnational associations crucially fill in the void, however modest and limited their means of assistance. The following is a close examination of the activities and impacts of one such organization—the Disabled Veterans and Widows Relief Association, or DVWRA.[16]

Mutual Assistance, Camaraderie, and the DVWRA

Established in 1992, the DVWRA originated from another RVNMF veteran group based in southern California—the Former Political Prisoner Mutual Assistance

Association (FPPMAA).[17] Active between 1989 and 1998, the FPPMAA assisted South Vietnamese veterans who resettled in southern California through the Program for Former Reeducation Camp Detainees.[18] Fueled by the motto "Those who leave Vietnam first take care of those who leave later. Those who leave later do not forsake those who are left behind," this organization fostered the spirit of mutual assistance that eventually led to the creation of the DVWRA.[19] The latter emerged from the desire of FPPMAA members to help fellow disabled veterans and widows of deceased veterans who remain in Vietnam. Upon its founding, the DVWRA assisted a dozen individuals through personal connections and on an ad hoc basis. Over a decade, the number of people who sought and received assistance from the association has increased exponentially, nearing some thirty thousand cases by 2014. In response to the demand for assistance, DVWRA leadership has grown from a handful of volunteers to over two dozen individuals.[20] At the same time the association's operation has also become more large-scale and systematic.

The DVWRA's scope of operation is multifaceted and transnational. It includes identifying and classifying eligible disabled RVNMF veterans and widows of deceased veterans in Vietnam as well as securing and distributing funds to those individuals. However, due to its mission to help individuals affiliated with the old regime, the current Vietnamese government considers the DVWRA as a "reactionary organization" and bars it from officially operating in Vietnam.[21] The SRV's antagonism toward the DVWRA suggests that although some four decades have passed, the attention of diasporic Vietnamese to disabled RVNMF veterans in Vietnam poses a threat to socialist nation-building agendas. Given its blacklisted status, the DVWRA thus has to rely on a word-of-mouth approach to reach out to potential beneficiaries in Vietnam.[22] Since anyone could claim to be a disabled RVNMF veteran, the DVWRA screens incoming applications to protect the association from fraudulent claims.[23] To be eligible, each applicant must furnish enlistment, discharge, and medical documents issued by the defunct South Vietnamese government prior to the collapse of the RVN. In addition, recent photographs showing injuries sustained during the war must also accompany the applications. Upon receiving the documents, DVWRA executive committee members further verify the submitted materials with an extensive network of RVNMF veterans who have resettled in the United States, such as the Southern California RVNMF Veterans Coalition.[24] Once authenticated by the DVWRA, the applicant's name is entered in the database of those eligible for financial assistance. Arguably, this formal verification process reinstates legitimacy and honor to those who were wounded while serving the RVN.

Since it does not have representatives in Vietnam, the DVWRA uses diasporic Vietnamese money transfer services to distribute monetary assistance. Based on a sliding scale, the amount dispensed depends on the types of wounds and the personal circumstances of those who sought assistance. Individuals who lost both arms or both legs or vision in both eyes during their military services would receive US$200 and appropriate medical equipment, such as a wheelchair or a pair of crutches, from the association. Those who lost one limb or one eye, or who suffered an internal injury would receive US$100. Widows of RVNMF veterans would receive US$50. Sometimes RVNMF veterans in Vietnam suffering from illnesses unrelated to combat would also receive assistance.[25] Although nominal, these one-time funds nonetheless help improve the lives of many beneficiaries, especially those who live in abject poverty. As a widow of an RVNMF veteran shares in a letter to the DVWRA: "The money that the association had sent helped me cover two months of living and medical expenses."[26]

The spirit of camaraderie is one of the forces sustaining the DVWRA's mission. Most of the association's volunteers are themselves RVNMF veterans. Its current president, for example, is an eighty-five-year-old woman who had served as a lieutenant colonel in the South Vietnamese Women's Armed Force Corps. Since she assumed leadership of the association in 2006, Nguyễn Thị Hạnh Nhơn's dedication to helping disabled RVNMF veterans has been noted by many. Once asked why she is so committed to the cause, the octogenarian emphasized, "Because our sense of camaraderie as soldiers is very strong."[27] Like many fellow RVNMF veterans, Nguyễn believes that RVNMF soldiers were bound together by the conviction that they were fighting for a righteous and legitimate cause—defending South Vietnamese democracy and freedom from communist encroachment.[28] Thus, the feeling of fellowship that Nguyễn references stems simultaneously from wartime military service, from a sense of shared fate among those who had fought for South Vietnam but ultimately lost, and from a South Vietnamese nationalist ethos that is grounded in a particular anticommunist ideology.[29]

If the misfortunes and discriminations that disabled South Vietnamese veterans have experienced in postwar Vietnam directly resulted from the defeat of the RVN, then contemporary efforts to assist the former by fellow veterans abroad constitute both an effort to resist the mistreatments of the Vietnamese government and an expression of camaraderie, which enable an attempt to restore the legitimacy of South Vietnamese veterans, citizenship, and nationalism in diaspora. Such redemptive endeavors reveal the implicit cultural politics that animate the DVWRA's benevolent mission and highlights the implications of exile nationalism.

Restoring Legitimacy and Honor through Gratitude

It is important to note that, besides former South Vietnamese veterans, ordinary diasporic Vietnamese also actively support the DVWRA's mission. Such support is discernable and quantifiable through the outdoor music concerts that the DVWRA organizes annually to raise money for its operation. Emphasizing the gratitude of diasporic Vietnamese toward the sacrifices of disabled RVNMF veterans, these concerts also embody concrete resistive and redemptive acts that help restore legitimacy and honor to RVNMF veterans (particularly disabled veterans), to South Vietnam, and, by extension, to South Vietnamese citizenship and nationalism—all of which have been dismissed and trivialized in the wake of American abandonment of South Vietnam and the communist victory that ended the Second Indochina War. As I show in the following, the gratitude expressed by diasporic Vietnamese toward disabled South Vietnamese veterans differs from the kind of gratitude directed toward Americans for "rescuing" Vietnamese refugees that scholars have noted in the past.[30] Whereas the grateful Vietnamese American refugee figure is often co-opted by American mainstream media and politicians as well as deployed by Vietnamese Americans themselves to perpetuate the myth of U.S. liberal narrative of Vietnamese assimilation, diasporic Vietnamese remembrance and gratitude toward disabled RVNMF veterans serve to affirm the legitimacy of South Vietnam and the defunct state's own quest for self-determination based on a noncommunist nationalist ideology.

Between 1992 and 2005 the DVWRA employed small-scale fundraising efforts such as benefit dinners to raise money. However, since 2006, the association has turned to large-scale fundraising efforts in order to meet increasing demands for assistance from disabled RVNMF veterans in the homeland. Under the leadership of Nguyễn, the DVWRA has collaborated with over forty other Vietnamese American organizations to organize annual fundraising concerts known as "Thank You, Disabled Veterans of the Republic of Viet Nam Concert."[31] Each of these five- to seven-hour-long events has a local live audience and is also broadcast live across the Vietnamese diaspora in the form of a telethon. The inaugural concert took place in the summer of 2006 at the stadium of Bolsa Grande High School in Garden Grove, California. With more than ten thousand people attending in person and tens of thousands of others pledging their support via telephone, the event brought US$379,085 in donations to the DVWRA that year.[32]

To date, eight annual Thank You concerts have taken place alternatively in Southern and Northern California. Together these events have brought the DVWRA over US$7 million in donations, making them the most successful and high-profiled charitable occurrences in the diaspora. Three factors contribute to these concerts' success. First, despite its modest means, the DVWRA has managed to secure assistance from reputable partners including diasporic media outlets, veteran's associations, and popular public figures. All these entities share in common an affinity for the defunct RVN. For instance, the Saigon Broadcasting Television Network (SBTN)—a wide-reaching satellite broadcast network founded by a group of former South Vietnamese civilians—brings the live concerts to diasporic Vietnamese audiences in the form of telethons. In addition, Asia Entertainment Incorporation, an internationally renowned diasporic Vietnamese music and video production company, lends its professional expertise in producing and promoting variety shows to the DVWRA's cause. Asia Entertainment's history of advocating for South Vietnamese veterans through past music video productions has proven particularly advantageous to the DVWRA fundraising efforts.[33] Furthermore, over fifty popular diasporic Vietnamese entertainers have also consistently donated their talents and time to benefit disabled RVNMF veterans in Vietnam.[34]

The second factor contributing to the DVWRA's fundraising success has to do with the accessibility of the concerts. Since the inaugural show, organizers have strategically kept tickets at an affordable price—US$10 each. Tickets could be purchased through a variety of outlets—local Vietnamese markets, temples, churches, restaurants, bookstores, music stores, and numerous Vietnamese American associations based in California.[35] As telethons, the concerts further reach audiences beyond California. Financial records from these events reveal the effectiveness of such strategies. For example, the fourth annual concert, which took place in southern California in August 2010, brought in a total of US$828,041. Of this amount, 12 percent came from ticket sales and 15 percent from cash donations received on the day of the concert via on-the-spot cash contributions; 73.2 percent were donations sent to DVWRA and SBTN offices both before and after the concert from all over the Vietnamese diaspora—most of which were telethon pledges. The donations collected that year enabled the association to assist approximately five thousand eligible applicants.[36]

The diversity of those who attended and donated to the concerts is the third factor behind the DVWRA's fundraising success. The participation of the very old to the very young and all age groups in between, of the rich and poor, of RVNMF veterans as well as their descendants, and of ordinary former South Vietnamese civilians reflect the broad appeal of the DVWRA's mission.[37] The association has managed to garner such a broad support base by framing these fundraising efforts as opportunities for diasporic Vietnamese, particularly those who had fled from communism, "to show that [they] care about the conditions of disabled RVNMF veterans," "to express their gratitude to those who had fought and sacrificed a part of their body to protect the freedom of South Vietnam," and "to show the strength and unity of Vietnamese refugees in this community event."[38] Through the tropes of gratitude, sacrifice, and unity, concert organizers thus underscore multilayered significance and urgency to the collective mission of helping disabled RVNMF veterans in Vietnam.

By depicting and recognizing South Vietnamese veterans as selfless and heroic figures, these concerts serve similar functions as the cenotaphs and tombs of unknown soldiers that Benedict Anderson has noted in his ground-breaking study of nationalism.[39] Anderson writes, "The public ceremonial reverence accorded these monuments precisely because they are either deliberately empty or no one knows who lies inside them, has no true precedents in earlier times. The empty tomb represents the ideal everyman, willing to sacrifice himself for the glory of the nation."[40] The eighth Thank You concert held in Southern California on August 1, 2014, offers an illuminating example. It began with an opening ceremony in which a dozen South Vietnamese veterans in full military uniforms escorted the South Vietnamese and American flags to the stage area. Event organizers and participants then collectively saluted the flags and sang the South Vietnamese and the American national anthems, signaling their affiliations with both the RVN and the United States as Vietnamese Americans. Thereafter, the concert participants observed a moment of silence "to commemorate predecessors who founded and defended [Vietnam]; military and government personnel who sacrificed their lives to protect the just cause, the nation, and the people of South Vietnam; compatriots who died at sea and in the jungle in search for freedom; and allied forces' personnel who sacrificed their lives in the Vietnam War."[41] As these rituals and their participants commemorated those who had died defending South Vietnam, they also rekindled the spirit of South Vietnamese nationalism. At the same time, the inclusion of "allied forces" in the commemorative ritual emphasizes the wartime alliance between the RVN and the United States and starkly contrasts the habitual forgetting of South Vietnam in official and popular American discourses about the war.

Whereas other efforts commemorating the loss of South Vietnam in the Vietnamese diaspora tend to focus only on the symbolic significance of South Vietnamese war dead, the Thank You concerts emphasize the living and generate practical results alongside symbolic values. For instance, after the opening ceremonial rituals, concert organizers acknowledged the sacrifices of disabled South Vietnamese veterans. Describing the latter as "soldiers who had fought courageously to protect the ancestral land and to bring freedom and peace to those living in South Vietnam," the DVWRA president reminded the audience that disabled veterans have suffered the greatest disadvantages as they live with their wounds for the rest of their lives. Further lauding past and ongoing support of diasporic Vietnamese toward the mission to help disabled RVNMF veterans in Vietnam, the DVWRA president informed the audience that donations sent by diasporic Vietnamese have brought happiness, consolation, and pragmatic help to disabled RVNMF veterans and dependents of deceased veterans.[42]

Featuring over fifty performances, the eighth annual concert highlighted the glories as well as the trials and tribulations of South Vietnamese soldiers.

The opening performance, for instance, reenacted the historical battle between the Vietnam People's Army and the RVNMF for the control of Quang Tri City in the summer of 1972.[43] In that battle, South Vietnamese soldiers—backed by American troops—emerged victoriously and recaptured the city from communist forces after eighty-one days of fighting. The upbeat song "The Flag Flies on Beloved Quang Tri" celebrates their heroism and highlights that costly victory: "The flag flies, flies mightily over the beloved city, recaptured last night through bloodshed."[44] Other performances further underscored RVNMF soldiers' pride and patriotism. Singing the song "I Am a Soldier" in a later part of the concert, members of a choir made up of former South Vietnamese veterans conveyed: "I want to let friends near and far know that I am a soldier / . . . As long as my country still suffers / I still go to war / Soldiers love their country more than themselves / As long as there is no peace / I will continue army life and therefore I am still a soldier / a soldier of the Army of the Republic of Vietnam."[45] Other performances emphasized the humanity of RVNMF soldiers. The song "Farewell to Arms" sung by singer Ngoc Quang Dong articulates the aspirations of an RVNMF soldier who longs to return to his ancestral land once the fighting ends. In the song's refrain, the soldier professes to his girlfriend on the home front: "I will rebuild the old house / I will invite my parents to live with me / I will visit your house / and bring with me areca nuts and betel leaves, / we will start anew."[46]

However, the dream of a peaceful postwar civilian life did not materialize for many RVNMF veterans. Throughout the concert, ample audio and visual cues reminded the audience of disabled RVNMF veterans' suffering in postwar Vietnam and the moral obligation of diasporic Vietnamese as former RVN citizens to assist them. For example, two large banners hung at the concert's entrance stated: "We cannot fully repay our debt to disabled veterans, their struggles pain us" and "From abroad, we do not forget the camaraderie, fellow compatriots will forever remember the virtues of disabled veterans."[47] Images of wounded, amputated, and blinded soldiers also appeared on concert promotional materials and stage backdrops. These powerful visuals were accompanied by equally compelling performances that further called attention to the misfortunes of disabled RVNMF veterans. The song "On the Hau Giang Ferry One Evening," performed by singer Bich Dao, was one such example. Recalling a chance encounter on a ferry between the songwriter and a homeless disabled RVNMF veteran, who made a living by singing on the streets, the song's poignant lyric and sad melody recounted: "On the Hau Giang Ferry one evening, a street singer sings sadly / His sorrowful voice arouses the pains of past time / Leaning on crutches, his uneven steps drag along with the melody / His faded uniform invokes endless sadness / . . . Oh, passersby, have you any idea / that there are those who had quietly / sacrificed their youth on the battlefields / Now this is what is left of them."[48]

As a whole, the DVWRA's mission to help disabled RVNMF veterans and the concerts organized to raise funds on their behalf ensured that these marginalized figures do not fade into obscurity and that they are not forsaken. Through the concert, the battle scars of disabled RVNMF veterans are not symbols of shame. Rather, they are symbols of pride, heroism, and patriotism. The enthusiastic supporters of both diasporic Vietnamese veterans and civilians via their donations and participation in the Thank You concerts have affirmed both the value and significance of the DVWRA's mission as well as that of disabled RVNMF veterans. Reflecting on the successes of the concerts, one observer has noted, "This demonstrates that the camaraderie among RVNMF soldiers is genuine and not just something romanticized in songs. It also proves that Vietnamese refugees in different parts of the world are truly grateful and cognizant of their debt to RVNMF veterans, those who had sacrificed their lives so that the people on the home front can enjoy peace."[49] Such collective expressions of diasporic Vietnamese gratitude and acknowledgment of debt thus refute the negative characterizations of RVNMF veterans in dominant narratives expounded by both the Vietnamese communists and the American states. The gratitude expressed by diasporic Vietnamese toward disabled South Vietnamese veterans also acknowledges that the sacrifices of the latter were vital to the existence of South Vietnam and its citizens both during the war and later in diaspora.

Conclusion

In the four decades after the Second Indochina War ended, scholars have only begun to attend to the roles of the South Vietnamese government, soldiers, and civilians in that war and the postwar fates of these entities.[50] This essay contributes to this body of emerging scholarship by offering a glimpse into the complex postwar experiences of South Vietnamese veterans and civilians. It shows that transnational expressions of mutual assistance, camaraderie, and gratitude of diasporic Vietnamese toward disabled RVNMF veterans constitute powerful resistive and redemptive acts which remind us that those who had supported the RVN during the war had their own stakes in the conflict as well as in postconflict remembrances. In attending to the needs of disabled RVNMF veterans in Vietnam and acknowledging the sacrifices of those veterans, diasporic Vietnamese have shown that although the RVN lost the war, South Vietnamese moral sensibility and nationalist values continue to exist. The broken but not forsaken RVNMF veterans and the DVWRA and its Thank You concerts are all indicators of such existence.

NOTES

1. In this essay, I use the terms "RVNMF veterans" and "South Vietnamese veterans" interchangeably to mean those who had served in the three different branches of the Republic of Vietnam Military Forces—Army, Air Force, and Navy. I refrain from using the more popular but imprecise term, Army of the Republic of Vietnam (ARVN), to collectively refer to all South Vietnamese military forces since the ARVN depicts only one branch of the RVN armed forces.

2. This estimate is based on the South Vietnamese military wounded figure noted by the U.S. Department of Defense between 1960 and 1972 (411,501). See "South Vietnamese Casualties, Wounded, and Refugees, Civilian and Military—Department of Defense Table," Douglas Pike Collection: Unit 03—Statistical Data, Item No. 2234403005, accessed December 1, 2014, http://www.virtual.vietnam.ttu.edu/cgi-bin/starfetch.exe? QDxMBQ7NxdRCXQLaYvmGlfhN5GvElHVD3Xh@O.afAJguKlD8T7M1T7brxxbc MZAEHrY@@GIToR71UVwlZtWvnqjzFPr621cSsfJiD6.Wf3o/2234403005.pdf.

3. The Vietnamese communist government has deployed the derogatory terms *ngụy quân* [puppet army] and *ngụy quyền* [puppet government] during and after the war to discredit both the army and government of the Republic of Vietnam. Henceforth, all translations of Vietnamese sources into English are my own unless noted otherwise.

4. For examples, see: Hồ Tài Huệ Tâm, ed. *The Country of Memory: Remaking the Past in Late Socialist Vietnam* (Berkeley: University of California, 2001); Nguyễn-võ Thu-hương, "Forking Paths: How Shall We Mourn the Dead?," *Amerasia Journal* 31, no. 2 (2005): 157–175; and Yến Lê Espiritu's essay in this collection.

5. I thank Jeehyun Lim for encouraging me to foreground and elaborate on this argument.

6. For examples, see Yến Lê Espiritu, *Body Counts: The Vietnam War and Militarized Refuge(es)* (Berkeley: University of California Press, 2014); Thúy Võ Đặng, "Anticommunism as Cultural Praxis: South Vietnam, War, and Refugee Memories" (Ph.D. diss., University of California, San Diego, 2008); Nguyễn-võ, "Forking Paths"; Phương Nguyễn, "The People of the Fall: Refugee Nationalism in Little Saigon, 1975–2005" (Ph.D. diss., University of Southern California, 2009); Karin Aguilar-San Juan, *Little Saigons: Staying Vietnamese in America* (Minneapolis: University of Minnesota Press, 2009); and Evyn Le Espiritu, "Who Was Colonel Ho Ngoc Can? Theorizing the Relationship between History and Cultural Memory" (Senior thesis, Pomona College, 2013).

7. Nguyễn-võ, "Forking Paths," 159.

8. Nguyễn, "The People of the Fall," 2.

9. As Phương Nguyễn reminds us, "Refugee nationalism—the culture of the stateless exile—has to find ways to survive in foreign countries, thus inevitably changing over time in relation to the host society. Because of the narrative of rescue inherent to refugee identity, there exists a strong dependence on the goodwill of the new homeland to support the interests of the exile." Nguyễn, "The People of the Fall," 7.

10. Phạm Phong Dinh and Trần Việt Hải, "Cảm Ơn Anh—Người Thương Binh Việt Nam Cộng Hòa [Thank You, Disabled RVNMF Veteran]," July 2007, accessed May 12, 2014, http://camonanh.blogspot.com/2007/07/cm-n-anh-ngi-thng-binh-vnch.html.

11. Ibid.

12. Nguyễn Văn Huy and Phan Minh Hiển, eds., *Những Mảnh Đời Rách Nát* [*Tattered Lives*] (Paris, 1999), accessed May 3, 2014, http://www.dactrung.com/Bai-bv-1255-Nhung_ Manh_doi_Rach_Nat.aspx.

13. "Những thương phế binh sống sót sau cuộc chiến cảm thấy bơ vơ, không còn biết xoay sở làm sao để bảo toàn mạng sống. Chúng tôi có cảm tưởng như những đứa trẻ bị tật nguyền vừa mới sinh ra đã mồ côi cha mẹ. [. . .] Ở những vùng xa đô thành Sài Gòn, những người cộng sản [. . .] ra lệnh tịch thu những căn nhà cứu tế của phế binh do chính phủ Việt Nam Cộng Hòa cấp. Ở làng Mỹ Thới, anh em phế binh phải đi ra khỏi nhà trong vòng 24 tiếng đồng hồ. Vì không còn nơi nương tựa, nhiều người đã bỏ miền Tây lên Sài Gòn sống lang thang trên các đường phố, đêm ngủ ở các sân ga, bến xe, sạp chợ và những nghĩa địa bỏ hoang. . . Anh em chúng tôi đã gặp nhau, hỏi thăm và thông cảm lẫn nhau. Chúng tôi họp nhau thành những nhóm nhỏ và hàng ngày đến các đình chùa để lãnh nhang đi bán dạo khắp các phố phường. [. . .] nhiều anh phế binh bị tàn phế nặng, gia cảnh lại nghèo không đi bán nhang nổi, đã phải đi ăn xin." Nhất Chi, "Chương 9: Bạo Tàn và Nhân Nghĩa [Chapter 9: Cruelty and Humanity]" in *Những Mảnh Đời Rách Nát* [*Tattered Lives*], ed. Nguyễn Văn Huy and Phan Minh Hiển (Paris, 1999), accessed May 3, 2014, http://www.dactrung.com/NoiDung.aspx?m=bv&id=1264.

14. Among the volume's sixteen chapters, only one narrative is told from the perspective of a RVNMF veteran's widow; the others are firsthand accounts from disabled South Vietnamese veterans.

15. For more on diasporic Vietnamese philanthropic activities in Vietnam, see Mark Sidel, "Vietnamese-American Diaspora Philanthropy to Vietnam," May 2007, accessed August 1, 2014, http://www.tpi.org/sites/files/pdf/vietnam_diaspora_philanthropy_final.pdf. Examples of such charitable organizations in the United States include Hội Huynh Đệ Chi Binh [Military Brotherhood Association] and Tổng Hội Cựu Sinh Viên Sĩ Quan Thủ Đức-Nam Định [Union of Former Cadets of the Reserve Officers Schools in Thu Duc and Nam Dinh] in northern California; Hội H. O. Cứu Trợ Thương Phế Binh and Quả Phụ Việt Nam Cộng Hòa [Disabled Veterans and Widows Relief Association] in Southern California; and Hội Cứu Trợ Thương Phế Binh Quân Lực Việt Nam Cộng Hòa [Republic of Vietnam Military Forces Disabled Veterans Support Association] in Texas. Other similar associations outside of the United States include Hội Bạn Thương Phế Binh Việt Nam Cộng Hòa [Friends of Disabled Republic of Vietnam Veterans] in France and Hội Yểm Trợ Thương Phế Binh Việt Nam Cộng Hòa [Association to Support Disabled RVNMF Veterans] in Australia.

16. Among diasporic Vietnamese, this association is better known by its Vietnamese name: Hội H.O. Cứu Trợ Thương Phế Binh và Quả Phụ Việt Nam Cộng Hòa. In this essay, I use the English name of the association as it appears on the association's website.

17. This association's Vietnamese name is Hội Tương Trợ Cựu Tù Nhân Chính Trị.

18. More commonly known as the H.O. Program (or Humanitarian Operation), the Program for Former Reeducation Camp Detainees is an agreement between the United States and Vietnam that allowed eligible RVNMF veterans (those who were imprisoned for at least three years in Vietnamese communist reeducation camps) to immigrate with their dependents to the United States as political refugees. An estimated three hundred thousand people have resettled in the United States through this program.

19. Original Vietnamese: "Người đi trước lo cho người đi sau—Người đi sau không quên người ở lại." See Huy Phương, "Nhớ Ông Nguyễn Hậu và Hội Tương Trợ Cựu Tù Nhân Chính Trị" [Remembering Mr. Nguyen Hau and the Former Political Prisoner Mutual Assistance Organization], *Người Việt Daily News*, December 5, 2011, accessed July 12, 2014, http://www.nguoi-viet.com/absolutenm2/templates/viewarticlesNVO.aspx?articleid=141153&zoneid=3#.U9LG8LHCdJw.

20. Nguyễn Thị Hạnh Nhơn, Interview by Nancy Bui and Triều Giang Vietnamese American Heritage Foundation 500 Oral Histories, November 9, 2010, Transcript, 9–12. Vietnamese American Oral History Project, University of California, Irvine, accessed June 2, 2013, http://ucispace.lib.uci.edu/handle/10575/5243.

21. The Vietnamese government uses the label "*tổ chức phản động*" (reactionary organiza- tion) to classify a wide range of diasporic organizations including those that are vocally anticommunist, those that advocate for democracy and human rights in Vietnam, and those that reach out to former South Vietnamese military service per- sonnel. See Vi Anh, "Đền ơn đáp nghĩa thương phế binh" [Expressing Gratitude to Disabled Veterans], *Việt Báo Online*, August 10, 2010, accessed December 19, 2014, http://vietbao.com/a140410/den-on-dap-nghia-thuong-phe-binh.

22. Nguyễn Thị Hạnh Nhơn, "Interview," 10.

23. The DVWRA has seen its fair share of fraudulent applications sent from Vietnam. See Bắc Đẩu Võ Ý, "Viết về một người hết lòng với Thương Binh VNCH" [About an Individual So Dedicated to Disabled RVNMF Veterans], *Người Việt Daily News*, August 14, 2012, accessed June 23, 2014, http://www.nguoi-viet.com/absolutenm2/templates/ viewarticlesNVO.aspx?articleid=153376&zoneid=271#.VCoHEWOC-uk.

24. Also known in Vietnamese as Liên Hội Cựu Chiến Sĩ Việt Nam Cộng Hòa. See Nguyễn Thị Hạnh Nhơn, "Interview," 10.

25. Ibid.

26. The letter acknowledging donation sent by the DVWRA reads: "Vào ngày 6 tháng 1, 2011 tôi có nhận được $50 USD từ Hội Cứu Trợ TPB&QP/VNCH. Tôi rất mừng và hạnh phúc, không sao cầm được nước mắt. Vì quí hội đã quan tâm đến các anh em tử sĩ, những TPB hy sinh vì đất nước và những quả phụ còn lại sau chiến tranh. Số tiền mà quí hội đã gởi cho tôi, đã đủ cho tôi sinh hoạt và uống thuốc được 2 tháng." Quoted in Bắc Đẩu Võ Ý, "Viết về một người hết lòng với Thương Binh VNCH."

27. "Vì tình huynh đệ chi binh. Là lính, tình cảm ấy nặng lắm." See Linh Nguyễn, "Bà Hạnh Nhơn và tình chiến hữu của một nữ quân nhân" [Mrs. Hanh Nhon and the camarade- rie of a female soldier], April 21, 2011, accessed August 4, 2014, http://www.nguoi-viet .com/absolutenm2/templates/viewarticlesNVO.aspx?articleid=129902&zoneid=3# .VAkZP2PCdJw.

28. Nguyễn Thị Hạnh Nhơn, "Interview," 4.

29. It is important to note, as growing numbers of scholars have done in the recent decade, that although they converged at one point, the anticommunism that influ- enced South Vietnamese nationalism differs from the kind of bipolar logic and for- eign policies that guided U.S. Cold War involvement in Southeast Asia. Tuan Nguyen, for example, points out that urban South Vietnamese anticommunism was shaped by earlier differences about modernity and postcolonialism and was intensified through intra-Vietnamese experiences of the First Indochina War. Nu-Anh Tran asserts that South Vietnamese anticommunism was a core value that sustained Republican nationalism in South Vietnam. See, respectively, Tuan Nguyen, "Ideology in Urban South Vietnam, 1950–1975" (Ph.D. diss., University of Notre Dame, Indiana, 2013); and Nu-Anh Tran, "Contested Nationalism: Ethnic Identity and State Power in the Republic of Vietnam, 1954–1963," ISSI Fellow Working Paper, 2012, accessed December 15, 2014, https://escholarship.org/uc/item/1kb7z2vh.

30. For examples, see Mimi Thi Nguyen, *The Gift of Freedom: War, Debt, and Other Refugee Passages* (Durham, NC: Duke University Press, 2012); and Nguyễn, "The People of the Fall."

31. Popularly known in Vietnamese as *Đại Nhạc Hội Cảm Ơn Anh—Thương Phế Binh Việt Nam Cộng Hòa*.

32. Nguyễn Hiền, "Ban tổ chức Nhạc hôi "Cảm Ơn Anh" giúp 3,600 TPB Quả Phụ ở VN" [Concert to thank RVNMF veteran organizers help 3,600 disabled veterans and deceased veterans' widows in Vietnam], *Viet Bao Online*, August 23, 2006, accessed August 21, 2014, https://vietbao.com/a64709/btc-nhac-hoi-39-cam-on-anh-giup-3-600-tpb-qua-phu-o-vn.

33. Examples include thematic music productions such as "War and Peace" (2000), "Love Songs during Wartime" (2000), and "The Soldier" (2002). See Asia Entertainment, "About Us," accessed August 3, 2014, http://trungtamasia.com/index.php/about-us.

34. Nguyên Huy and Đỗ Dzũng, "Món nợ ân tình chưa trả hết [An Unpaid Debt of Love]," *Người Việt*, August 7, 2011, accessed August 12, 2014, http://www.nguoi-viet.com/absolutenm2/templates/viewarticlesNVO.aspx?articleid=135335&zoneid=177#.VEpThBbCdJw.

35. Ibid.

36. DVWRA, "Bản Tổng Kết Tài Chánh Đại Nhạc Hội 'Cảm Ơn Anh Kỳ 4' [4th Concert to Thank RVNMF Veteran Concert Financial Report]," August 2010, accessed August 4, 2014, http://camonanhtb.com/hypeblog/contact/advertisers/b%E1%BA%A3n-t%E1%BB%95ng-k%E1%BA%BFt-tai-chanh-dnh-4/.

37. Examples include Nguyên Huy and Đỗ Dzũng, "Món nợ ân tình chưa trả hết [An Unpaid Debt of Love]"; SBTN, "Đại Nhạc Hội Cảm Ơn Anh Kỳ 8 Thành Công với 520 USD Quyên Góp [8th Concert to Thank Disabled RVNMF Veterans Successful with 520 USD in Donation]," August 4, 2014, accessed August 21, 2014, http://www.sbtn.tv/vi/tin-c%E1%BB%99ng-%C4%91%E1%BB%93ng-h%E1%BA%A3i-ngo%E1%BA%A1i/%C4%91%E1%BA%A1i-nh%E1%BA%A1c-h%E1%BB%99i-c%C3%A1m-%C6%A1n-anh-k%E1%BB%B3-8-th%C3%A0nh-c%C3%B4ng-v%E1%BB%9Bi-520-ng%C3%A0n-usd-quy%C3%AAn-g%C3%B3p.html. Photos and videos of the various concerts can be found at the DVWRA's website: http://camonanhtb.com/publishers/ and at SBTN Official YouTube site: https://www.youtube.com/user/SBTNOfficial/videos.

38. "Sự tham dự đông đảo của tất cả quý vị không những thể hiện mối quan tâm đối với tình trạng anh em Thương Phế Binh tại quê nhà, mà còn tỏ lòng biết ơn đối với những chiến sĩ đã chiến đấu và hy sinh một phần thân thể để bảo vệ tự do cho Miền Nam Việt Nam một thời đáng kể. Đồng thời cũng chứng tỏ sức mạnh và tinh thần đoàn kết của người Việt tỵ nạn chúng ta trong sinh hoạt cộng đồng." See Ban Tổ Chức Đại Nhạc Hội Cảm Ơn Anh—Người Thương Binh VNCH Kỳ 7 Bắc Cali, "Thông Báo [Announcement]," May 1, 2013, accessed August 2, 2014, http://camonanhtb.com/.

39. I thank Jeehyun Lim also for pointing out this important connection.

40. Benedict Anderson, *Communities: Reflections on the Origins and Spread of Nationalism* (New York: Verso, 1982), 9.

41. SBTN Official, "Đại Nhạc Hội Cảm Ơn Anh Kỳ 8, Phần 1 [8th Concert to Thank Disabled RVNMF Veterans, Part 1]," Posted August 13, 2014, accessed August 21, 2014, https://www.youtube.com/watch?v=MCnhSmSmkiE, 00:06:48–00:08:30.

42. Ibid., 00:13:25–00:13:49.

43. Ibid., 00:40:40–00:54:07.

44. "Cờ bay trên thành phố Quảng Trị": "Cờ bay, cờ bay trên thành phố thân yêu vừa chiếm lại đêm qua bằng máu." Ibid.

45. "Ta là lính": "Ta muốn nói với bạn bè gần xa mình đang là lính / . . . Đất nước ta còn khốn khổ điêu linh / Ta vẫn còn rong đuổi chiến chinh / Lính yêu non sông hơn chính thân mình / Khi quê hương chưa có yên bình / Ta vẫn sống mãi cuộc đời nhà binh nên ta vẫn là lính / Người lính Việt Nam Cộng Hòa." See SBTN Official, "Đại Nhạc Hội Cảm Ơn Anh Kỳ 8, Phần 2 [Concert to Thank Disabled RVNMF Veterans, Part 2]," Posted August 13, 2014, accessed August 21, 2014, https://www.youtube.com/watch?v=vdlHfDKELig, 00:29:20–00:33:55.

46. "Giã từ vũ khí": "Rồi anh sẽ dựng căn nhà xưa / Rồi anh sẽ đón cha mẹ về / Rồi anh sẽ sang thăm nhà em / Với miếng cau với miếng trầu/ ta làm lại từ đầu." Ibid., 00:22:50–00:25:20.

47. "Hải ngoại không quên tình chiến sĩ / Đồng hương nhớ mãi nghĩa thương binh." See Vietnam Nation Council Television, "Cảm Ơn Anh Kỳ 8, Phần 3 [Thank You Disabled RVNMF Veterans, Part 3]," Posted August 4, 2014, accessed August 21, 2014, https://www.youtube.com/watch?v=EcMILI9tCVI, 00:00:01–00:01:00.

48. "Chiều qua phà Hậu Giang": "Chiều qua phà Hậu Giang tiếng ai hát dạo buồn thay / Tiếng ca sầu mênh mang như khơi niềm đau năm tháng xưa / Chân nạng gỗ thấp cao kéo lê đời theo dòng nhạc đưa / Manh chiến y phai màu khúc ca nào gợi sầu khôn nguôi / Hò . . . ơi nào ai biết chăng / Những kẻ ngày xưa đã âm thầm / Hiến dâng cả đời trai giữa sa trường / Giờ còn lại chi đây." See SBTN Official, "Đại Nhạc Hội Cảm Ơn Anh Kỳ 8, Phần 8 [Concert to Thank Disabled RVNMF Veterans, Part 8]," Posted August 13, 2014, accessed August 21, 2014, https://www.youtube.com/ watch?v=gnr8QrQinKM, 00:15:27–00:20:15.

49. "Điều đó minh chứng rõ rệt tình của lính VNCH là một thứ tình có thật không chỉ trong lời ca tiếng hát. Điều đó cũng chứng minh rằng cộng đồng người Việt tị nạn ở khắp nơi hết lòng tri ân trả nghĩa đến TPB/VNCH, những người đã hy sinh cho người dân được yên ấm ở hậu phương." See Nguyên Huy and Đỗ Dzũng, "Món nợ ân tình chưa trả hết [An Unpaid Debt of Love]."

50. For examples, see Edward Miller, *Misalliance: Ngo Dinh Diem, the United States, and the Fate of South Vietnam* (Cambridge, MA: Harvard University Press, 2013); Nu-Anh Tran, "Contested Identities: Nationalism in the Republic of Vietnam (RVN), 1954–1963" (Ph.D. diss., University of California, Berkeley, 2012); Tuong Vu and Edward Miller, "The Vietnam War as a Vietnamese War: Agency and Society in the Study of the Second Indochina War," *Journal of Vietnamese Studies* 4, no. 3 (Fall 2009): 1–16; and Tuan Hoang, "The Early South Vietnamese Critique of Communism," in *Dynamics of the Cold War in Asia: Ideology, Identity, and Culture*, ed. Tuong Vu and Wasana Wongsurawat, 17–32 (New York: Palgrave Macmillan, 2009).

3

What Is Vietnamese American Literature?

VIET THANH NGUYEN

Like others who came before them to America, the Vietnamese have sought to claim their voice in the land they have adopted or found themselves born into. Speaking up and speaking out are fundamental to the nature of the American character, or so Americans like to believe. The immigrant, the refugee, the exile, and the stranger who comes to these new shores may already have a voice, but it is usually a voice that speaks in a different language than the American lingua franca, English. While those who live in America speak many languages, America as a whole—the America that rules—prides itself on its monolingualism. The immigrant, the refugee, the exile, and the stranger can be heard in high volume only in the enclaves they carve out for themselves and in their own homes. But outside those ethnic walls, facing an indifferent America, the other clears her or his throat, hesitates, struggles to speak, and, most often, waits for the next generation raised or born on American soil to speak for them.

So it is with Vietnamese American literature, which also follows this ethnic cycle of silence to speech. In that way, Vietnamese American literature fulfills the most basic function of ethnic writing, to serve as proof that regardless of what has happened in the past to bring these others to America, they or their children have become accepted, no matter how grudgingly, by other Americans. This move from silence to speech is the form of ethnic literature in America, the box that contains all sorts of troubling content. After all, what brings these so-called ethnics to America is usually a difficult experience—more often than not, a terrible and traumatizing one. Stories of Old World poverty, starvation, persecution, and war are the most salient characteristics of the ethnic literature written by those who have come to America. For those forced to come to America, or for those whom America settled on, slavery, exploitation, and expropriation are the notable features, although poverty, starvation, persecution, and war are common as well.

The academic distinction one could draw between the form or the box, on the one hand, and its contents, on the other, is that the form is ethnic and the content is racial. The ethnic is what America can assimilate while the racial is what America cannot digest. In the American mythology, one ethnicity is the same, eventually, as any other ethnicity: the Irish, the Chinese, the Mexican, and even, eventually—hopefully—the black, who remains at the outer edge as the defining limit and the colored line of ethnic hope in America. But the racial continues to roil and disturb the American Dream and divert the American Way from its road of progress. If form is ethnic and content is racial, then the box one opens in the hopes of finding something savory may yet contain that which refuses to be consumed so easily.

The form of Vietnamese American literature has, over the fifty years or so of its existence, become increasingly aesthetically refined, but its content remains potentially, uneasily troublesome, even volatile. At the center of it all is the war. One does not need to name this war. There is only one war when it comes to Vietnamese Americans, both for them and for other Americans. This war is where race matters, the indelible stains of red blood and yellow skin, of the inequity of 58,000 or so American deaths versus 3 million Vietnamese deaths and more than 2 million Laotian and Cambodian deaths, if one were to count what happened in Laos and Cambodia as part of this war (as I do), and if one counts what happened in the years after the so-called end of the war as part of the war (which I do). The American misadventure in Indochina was the sequel to a French colonial calamity, and if there is no doubt that the French ideals of the *mission civilisatrice* (civilizing mission) masked the racist exploitation and domination of their Indochinese colonies, then what should one make of the nasty, brutal, and short American occupation?

Race mattered but also continues to cause disagreement among Americans and Vietnamese. One can draw another distinction here between the two faces of one country, the United States and America. If the United States is the reality, then America is the mythology. Even the Vietnamese who fought against the Americans drew this line, appealing to the hearts and minds of the American people to oppose the policies of the United States and its un-American war. As for Americans, they too—then and now—see this line, although what it means exactly is a subject of intense debate. Many Americans experienced and remember the war as an unjust, cruel one that betrayed the American character. Many other Americans see the war less as a betrayal and more as a failure of the American character, where Americans did not do bad in so much as they did not do enough good. But the number of Americans who think of the war as expressing a fundamental flaw in the American character, as being the culmination of a long history of racial domination and imperial expansion since the seventeenth century, is probably a minority.

Vietnamese American literature is thus published in a country that has no consensus on what to make of this war and what it says about the United States, America, or the American people. Was the war a mistake and a failure? Or a noble but flawed endeavor carried out with the best of intentions? Or even the naked throbbing of the heart of darkness? If Vietnamese American literature could avoid the war, then it could avoid this challenge of confronting the mythology and the contradictions of an America toward which Vietnamese Americans feel both gratitude (for being rescued and brought to America) and resentment (for being abandoned during the war). But the literature cannot avoid the war because the literature is inseparable from the Vietnamese American population itself, which exists only because of the war.

Insofar as any literature is ethnically defined, it finds itself bound up with the history of that ethnic group in America. Race again is key here. For those ethnic groups that have shed racial difference, such as the Irish, who were once seen as akin to black, or the Jews, once seen as beyond the pale, ethnicity becomes, as Mary Waters says, an option, a choice to be taken or not, a mask to be worn or not.[1] Those ethnic groups that remain marked or stained by race have a choice too, but they also have no choice about the fact that others thrust their ethnicity on them, thereby turning it into race. Thus, the choices made by racially defined people always run up against the hard expectations of other Americans. Bumping up against these expectations, the literatures of ethnic groups bound by race take on hard lines and defined shapes—the box of form assuming the name of the ethnic group, such as Vietnamese American literature. In contrast, Irish American literature or Jewish American literature exists but has considerably less traction, visibility, or durability. John O'Hara, Mary McCarthy, Saul Bellow, Philip Roth—they are American writers first and ethnic writers second, if at all.

For the racially straitjacketed ethnic writer, the necessity of speaking up, speaking out, and speaking for remains lashed to the name of the ethnic population. America will not let this ethnic other forget her or his racial past, as much as this person might want to and struggle to do so. For the Vietnamese, the realization of being committed to American memory in this way is expressed in the defiant and sad statement some have made that Vietnam is a country, not a war. If so, the boundary of Vietnamese American people and literature would seem to be historical, defined by an event that shocked the world. But that event would not have been so shocking if it was not for race, seeded by the orientalism and colonialism of the French, then elaborated on by the Americans. Free fire zones, body counts, the only good gook is a dead gook, the land as Indian country—all of this was the accumulation of American rhetoric, policy, and fantasy about a war that was always about the racial superiority Americans felt toward Asians. This is the history that Isabelle Thuy Pelaud speaks of when she characterizes Vietnamese American literature as being located between the poles of history and hybridity.[2] Hybridity is what America promises to the immigrant, the refugee, the exile, and the stranger, the dream of becoming something new and different on American soil. But history is the nightmare from which Americans cannot awaken, assuming the shape of this war, which Americans continue to evoke forty years after its end whenever the United States ventures again abroad.

Each racially defined ethnic group in the United States has its own notable instance of history for which it is remembered by Americans. Blacks have slavery and the plantation as well as the legacies they leave in blackness and the ghetto. Latinos have the ambiguous status of being of the Americas but not being white and North American, their lives supposedly marked by barrios and the border. Native Americans have genocide, dispossession, and the reservation. Vietnamese Americans have the war, or perhaps the war has them. These historical events are the hinges on the doors by which these racial and ethnic others can both enter America and are kept out of it. The American public, typically familiar with the history of these racial others in generic ways, expects them to speak about these events. These racial others know these expectations, and may certainly feel themselves obligated to speak on these events. Literature as art, education, and industry, all being a part of this American public, does not escape from the web of these expectations and reactions. So it is that racially marked ethnic writers discover that they are most easily heard when they speak about the historical events that defined their populations. At the same time this opening of one door for the writer, her or his entrée into the literary world, is the closing of other doors to other rooms not marked by history and by race.

It is not that these writers cannot speak of something else. It is simply that they are rewarded for speaking about their history and their race, and the history of their racial difference instills in (some of) them the desire to speak about their past. Nam Le captures this dynamic of racially marked ethnic silence and speech in his story "Love and Honor and Pity and Pride and Compassion and Sacrifice."[3] A writer named Nam is studying at the fabled University of Iowa writing program. He does not want to write about Vietnamese experiences, but when his father visits, he decides to write the ethnic story based on his father's harrowing life during the war. The father survived a massacre, and not just any massacre but the most horrible event of the war for the American conscience—the My Lai massacre. Nam knows he can make a reputation for himself out of this story, but when he proudly shows it to his father, his father responds by burning the manuscript.

Ironically, this was the story that first brought Nam Le to visibility. He accurately predicted that writing the ethnic story would make his name in the literary scene, and yet both he and his character Nam are troubled by the lure of history and race. Once the writer is hooked, he can be put on display as the ethnic writer of ethnic stories, but he might find it hard to get off that hook. Has he been rewarded with prizes, as Nam Le was for the book which eventually featured his story, *The Boat*? Or is the author himself the prize? If the literary world allows ethnic authors inside, even if only to one corner, then surely this proves that the larger world is also accommodating them and the people they speak of and speak for. This is perhaps the most troubling tension running throughout Vietnamese American literature. On the one hand, this literature speaks of the war and the terrible things that happened to the Vietnamese and that the Americans did in the name of supposedly defending freedom. On the other hand, the existence of Vietnamese American literature proves that America, in the end, is a beneficent country that ultimately fulfilled its promise of freedom.

Le's story hesitates about whether being an ethnic author writing ethnic stories is really liberatory. While a pigeonhole can be home, it is a very small one, no matter how nicely feathered. But the story questions more than the confinement of the author by the literary and larger world. The father's reaction illustrates another danger—that the ethnic author is not only speaking of and speaking for the ethnic population but may be betraying them, may be deserving not of the spotlight but the bonfire. The literary world hungers for secrets and calls on the ethnic author to work as tour guide, ambassador, translator, and insider, to deliver the exotic or mysterious unknown to an audience that wants to know. But the ethnic population may want to keep its secrets or may feel that its stories and its lives are being used or misused for the benefit of the author, who is a thief and a traitor. The tension between the ethnic writer and the ethnic population is also a legacy of race and subjugation, for the reason for the tension is an inequity of stories that compels the writer and the population to be at odds.[4]

White Americans experience this inequity from the side of the narratively wealthy. The airwaves and the pages are full of stories about Americans of the dominant class, discussed in all their glorious Whitmanian diversity and individuality. And when these Americans want to know about their others, they can often find the stories they want to consume, written to cater to their expectations. But this relationship does not work equally in reverse. If dominant Americans exist in an economy of narrative plenitude, their ethnic and racial others live in an economy of narrative scarcity. Many fewer stories exist about them, at least ones that migrate outside their enclaves and into the larger American life. Because of this, great pressure is put on those few stories and those few writers who emerge to stand on the American stage, a pressure exerted both by the larger American public and by the ethnic community.

These pressures shape ethnic literature in general and Vietnamese American literature in particular, providing them with some common generic features.

One feature is the sign of translation within the story, when the author or the narrator explains some feature of the ethnic community, such as its language, food, customs, or history. The insiders of an ethnic community do not need these things explained or translated to them because they already know. Thus, the existence of the explanation or the translation, as Sau-ling C. Wong argues in the case of Amy Tan, implies an audience for the story that needs to have something translated to them, the outsiders.[5] Sometimes the address to an outside audience is explicit, as in Le Ly Hayslip's *When Heaven and Earth Changed Places*, where she speaks directly at beginning and end to Americans, especially veterans, and absolves them of any guilt they may feel about the war.[6] Sometimes the address is implicit, as in Lan Cao's *The Lotus and the Storm*.[7] In one example early in the novel, the character Mai recounts an episode from the classic *The Tale of Kieu* and says that "every child in our country grows up with this story."[8] One does not explain such a story to one's countrymen, only to those who did not grow up with it. Authors accrue a certain kind of power here as those who can speak for the community, and this power can be rewarded greatly, with publication, sales, prizes, and accolades. But in an economy of narrative scarcity and inequity, the ones with the real power are the outsiders to the ethnic community who already have so many more stories and who are the real insiders: the readers, agents, editors, publishers, reviewers, and critics who demand that things be translated to them. This is the literary industry, and the ethnic writer is only its employee, a status no better or worse than those of all writers in America.

Another generic feature of ethnic literature that is related to translation is affirmation, which also has implicit and explicit versions. Now it is hardly a surprise that translators affirm those whom they serve. While translators serve both sides of the translating relationship, the most important side is the one that pays. How much, exactly, does the person asking for the translation really want to know? Does the translator ever soften the blow of the translation? Does the translator ever silence the side that does not pay? These questions haunt Vietnamese American literature, as they do all ethnic literature. Like ghosts, these questions are not usually visible. They lurk at the edges of the text, as shadows in the reader's peripheral vision. The most subtle and excellent kinds of affirmation are invisible, so ingrained that both the person affirming and the person affirmed simply take for granted what is being said.

This implicit version of affirmation in ethnic literature endorses the American Dream, the American Way, and American exceptionalism. But that endorsement takes place in stories that also criticize those mythological American ideas. Vietnamese American literature will often bring up the failure

of American ideals in the conduct of the war but at the same time affirm
American possibility for refugees from that war. The historian Phuong Nguyen
calls this tricky maneuver "refugee nationalism," where the refugee feels bound
to America in both resentment for being betrayed and gratitude for being
saved.[9] The contradiction of failure and idealism is part and parcel of the
ideological power of the American Dream, the American Way, and American
exceptionalism, all of which profess that while Americans may falter, they
always strive.

It is arguably the case that the majority of Vietnamese American literature
engages in endorsing this kind of American self-regard, partially through what
it depicts and more so through what it does not mention or criticize. Most of
Vietnamese American literature, having given up on revolution, does not offer
a radical threat to American mythology. Revolution was tainted for most
Vietnamese Americans by communism and its impact on their families and
their lost republic, and revolution is a difficult topic for them to raise in
America, which accepts only one revolution, its own. Revolution exists as the
horizon for most Vietnamese American literature, the line that cannot be met
or crossed, forbidden in the United States and foreclosed in Vietnam. What
remains is either a curdling resentment that continually returns to the bitter
past, which is more likely to be spoken of in the kind of literature that
Americans cannot read—written in Vietnamese—or the desire for some kind of
reconciliation and closure. Reconciliation and closure are foregrounded in the
endings of Hayslip and Cao's books and in the literature that is explicit in its
affirmation, as in Andrew Lam's collection of essays, *Perfume Dreams*.[10] Here the
Viet Kieu—the overseas Vietnamese—become the embodiment of American
possibility, a successful model minority who returns to Vietnam displaying the
kind of American wealth that the Vietnamese could have had except for
communism.

Vietnamese American literature's political position on the American landscape as a literature of translation and affirmation might best be described as
anticommunist liberalism. As Yến Lê Espiritu says, "Otherwise absent in U.S.
public discussions on Vietnam, Vietnamese refugees become most visible and
intelligible to Americans as anticommunist witnesses, testifying to the communist Vietnamese government's atrocities and failings."[11] In their literature
there is faith in America but also awareness that America needs encouragement and reminders to protect it from its worst instincts. There is sympathy for
others, bred from the experience of being others. There is an awareness of history, given that the authors are produced from a history they cannot forget.
There is an investment in the individual, in education, in free speech, and in
the marketplace. All of these liberal gestures take place against the backdrop of
anticommunism, not of the rabid, demagogic kind found on the streets of Little

Saigon but the reasonable, intellectual kind that allows for conversation with former enemies and for returns to the homeland.

The movement from the homeland to the adopted land, as refugees and exiles, and then the return, marks much of the literature. In academic terms, the literature is "diasporic," "transnational," and "transpacific," as in Andrew X. Pham's *Catfish and Mandala*, about a Viet Kieu who returns to the homeland during the early, difficult years of economic reform in the 1990s, or Monique Truong's *The Book of Salt*, which follows the story of a young peasant in French colonial Vietnam who migrates to France to become the cook for Gertrude Stein and Alice B. Toklas.[12] Or the literature could be set in ethnic enclaves like Little Saigon, itself a diasporic, transnational trading post no matter where it is located, as is the case with Aimee Phan's *We Should Never Meet*, about orphans who have no choice in being moved to America.[13] The literature overall is marked by the stamp that says to America "we are here because you were there."

This is a powerful stamp, but while its message is not to be disregarded, its implications can be contained. The encouragement and the adoption of an anticommunist liberalism is one way to manage the disruptive possibilities expressed in "we are here because you were there." Another mode of management is education, especially higher education, the invisible infrastructure of Vietnamese American literature. Throughout the fifty or so years of the literature in English, there is only one author who is not college educated or from the upper classes, Le Ly Hayslip. Her two memoirs are also cowritten, which leaves some doubt as to the "literary" quality of her work. But outside of oral histories, hers is also the only major work, besides *The Book of Salt*, that focuses mainly on the life of a peasant. Most of the literature deals with those from the political, merchant, military, mandarin, elite, or middle classes. All of these positions imply some kind of educational background in Vietnam for the protagonists or their parents. This shapes the concerns of the protagonists, their worldviews and the settings of their books, and their amenability to an anticommunist liberalism once they have moved to the United States (or once the American-born or -raised protagonists come to consciousness). But given that the overwhelming majority of the Vietnamese are peasants, and that the war was fought ostensibly to liberate and protect them, it is ironic that almost all of the literature focuses on the classes above them.

Vietnamese American literature in English, produced mostly by the 1.5 or second generation in the United States, magnifies the underlying educational influence. While Vietnamese Americans are socioeconomically diverse, Vietnamese American authors are not, at least in terms of their education. This is especially evident with the wave of Vietnamese American literature that commences in the 1990s with *Catfish and Mandala* and that gained momentum with *The Book of Salt* in 2003 and le thi diem thuy's *The Gangster We Are All Looking For* in 2004.[14] These works appeared in the decade or so after Hayslip's two memoirs, her second being *Child of War, Woman of Peace* in 1993.[15] Hayslip was the most visible Vietnamese American author until the arrival of this younger generation, who, unlike her, could clearly claim to be authors as auteurs. They won major prizes and received wide recognition from the literary industry, their works considered "literary" in a way that Hayslip's was not. While none of these authors had a master of fine arts in creative writing, more and more of the new authors emerging would, such as Aimee Phan and Nam Le. The impact of college and creative writing education on writers is hard to measure and quantify, but, as Mark McGurl argues, the master of fine arts program has helped to shape twentieth-century American literature. Vietnamese American literature is no exception, for it is the expression not of Vietnamese Americans in general, but of their most educated class.[16]

Class markers are sometimes evident in what the literature does not deal with (the peasantry) as well as in an array of stylistic features that mark the anxiety of being the educated elite of a racial minority. Translation and affirmation, in various degrees, are some of those features. But the most significant or explicit anxiety has to do with voice. The college-educated writer, and especially the American-raised one, is aware of her or his status as the person who has the voice to speak of and speak for Vietnamese or Vietnamese Americans. This is both a responsibility and a burden, as Monique Truong shows in her essay on "Vietnamese American Literature."[17] The greatest of responsibilities and burdens is the need for Vietnamese American authors to speak for Vietnamese Americans. This call on Truong's part takes place against two notable acts of speaking of and for Vietnamese Americans. In 1993 Robert Olen Butler won the Pulitzer Prize for his collection of short stories written from the perspective of Vietnamese Americans, *A Good Scent from a Strange Mountain*.[18] Earlier in 1986 Wendy Wilder Larsen had cowritten a collection of poetry with Tran Thi Nga, *Shallow Graves: Two Women and Vietnam*.[19] For Truong, both works are problematic. Butler's is either a deep act of empathy or a kind of ventriloquism that takes on Vietnamese voices. The acclaim given to his work raises the issue of whether American audiences would rather hear an American speaking for the Vietnamese rather than the Vietnamese themselves (or whether Vietnamese American writers simply were not good enough at the time to interest American audiences). In Larsen's case, Truong objects to the collaboration that gives greater credence to Larsen's voice. In the remarkable image that Larsen deploys, Nga is the inert violin and Larsen is the active bow.

Against these American literary acts that appropriate or subordinate Vietnamese voices, Truong calls for a Vietnamese American literature written by Vietnamese Americans. This urge for self-representation and self-determination is deeply embedded in ethnic literature in general. If "ethnic" means anything in relation to literature, it is the sign of the ethnic author speaking of and for the ethnic population. But the issues Truong raises in terms of appropriation and subordination are important not just for outsiders but for insiders as well. The ethnic author as an insider is not immune to the charges or the dangers of appropriation and subordination, of the risks found in speaking for and speaking of others, even the others of one's own community. Truong's *The Book of Salt* both dramatizes these risks and embodies them. In the novel, the peasant cook for Stein and Toklas—Binh—discovers that Stein has secretly written about him. He has been spoken for and about, and in revenge he steals the book. But in depicting these acts of mutual theft, Truong also depends on speaking for and speaking of Binh. The relationship of author to fictional character here parallels the relationship of author to a real community. Does Truong—and any other Vietnamese American author—also run the risk of ventriloquizing through the creation of fictional characters that are also rather distant to them? If Larsen's bow plays on Nga's violin, then does Truong do the same to Binh?

No, because Nga is a real person and Binh is a character of Truong's imagination. She has created both the bow and the violin. But the risks in speaking for and of others are not erased because the other is fictional. In the case of ethnic literature, the "ethnic" label collapses the distinction between ethnic author and ethnic character so that an ethnic author using ethnic characters somehow appears more "authentic" than a non-ethnic author doing the same. There is good reason to think that an ethnic author would be more sensitive in depicting ethnic characters and that ethnic authors should have the opportunity to do so. In an economy of narrative scarcity where literary representation cannot be separated from larger social issues of equity and justice, ethnic authors should have equal opportunity to represent both themselves and ethnic characters. But the drawbacks to this necessary move are twofold. One is the reinforcement of authenticity, the belief that an author who shares a background with those whom he or she represents will tell a more truthful story. This claim is doubtful aesthetically. If Butler's short stories had appeared with a Vietnamese American author's name on them, few would question their authenticity. The stories are at least as good as what many Vietnamese American authors have written, which is also to say that if one finds them problematic in how they represent the Vietnamese, then some Vietnamese American literature is guilty of the same problem. Nevertheless, the author's identity and body still has relevance because art exists in a social world where readers and writers bring prejudices and injustices to the act of reading. Thus, it is necessary for ethnic authors to speak for and of ethnic characters, although they must do so aware of the risks of claiming an authenticity that is fictional at best and illusory at worst. But since race is forced on ethnic authors, having ethnic authors is necessary to address the preexisting condition of race.

The other drawback to ethnic authorship concerns betrayal, even for characters in a fictional world. In that world, Binh steals the book written about him, and Nam's father burns his story. They have been played on, as Larsen plays on Nga in real life, and the authors stage those feelings of resentment. What authors risk, both in relationship to their characters and their communities, is exploiting those people through telling their stories. Betrayal is hence an omnipresent theme in Vietnamese American literature, but not only for these formal and racial reasons. Betrayal is a part of Vietnamese history as well, particularly in the era of war and revolution, when politics encouraged partisans to betray each other, or to betray family members of different political stripes, or to betray certain sides or even the nation.

As Lan Duong says, however, betrayal in Vietnamese culture is the other side of collaboration. On the one hand, Duong argues, collaboration is fundamental to artistic work and to building the nation. On the other hand, collaboration risks being seen as an act of treachery, of working with foreigners to betray the nation.[20] Likewise, the depiction of others by authors is an act of collaboration—explicitly so when those are "real" others, people like Nga and implicitly so when they are fictional others, as in the cases of Truong and Le. Their fiction shows what can happen when the others who are spoken for do not desire this collaboration.

Throughout Vietnamese American literature, however, collaboration's positive aspect is also present. Nguyen Qui Duc wrote his memoir *Where the Ashes Are* very much as a story about his father, in a sense turning a self-oriented genre into one about others, deploying his father as a character in the way Truong and Le do.[21] Andrew X. Pham in *The Eaves of Heaven* goes a step further and writes that book in his father's voice, depicting a kind of man rarely seen in American literature, the Southern Vietnamese soldier of a lost regime.[22] He and his father would collaborate on the translation of Dang Thuy Tram's diary, *Last Night I Dreamed of Peace*, the personal document left behind by an idealistic Northern Vietnamese military doctor before American troops killed her.[23] Even the self can be the site of collaboration, as Lan Cao shows in *The Lotus and the Storm*. One of the central characters has multiple personalities produced by terrible trauma, but even they eventually move from conflict to cooperation.

The ambivalence between collaboration and betrayal as strong themes in Vietnamese American literature are signs of ambivalence in the literature itself. Vietnamese American literature can be seen as collaborative in its relationship to American culture, engaged in tactics of translation and affirmation, fulfilling a role it shares with ethnic literature in general: that of America's loyal opposition. As such, the literature can bring up the troublesome past of war and even the difficult present of racial inequality so long as it also promises or hopes for reconciliation and refuge. But scattered throughout the literature of loyal opposition are signs of betrayal, of criticisms so serious that they threaten American culture and the ways that Americans like to see themselves. Sometimes the impulses toward collaboration and betrayal are found in the same works, like *The Lotus and the Storm*, which ends on notes of reconciliation between Vietnamese and Americans but which also indicts America for not learning from its war with Vietnam as it fights new wars in the Middle East. Sometimes the betrayal is hinted at obliquely, through ruptures where the past cannot be forgotten, as in G. B. Tran's *Vietnamerica*, where the frenetic, color-saturated narrative ends in the blackness of an airplane hold as the cargo doors shut on frightened refugees fleeing the fall of Saigon.[24] Even though *Vietnamerica*'s timeline continues in the plot of the book, the book's ending on this note suggests that the loss of their nation and their betrayal by Americans will always entrap Vietnamese refugees.

So war returns as the sign of race—a war that would not have been fought except for race as a central factor in the American imagination. Vietnamese American literature that avoids a direct confrontation with the war is growing slowly, such as might be found in the writing of Bich Minh Nguyen, but even here the literature's refusal to discuss the war has to be seen in light of the war itself.[25] Just as it is impossible for an ethnic author to refuse to talk about race without having that decision seen in the light of race, so it is with the war. The traces of war and race continue to haunt Vietnamese American literature, as le thi diem thuy's *The Gangster We Are All Looking For* shows. In this book the narrator survives the experience of fleeing by boat from Vietnam, but her brother does not. His ghost shadows her and becomes one sign of the past that will not go away. The author's postscript to the paperback edition makes that haunting even more explicit when she recounts how her name is not her own but her drowned sister's, transferred to her by her father when she entered America.

The ghost that continues to tie Vietnam to America must be dealt with if Vietnamese American literature is to be more than an ethnic literature that ultimately affirms America. Perhaps not surprisingly, the literary works that eschew affirmation and most directly confront the limits of America are the ones that appear from small presses rather than the major trade houses. Linh Dinh's *Love Like Hate* is raw, sometimes rough, almost always impolite, but it depicts, satirizes, and criticizes both Vietnam and America unrelentingly. "Saigon is often squalid but it is never desolate," he writes. "Vietnam is a disaster, agreed, but it is a socialized disaster, whereas America is—for many people, natives or not—a solitary nightmare."[26] This double-edged writing cuts both ways in order to slice open the ethnic box, and it does so by not affirming either of the nations or their nationalisms. A more radical Vietnamese American literature that struggles to break out of the ethnic box must confront the way history, ideology, and nationalism has formed it in at least two countries.

Such a literature can also turn with great passion and righteous indignation to the American landscapes that have been populated by refugees and ghosts and then forgotten. This is what the poet Bao Phi does in *Sông I Sing*, mixing lyricism with obscenity because war and racism are obscene. In his poetic "refugeography," the refugee in America is produced by the war and is its constant, uncomfortable reminder to those who would rather forget it.[27] Many refugees also try to forget, turning themselves into immigrants and sealing over their refugee past in an effort to soothe their own feelings and those of the Americans around them. Unlike these forgetful refugees and Americans, Bao Phi both brings up the war-torn past and connects it to the racially troubled present. Of Vietnamese refugees rendered homeless once again by Hurricane Katrina, he writes, "It's like this country only allows us one grief at a time. Your people, you had that war thing. That's all you get. Shut. The fuck. Up."[28] He directs grief and rage both outward toward America and inward toward those people of color who have absorbed the racism directed at them and internalized it. What happens, he asks,

> When you can no longer tell
> if you're liberating yourself through expression
> or selling your oppression.[29]

This is the challenge that can be leveled at any ethnic author in America.

NOTES

1. Mary C. Waters, *Ethnic Options: Choosing Identities in America* (Berkeley: University of California Press, 1990).

2. Isabelle Thuy Pelaud, *This Is All I Choose to Tell: History and Hybridity in Vietnamese American Literature* (Philadelphia: Temple University Press, 2011).

3. Nam Le, *The Boat* (New York: Alfred A. Knopf, 2008).

4. On betrayal and ethnic literature, see Leslie Bow, *Betrayal and Other Acts of Subversion: Feminism, Sexual Politics, Asian American Women's Literature* (Princeton, N.J.: Princeton University Press, 2001); and Crystal Parikh, *An Ethics of Betrayal: The Politics of Otherness in Emergent U.S. Literature and Culture* (New York: Fordham University Press, 2009).

5. Sau-ling Cynthia Wong, "'Sugar Sisterhood': Situating the Amy Tan Phenomenon," in *The Ethnic Canon: Histories, Institutions, and Interventions*, ed. David Palumbo-Liu (Minneapolis: University of Minneapolis Press, 1995), 174–210.

6. Le Ly Hayslip, with James Wurts, *When Heaven and Earth Changed Places* (New York: Doubleday, 1989).

7. Lan Cao, *The Lotus and the Storm* (New York: Viking, 2014), e-book version.

8. Ibid., location 80 of 6082, e-book version.

9. Phuong Nguyen, "The People of the Fall: Refugee Nationalism in Little Saigon, 1975–2005" (PhD diss., University of Southern California, 2009).

10. Andrew Lam, *Perfume Dreams: Reflections on the Vietnamese Diaspora* (Berkeley, Calif.: Heyday Books, 2005).

11. Yến Lê Espiritu, *Body Counts: The Vietnam War and Militarized Refugees* (Berkeley: University of California Press, 2014), 101.

12. Andrew X. Pham, *Catfish and Mandala: A Two-Wheeled Voyage through the Landscape and Memory of Vietnam* (New York: Picador, 2000); and Monique Truong, *The Book of Salt* (New York: Houghton Mifflin Harcourt, 2003).

13. Aimee Phan, *We Should Never Meet* (New York: Picador, 2005).

14. le thi diem thuy, *The Gangster We Are All Looking For* (New York: Anchor Books, 2004).

15. Le Ly Hayslip, with James Hayslip, *Child of War, Woman of Peace* (New York: Doubleday, 1993).

16. Mark McGurl, *The Program Era: Postwar Fiction and the Rise of Creative Writing* (Cambridge, Mass.: Harvard University Press, 2011).

17. Monique T. D. Truong, "Vietnamese American Literature," in *An Interethnic Companion to Asian American Literature*, ed. King-Kok Cheung, 219–246 (New York: Cambridge University Press, 1997).

18. Robert Olen Butler, *A Good Scent from a Strange Mountain* (New York: Henry Holt, 1992).

19. Wendy Wilder Larsen and Tran Thi Nga, *Shallow Graves: Two Women and Vietnam* (New York: Random House, 1986).

20. Lan Duong, *Treacherous Subjects: Gender, Culture, and Trans-Vietnamese Feminism* (Philadelphia: Temple University Press, 2012), 1–22.

21. Nguyen Qui Duc, *Where the Ashes Are* (Reading, Mass.: Addison-Wesley, 1994).

22. Andrew Pham, *The Eaves of Heaven* (New York: Broadway Books, 2009).

23. Dang Thuy Tram, *Last Night I Dreamed of Peace* (New York: Harmony Books, 2007).

24. G. B. Tran, *Vietnamerica: A Family's Journey* (New York: Villard, 2011).

25. Bich Minh Nguyen, *Pioneer Girl* (New York: Viking, 2014).

26. Linh Dinh, *Love Like Hate* (New York: Seven Stories Press, 2010), location 113, e-book version.

27. Bao Phi, *Sông I Sing* (Minneapolis: Coffee House Press, 2011), 9.

28. Ibid., 39.

29. Ibid., 78.

4

Việt Nam and the Diaspora

Absence, Presence, and the Archive

LAN DUONG

During my last days of doing research at the Film Institute (Viện Phim) in Hà Nội, I watched *Battle at Moc Hoa* (1945) on a small editing bay.[1] Made by one of Việt Nam's most esteemed directors, Mai Lộc, the film is one of the few films to survive from the colonial period. Many film reels in Việt Nam were destroyed or damaged during the country's long war with the French, Japanese, and Americans in the second half of the twentieth century. While similar to other films about the anticolonial resistance, Lộc's film was especially compelling because of the state of the film it was in: framed between two whirring reels as I had screened it, *Battle at Moc Hoa* was without sound, the images blurry and unclear. Situated against the commercial streets that were just outside the archive's doors, the film's imagery of revolution seemed archaic and "out of joint," to use Jacques Derrida's term. Exquisitely shot and yet strangely spectral, *Battle at Moc Hoa* is a moving composite of light and dark, appearing ghostly in its details of another time of war, another era of sacrifice. Watching *Battle at Moc Hoa* in this way was a doubled sign of the poor material conditions under which the film was made in the past and screened in the present. This moment was symbolic of how the Vietnamese film archive is a jarring experience of both absence and presence.

I begin with these details about Việt Nam's Film Institute to delineate the ways that the archive—the country's most important cinematic trove—serves as a technology of state power in the postsocialist era and is perforated by absence. For the archive attempts to make legible the country's history through its collection of films, catalogues, journals, and ephemera, repressing texts that run counter to its narrative about nationhood, sacrifice, and revolution. It is at once rich and full of elisions. Southern Vietnamese films produced during the Second Indochinese War; diasporic Vietnamese films about the refugee or reeducation experience of the four million overseas Vietnamese, many of whom fled the revolutionary regime; and the large number of colonial films produced before the founding of the Democratic Republic of Việt Nam in 1945 are missing or not included its collection. Some of these films instead circulate on the Internet, are sold in DVD stores in Vietnamese community enclaves, or are screened at local film festivals in the United States. Compounding the Film Institute's omissions is a central problem: film preservation remains a developing art in the country and a vastly underfunded state effort. These uneven developments in the country's cultural infrastructure are symptomatic of contemporary state politics; hobbled by a long history of war, Việt Nam is impoverished but also rapidly developing in its embrace of global capitalism. Việt Nam has become a major player in the Southeast Asian region in the wake of major developments: the country's implementation of market reforms in 1986 and World Trade Organization membership in 2004.

Even as the country's cultural institutions lack funding and organizational structure, the state nonetheless has the ability and authority to develop its archives as one way to commemorate the past and grow its futurity. On this point, I posit that what counters the statist impulse to document the past in perpetuity is a diasporic film archive. Virtual, decentralized, and provisional, this archive is vital to the remembrance of "South Việt Nam." Uploaded by film enthusiasts or digitized by production companies and sold at market, images of a prewar Saigon constitute a tenuous archive and contradict the state's gestures to erase the "disappeared history" of the southern Vietnamese.[2] This history begins with the formation of a Vietnamese diaspora following the war's end in 1975 when millions of Vietnamese and ethnic Chinese fled Việt Nam in fear of communist persecution. In response to those who left the country in staggered numbers from the 1970s to the late 1980s, the state denounced this group as "traitors" for having collaborated with the United States during the war and abandoning the country. Forty years since the "reunification" of the country, the state now embraces the return of diasporic Vietnamese as investors, artists, and tourists, having recently promulgated a series of legislation that seek to welcome the diaspora back into the fold of the nation. At the same time, the state dismisses the history of refugees and reeducation camp prisoners as well as a South Vietnamese culture that are central aspects of this community and its politics. Such a disavowal manifests itself in the space of the archive.

This study looks at state and diasporic archives in tandem since they embody what Françoise Lionnet and Shu-mei Shih term "minor transnationalisms," or that which scores the relations of power between minority cultures in an era of global capital.[3] Here the concept of a "minor transnationalism" names the vexed historical relations between Việt Nam and the diaspora as an enduring contest of power about representation. More specifically, a "minor transnationalism" pinpoints the terrain constituting the transnational production and distribution of Vietnamese movies—in particular, Vietnamese war films. My argument is premised on the fact that Vietnamese and diasporic cinemas cannot compete with the spectacular ways that major countries like the United States and France have represented the wars that pockmark the country's history and its relations with its foreign others. The country is a site of trauma and recovery for those in the West, circulating and recirculating as such in the Global North.

In contrast, few Vietnamese films and images about the war are discussed or disseminated outside of Việt Nam and the diaspora. Even within these contexts, however, the terms of representation are problematic; the state has banned some diasporic films while some in the diaspora have treated with suspicion films made in collaboration with the government. While the Vietnamese state has revamped its film industry policies to include the work of diasporic filmmakers, it has also banned some of the diaspora's key filmic texts from circulating in the country. For Vietnamese diasporic filmmakers, they wield some cultural and financial capital in producing films in Việt Nam, but they must also work within the constraints of the state's cultural politics. Foregrounding the shifting postwar relations of power between Việt Nam and the diaspora, I investigate how a minor transnationalism inflects the ways that two films—*Land of Sorrows* (1971) and *Journey from the Fall* (2007)—are received in the Vietnamese American community.[4] While made in different time periods, the films exemplify state practices of regulating and censuring films in the past and present moment. Tracking the films' reception and their circulations, I gesture toward an archive formulated by new media technologies and shaped by local practices of commemoration, an archive that stands outside of the state's domain of control.

Besides speaking to the archive, another point of this essay is to demonstrate that images of war by the Vietnamese are greatly understudied within Euro-American film scholarship. Addressing these elisions in the production of knowledge about Việt Nam and its cinema, my essay highlights issues of memory, power, and capital underpinning the making and study of Vietnamese films. I underscore especially the formations of what I call the "archives of memory" as transnational sites that symbolize both absence and presence. On the one hand, the Film Institute in the country's capital represents state hegemony and its exercise of power in material form. On the other, an archive of memory can also be virtual, shared and screened by multiple users across transnational sites in the digital age. I underscore these differences between the archives to outline a different topography of the country, one that stands in contrast to the "Vietnam" that has been traditionally configured in the Global North. In the Western filmic archive, "Vietnam" functions as an enduring symbol of war and suffering. Mapping the nodes of production and reception of films across Việt Nam and the diaspora, I show how archives of memory are buttressed by power and a deep investment—one that is both affective and material—in the cinematic past and more specifically, in representations of war. To reveal how these archival sites operate as technologies of memory is to view Việt Nam anew. Contrary to the notion that Việt Nam remains a leftist fantasy of revolution and site of trauma, the country has tried to redefine the bounds of the nation through cinema and culture, with the archive symbolizing this gesture of domination within a minor key.

Archives of Memory

In thinking about the archives put forth by the state and by the diaspora, I turn to theorists who have framed the archive as both a symbol of (neo)colonial power and the location of an alternative archive. Investigating the archive-as-subject, Ann Laura Stoler argues that scholars must regard the archive not as an "extractive enterprise" but an ethnographic one. As she notes, colonial archives are not "merely sites of knowledge retrieval but of knowledge production as monuments of states as well as sites of state ethnography."[5] Vesting the archive with the authority to organize order, Jacques Derrida discusses the "institution-alization of the archival event" and the way in which archival fever—the *mal d'archive* or the *archive du mal*—bespeaks the state's feverish need to collect the past as well as the scholar's desire to recollect it.[6] Derrida reminds us of the necessity of viewing the archive as an institutional and juridical space, one that simultaneously houses the state's search for origin narratives and anticipates the future and future publics.[7] Temporality, therefore, constitutes a central part of the archive, whereupon the making and preservation of time becomes embedded in the project of modernity itself. Film scholar Mary Ann Doane emphasizes this point when she states, "what is at stake in modernity is not just a logic of mobility, circulation, and accelerated exchange but also a logic of the archive and especially the archivability of time."[8]

The Vietnamese state operates on an analogous "logic of the archive." Sited in Hà Nội (the country's other, smaller film archive is in Hồ Chí Minh City), the state's premier film archive showcases canonical works made by the country's most notable filmmakers from its inception to the present day. In their video library, which is open throughout the day and fairly accessible, a visitor can screen films on site using the institute's computers. On the second floor of the archive a reading library houses film journals and cinema books on a variety of different national cinemas. Most of these texts deal with Vietnamese cinema and its nationalist formations, however. In total, the Film Institute marginalizes a whole swath of filmic narratives about the others of communist Việt Nam. As a state-run archive that tries to guard itself against the intrusions of other histories, this space is indeed haunted by a "silenc[ing of] the past," to use Michel-Rolph Trouillet's words, an act that has implications for the future.[9] If situated within the *longue durée*, Vietnamese film historiography remains constricted for both present and future Vietnamese film scholars and students.

Despite its ambitions to archive time, however, the Film Institute is remarkably deficient in other areas. As a frequent visitor to this space for the past ten years, I have witnessed its structural improvements but have noted that it still lacks the kinds of monies that would sustain the project of film preservation over time. The Film Institute is burdened by an excessive bureaucracy and disorganized in terms of its display of materials and resources. While armed with a degree of power to narrate history via its curation of films, the Film Institute's "archival fever" seems limited in scope and degree. Thus, while the country's film archives are important sites of inquiry into film because these are the only places in the world that houses hundreds of Vietnamese films, they also symbolize the terrific changes within which the country is caught. In fundamental ways, such archival sites are very different from the colonial archives that theorists like Stoler and Derrida discuss and critique.

The diasporic archive I discuss here also stands in stark contrast from either the colonial archive or the Vietnamese state archive because of its ephemerality and the use of technology that drives it. This virtual archive hinges on contingency and transiency because the sites upon which the films appear can easily be shut down due to international copyright laws. The films themselves are not copyright protected either. Moreover, they do not officially circulate in Việt Nam because of an implicit state ban on films from this era and region. And yet the fact that these films can be accessible via the Internet speaks to the market and affective desires that underpin their circulation and redistribution.

Some of the most intriguing images and films of South Việt Nam are archived on the Internet. Some of these films have been sold on the market and repackaged as "pre-1975" films. The films are part of a collection of films that were made in the South during the American War, or the Vietnam War. Funded by private investors, they make up what I call a "forgotten cinema" and encompass a variety of genres like the melodrama, war film, and the comedy, genre films that were generally not made by filmmakers in the North in most of the nation's official film history. Such works are uploaded and shared among film enthusiasts on YouTube. On a number of Vietnamese film sites one can stream the films for free or a small fee. Most conspicuously, they are sold in Vietnamese American DVD stores in cities like San Jose and Garden Grove, California, having been redigitized by major Vietnamese American production companies like Thúy Nga and Asia. "Pre-1975" films are remarketed for a niche market today, as powerhouse production companies such as these commodify a diasporic, nostalgic love for the past. DVD covers proclaim that the films are "in color" and were made "before 1975," clearly drawing on how the year "1975" signifies for those in the diaspora the time that precipitated the exodus of many Vietnamese from South Việt Nam. Underpinned by these marketing strategies, the films' packaging promises the diasporic viewer a cinematic return to a colorful, unforgettable past.

Archived on the Internet and sold in community enclaves, these filmic texts are founded on nostalgia and desire and form an "alternative archive" to the state's own. As Mike Featherstone argues, alternative archives are significant because they shelter the "active aspirations for the reworking of desires and memories and the making of cultural identities" within the larger context of hegemonic power.[10] On the question of archive and affect, Ann Cvetkovich further contends that the making of an "archive of feelings" functions as a "[repository] of feelings and emotions, encoded not only in content but in practices that surround their production and reception."[11] Driven by market and affective desires, the user's makeshift and often illegal practice of digitizing and sharing Vietnamese films countermands how an official film archive operates in Việt Nam. These practices also counteract the Vietnamese state's own monumental memorializations of war and its gestures to preserve war memories in the face of globalization and tourism. In the years following the Second Indochinese War, the state has invested a great deal of money erecting monuments, museums, displays, cemeteries, and other war sites to commemorate the war dead and to generate tourism for domestic and international visitors.[12]

Just as significantly, an Internet-accessible diasporic archive of memory also contradicts the U.S. narrative about the loss of "Vietnam," which has so dominated Vietnam War discourse. File sharing and film uploading allow for a redistribution of a particular South Vietnamese affect about the war, one that hinges on nationalist feeling and melancholic commemoration of the war. Such feelings are often dismissed in dominant U.S. culture. Investigating refugee memorial sites on the Internet in this volume's essay and in her book *Body Counts*, Yến Lê Espiritu discusses the kinds of "new electronic media that are shaping remembrance practices."[13] Situating these practices against a U.S. national culture that denies the South Vietnamese American experience, Espiritu argues that the "public display of South Vietnam's war dead on the Internet is itself an instance of an oppositional political imaginary at work, an act of sedition" in which there is a collapse in the distinction between public and private: a private personal grief becomes part of a collective loss.[14] Espiritu looks at how the Internet has changed the terms of representation for marginalized groups within the United States as they relate to the Vietnam War.[15] Espiritu's arguments align with my claims about the affective circulation of diasporic Vietnamese films appearing on the Internet since this kind of filmic imagery—especially those that visualize for contemporary viewers the space and time before Sài Gòn's "fall"—work along similar registers of pleasure, nostalgia, and longing when they are uploaded online, shared, accessed, and sometimes commented on by users.

Elsewhere I have argued that "Vietnam" discourse as it has circulated in the Global North has been defined by an asymmetry of power relations and uneven access to culture making.[16] In what follows, I extend this argument to include an analysis of power in the Global South (Việt Nam) and for those who are a part of minoritized populations in the United States (Vietnamese Americans). In my readings of *Land of Sorrows* and *Journey from the Fall*, I demonstrate how the two films pivot on the trope of the national family and its dissolution. Thematically, the trope of the family has been vital for the retelling of the war from a point of view that falls outside of the North Vietnamese and American perspectives. Beyond these thematic concerns, however, the ways that the films locally travel and are received by the Vietnamese American community are fused with the stories of power that they (re)tell. This retelling speaks to the relations of power that Việt Nam and the diaspora share in the contemporary moment.

Land of Sorrows and *Journey from the Fall*: Remembrance and Reconciliation

Made in 1971, *Đất Khổ*, or *Land of Sorrows*, shows the rupturing of the national family and its devastating impact on civilian lives. The film's value as a historical document lies in the fact that it was made during the war and preserved when other wartime films made in the South were not. Dealing exclusively with the Tết Offensive in Huế in 1968, it also incorporates actual footage of villagers fleeing their homes during this time period. Moreover, it was the only film directed by Hà Thúc Cẩn, who originated from South Việt Nam and who collaborated with a number of artists and writers to make the film. Finally, *Land of Sorrows* remains the only movie that features the performance of legendary songwriter and antiwar activist Trịnh Cộng Sơn and his songs. Both in its production and in its content, the film brings together a constellation of fascinating, historical details about wartime Huế, a part of the country that often becomes occluded in discussions about how the war has been fought between North and South, the communists and nationalists.

The film focuses on the politically complex lives of those who were caught in the war's crossfire. Using rare archival footage, it retells the Battle for Huế for the people who had to experience it on the ground. Mixing Trinh's musician persona into the fabric of the film's narrative, *Land of Sorrows* centers on one family in particular. Its focus lies with antiwar musician Quân (Trịnh's character) and his family. As the film unfolds viewers witness the ways his family becomes increasingly divided; one brother fights for the North, the other for the South. Quân's younger sister tries to maintain a love relationship during a time of war, while another takes an antiwar position much like Quân himself. Amid the familial turmoil, Quân's mother tries to keep her family intact but fails to do so in the face of the many displacements that the (national) family experiences in wartime.

Land of Sorrows is partially based on Vietnamese writer Nhã Ca and her book, *Mourning Headband for Huế*, which provided the details for some of the film's more poignant moments, most notably when a woman (played by veteran actress Kim Cương) mourns the loss of her dead child in a church overrun by war refugees. Originally published in Vietnamese in 1969, Nhã Ca's *Mourning Headband for Huế* was recently published in English and translated by Vietnam studies scholar Olga Dror. As Dror details, the Tết Offensive in Huế was a significant battle in which "80% of the city was destroyed by ARVN [Army of the Republic of Vietnam] and American forces" and caused the "deaths of 5,000 North Vietnamese soldiers, 400 ARVN soldiers, and 216 American soldiers."[17] Despite such troubling numbers, the state continues to deny its role in the massacre of civilians and instead celebrates the event as a victory for the communist war effort. Placing responsibility of these deaths directly on the Party, Nhã Ca's writing was deemed subversive by the Communist Party after 1975. She spent thirteen months in a reeducation camp thereafter. In 1985 she was able to immigrate first to Sweden and then eventually to the United States with her son.[18]

Today *Land of Sorrows* serves as a trace of Nhã Ca's affective mode of writing and its impact. Both the book and the film are well regarded as accurate accounts of this historical event. Because of the works' notoriety and subject matter, these two texts have been banned in Việt Nam since the early 1970s. Even so, the Vietnamese version of her book as well as its English translation can be found and bought online. Similarly, one can purchase the English-subtitled film on Amazon and other bookselling sites, or one can watch the film for free on YouTube. While the details of the book and the film can be abundantly detailed, the film's screening history in Việt Nam has not been well documented. Online evidence, however, shows that in the United States, *Land of Sorrows* was screened for a short amount of time. As a website about the film's distribution states, the film "had its first commercial showing at Paris's Orient Theater in 1980 and its first U.S. showing in the Fall of 1996 at the American Film Institute's Kennedy Center location in Washington D.C.; then at The University of Maryland and George Mason University as part of the Asian American International Film Festival . . . in the Greater Washington D.C. area."[19]

Most recently *Land of Sorrows* was screened in Anaheim, California, at the Viet Film Fest in April 2015. Viet Film Fest (formerly the Vietnamese International

Film Festival) came into being in 2003 as a local film festival originating in Southern California that showcased the work of Vietnamese and Vietnamese diasporic filmmakers. Staffed by volunteers and supported by corporate funders such as Wells Fargo and Macy's, this festival has been the premier site for the screening of many Vietnamese contemporary films by those in the diaspora and in Việt Nam. Since its inception the festival has garnered national and international attention in the diaspora and Việt Nam and continues to be an important cinematic and cultural event for Vietnamese Americans in the region. Now annual, the film festival regularly attracts thousands of attendees each year. For Vietnamese American audiences, the film festival allows the community to see (sometimes for the first time) rare and popular films from all around the world. They are also afforded the opportunity to talk to actors, producers, and directors during panel discussions. At once expansive and intimate, the space of the Viet Film Fest emphasizes the notion of community, representation, and history in its formation and in the way it operates.

I have been chair of the screening committee for Viet Film Fest for three installments of the festival. In 2015 I was part of the organizers' plans to commemorate the fortieth anniversary of the end of the war vis-à-vis the screening of the film *Land of Sorrows*. For the occasion, we invited writer Nhã Ca and the other screenwriters who collaborated on the film, Hà Thúc Như Hỹ (the director's nephew), Trần Lê Nguyễn, and Phạm Viết Lịch to attend the screening. We also recognized their work with individual awards and asked them to take part in a panel discussion after the film screening. Finally, we facilitated a book signing for the English-language translation of Nhã Ca's book as well. Albeit a small gathering of about thirty people, it was a memorable event that brought together mostly older members of the community as well as some members of the Vietnamese-language local press. As the screening and panel discussion made clear to me, the interest in the film and the book is ongoing and driven in part by the state's continued disavowal of the Huế Massacre. Within the Vietnamese American community, the resentment for this renunciation is ever-present.

Just as I was privy to the discussions to fête the film and book, I was also a part of the struggles to find the film's producers and director and acquire the permission to screen it at Viet Film Fest. After months of making inquiries into *Land of Sorrows*, we discovered that the director, Hà Thúc Cần, had died in Singapore in 2004. Through some investigative work via social media outlets and various Internet searches, we found that the film's distributor is an eighty-five-year-old retired artist by the name of George Washnis, who currently lives in Florida. In a phone conversation with me, Washnis relayed how he bought the rights to the film soon after it was made.[20] Along with his ex-wife, he acquired the film through some connections he had in Việt Nam during the

war. Washnis noted that his interest in the film stemmed from his own pro-
found disenchantment with what he saw as the U.S. imperialist incursion into
Việt Nam. Later on he played a large role in screening *Land* in the United States.
In 2007 he and the distribution company, Remis, LLC, released the film on DVD.
By phone, Washnis consented to the screening of the film at the last minute—
right before the weekend the film festival opened. My renarration of Viet Film
Fest's efforts to reach out to those who made and distributed the film demonstrates that the film's afterlife is, indeed, present and can be traced through
these local efforts to preserve film outside of the Vietnamese state's purview.
It is in these details, moreover, that a minor transnationality expresses itself
within a minority culture.

In contrast to *Land of Sorrows*, *Journey from the Fall* has followed a more conventional pattern in its marketing and distribution practices. The film falls in
line with how Asian American films are usually made and circulated, especially
because the director, UCLA film graduate Ham Tran, is attuned to the networks
that inform this kind of independent filmmaking and the minority politics that
fuel it. Promoted as a Vietnamese American film, the film was released in movie
theaters in major cities such as San Jose and Houston, and in Orange Country
where the largest populations of Vietnamese Americans live in the United
States. As a result of this strategy, the film did fairly well during opening weekend (with receipts of approximately $87,000).[21] After it was released, the media
company ImaginAsian, which is known for distributing Asian American films,
bought the rights to the film and currently sells the film through websites like
Amazon.com; however, the company has been defunct since 2011.

When *Journey from the Fall* was screened in Orange County in 2007, it
showed to packed audiences, with lines for the film that snaked around the
movie theater. I was one of these viewers. I watched the film with a mostly
Vietnamese American audience and I witnessed their highly emotional
responses to the film. Though not a critical hit, the film won the adulation of a
Vietnamese American audience that appeared to me not only multigenera-
tional but also diverse in terms of class. Part of this positive reception has to do
with the story that the film tells. *Journey* paints a bleak and yet redemptive
portrait of postwar Việt Nam in the South, broaching topics that few Vietnamese
and Vietnamese diasporic films have been able to discuss. The film explicitly
deals with the plight of reeducation camp prisoners as well as that of boat
people, two taboo subjects for the Vietnamese state.

Restaging the moment of "reunification" between North and South Việt
Nam in 1975, *Journey* centralizes the profound divisions of the national family
during wartime and in its aftermath. A former high-ranking officer in the South
Vietnamese army, the patriarch of the family, Long, decides early on to stay in
the country as Sài Gòn falls to the communists in 1975. Not long after, Long is

imprisoned in a reeducation camp where he and his fellow soldiers are tortured and beaten. As the film makes clear, Long is surrounded by other fathers and uncles who come from a similar background. Consigned to the task of demining the land, they are subject to immediate death. One of the most poignant moments of the film occurs when Long's friend, Trai, dies in a landmine explosion. Within these sections of the film, the narrative is essentially a male melodrama, focused on the men who fought for the South Vietnamese army and whose tender relationships with one another form the emotional core of the film.

Running parallel to this narrative about men is a narrative about women. Tran, who served as both director and co-screenwriter, creates a second layer in the film that speaks to the gendered experience of being a boat person and making the journey from Việt Nam to the United States as a woman. This story involves Long's wife, Mai, who along with her mother-in-law (played by veteran Vietnamese American actress Kiều Chinh) and son (Lai), tries to leave Việt Nam after 1975. On the boat, Mai narrowly escapes being raped by Thai pirates when her mother-in-law throws scalding hot water on her body to repel her attacker. The scars on her body as a result of this traumatic encounter are actual and metaphorical; the things she carries to America from Việt Nam are the wounds that mark her body in the transition from escape to resettlement.

Throughout the film Mai's and Long's narratives of escape are spliced together, effectively scissoring between past and present, mother and father as well as between Việt Nam and the United States. Juxtaposing the past with the present along a discontinuous continuum, the film's crosscutting of time and space disrupts the teleological narrative of history often narrated by official Vietnamese history of revolution, reunification, and progress that occurred after the country's civil war. As with *Land of Sorrows, Journey* powerfully demonstrates how Việt Nam was a house divided. While Cần's film significantly took place during the war and captured actual footage of the war as it happened, Tran's film revealed that after the reunification of the country, the discord, hostility, and animosity between North and South, in fact, animated the postwar policies toward the South, policies that affected not only the lives of those who left but also of those who stayed behind. Those who stayed behind were sent to new economic zones or imprisoned in reeducation camps. Families who lived in the South had their properties confiscated; were afforded fewer education opportunities, especially if they were former members of elite military families; and were socially ostracized, particularly if they were of Amerasian descent.

For most of the film, *Journey* focuses on the suffering that the South Vietnamese and Vietnamese refugees experienced in the years following the war. Despite the tremors of pain running throughout the film, it nevertheless

ends with the notion of reconciliation as the diasporic family becomes recon-
stituted in the United States. The final images of the film memorialize Long's
death in important ways but also visualize for viewers the restoration of the
nuclear family in the diaspora. Mai, Lai, the mother-in-law, and Nam (a character who serves as a surrogate father to Mai's son by the film's end) make wishes
to Long's spirit in flying a kite along an open expanse of sun and sand. More
metaphorically, they say goodbye to a country that symbolized destruction, dissolution, and death for them. It is key here that the film concludes on a tenor
of reconciliation—not between Việt Nam and the diaspora but between the
United States and Việt Nam more exactingly. The traumas of (economic and
political) displacement that Vietnamese refugees faced in resettling in the
United States are resolved in the film's conclusion. The final note of the film is
premised on how, for those in the United States, a new beginning awaits. Such
hope for renewal in the diaspora may be one of the reasons why the Vietnamese
state banned the film soon after it was released, as well as barring the director
from making a film in Việt Nam.

The story of *Journey from the Fall* does not end here, however. While initially banned from returning to Việt Nam to make films, director Ham Tran
has since been back many times. Ironically, his filmmaking prospects have
only flourished in the country in the wake of the state's overtures to welcome the diasporic community "home." For example, in recent years, the
state has allowed for the diaspora to acquire dual citizenship, five-year visas,
and land-ownership in the country. These legislative acts followed Resolution no. 36, when in 2004 the state posited that the overseas Vietnamese
community was "an integral part of the nation."[22] This recognition on the
part of the state toward the diaspora has bolstered the return migration of
many diasporic filmmakers who work in Việt Nam today. Tran is one of
them. In 2010 Tran was asked by film officials to edit a historic film about the
origins of the country's capital, Hà Nội. Celebrating the millennial founding
of the country's political center, *Khát Vọng Thăng Long* [*The Prince and the
Pagoda Boy*] (2010), however, performed poorly at the Vietnamese box
office.[23] Yet it was through this collaboration that Tran was able to extend his
stay in Việt Nam and pursue his filmmaking projects. Funded by a Vietnamese
production company, Tran's next directing feature was a box office hit in
Việt Nam, a romantic comedy called *Âm Mưu Giầy Gót Nhọn*, or *How to Fight
in Six Inch Heels* (2013).[24] Ham then followed this comedy film with a high-
concept horror film called *Đoạt Hồn*, or *Hollow* (2014), which focuses on the
sex trafficking of young women at the Vietnam–China border.[25] Despite
having made a film extremely critical of communist ideology, Tran's filmmaking career in Việt Nam attests to the extent to which the state now
accommodates certain subject matter (sex trafficking) and genres (horror)

in order to expand on its own archive and repertoire of both film and culture.

Culture and the Reinvention of the Vietnamese State

Since 2002 the state has allowed for the establishment of private film studios in the country and the private funding of films. This moment paves the way for transnational coproductions to take place in the making of film in the country. It has also spurred the phenomenon of return migrations for Vietnamese Americans who make films in Việt Nam. Such developments tell a story of how directors find both the funding and inspiration to make films in the country. They also narrate a particular moment for the country as it moves from postwar country to a postsocialist one. Aspiring to be an Asian Tiger like some of its Southeast Asian neighbors, the country positions itself as a major geopolitical player. In so doing, the state constantly refurbishes its relations with France, the United States, and its own diaspora, parts of which still agitate for regime change and thus severely test the model of affiliative relations that the state envisions for itself and the overseas community. In the contemporary moment, Việt Nam, as Martin Gainsborough observes, "proves adept at reinventing itself."[26]

The state's decisions to embrace the diaspora's return also keys into this adaptability. But its gesture of inclusion toward the diaspora is perhaps best understood in economic terms, underscored by the way that remittances to Việt Nam total in the billions. At last estimate the Vietnamese diaspora sent US$11 billion to Việt Nam in 2013.[27] The annual incomes of those living abroad also represent a tremendous amount of money that can be tapped. The incentive to attract the Vietnamese diaspora to the homeland remains strong and cloaked in language that accents their ties to the national family, despite the state's dismissal of refugee histories and memories.

The vexed relations between the state and the diaspora and the imbalance of power that mark these relations serve as the context for my readings of two war films, *Land of Sorrows* and *Journey from the Fall*. Both films have been censured by the state and yet embraced by many in the Vietnamese American community. Both texts are part of a body of work that archives a certain southern Vietnamese nationalist and anticommunist sentiment. Framed against Việt Nam's turn toward neoliberalism, these films reflect on the losses that the Vietnamese in Central and South Việt Nam experienced during and after the war. *Land of Sorrows* and *Journey from the Fall* and other films like them constitute a cinematic memorial to the other narratives of the war that are decidedly not found in either Việt Nam's archives of memory or those of the United States. Through these films I have tried to elucidate the power relations that enable films of the prewar and postwar eras to circulate in Việt Nam and the diaspora via official and unofficial routes. The minor transnational relationships analyzed in this study dramatize how the archives and the memories contained within them are structured by an absent and present dynamic, one that is powered by capital and desire.

NOTES

1. *Trận Mộc Hóa* [Battle at Moc Hoa], dir. Mai Lộc, Film, Cinema Zone 8, 1948.

2. Ashley Carruthers and Boi Tran Huynh-Beattie point out that against a context of a South Vietnamese memory that is being "disappeared" by the state, the Vietnamese government has been actively "trying to woo the diaspora in the West to participate in a project of transnational nation-building." Ashley Carruthers and Boi Tran Huynh-Beattie, "Dark Tourism, Diasporic Memory, and Disappeared History: The Contested Meaning of the Former Indochinese Refugee Camp at Pulau Galang," in *The Chinese-Vietnamese Diaspora: Revisiting the Boatpeople*, ed. Yuk Wah Chan (New York: Routledge, 2011), 149.

3. Resisting a binaristic model that pits the center against those in the margins, Lionnet and Shih develop the notion of a "minor transnationalism" to speak to the creative expressions of minority cultures that are "products of transmigrations and multiple encounters." As they note, minor transnationality "points toward and makes visible the multiple relations between national and transnational." Shu-Mei Shih and Francoise Lionnet, "Introduction: Thinking through the Minor, Transnationally," in *Minor Transnationalism*, ed. Shu-Mei Shih and Francoise Lionnet (Durham, N.C.: Duke University Press, 2005), 10, 8.

4. *Đất Khổ* [Land of Sorrows], dir. Hà Thúc Cần, DVD, CreateSpace, 1971; and *Journey from the Fall* [Vượt Sóng], dir. Ham Tran, Film, Asia Entertainment, 2007.

5. Ann Laura Stoler, "Colonial Archives and the Arts of Governance," *Archival Science* 2, no. 1–2 (2002): 90.

6. Jacques Derrida, *Archive Fever: A Freudian Impression* (Chicago: University of Chicago Press, 1995), 18.

7. As Derrida notes, the archive is marked by an anticipation of the future, even as it dwells on the past. He writes: "The archive seems at first to point toward past, refer to signs of consigned memory, to recall faithfulness to tradition. . . . The archive also calls into question the coming of the future." Ibid., 33–34.

8. Mary Ann Doane, *The Emergence of Cinematic Time: Modernity, Contingency, Archive* (Cambridge, Mass.: Harvard University Press, 2002), 105.

9. I borrow this from the title of Michel-Rolph Trouillot's book, *Silencing the Past: Power and the Production of History* (Boston: Beacon Press, 1995).

10. Mike Featherstone, "Archive," *Theory, Culture & Society* 23, no. 2–3 (2006): 594.

11. Ann Cvetkovich, *Archive of Feelings: Trauma, Sexuality and Lesbian Public Culture* (Durham, N.C.: Duke University Press, 2003), 7.

12. In her book *The American War in Contemporary Vietnam*, Christina Schwenkel discusses the politics of commemoration and of war tourism sites in Việt Nam. See Christina Schwenkel, *The American War in Contemporary Vietnam* (Bloomington: Indiana University Press, 2009).

13. Yến Lê Espiritu, *Body Counts: The Vietnam War and Militarized Refuge(es)* (Berkeley: University of California Press, 2014), 112.

14. Ibid., 114.

15. Ibid., 113.

16. Lan Duong, *Treacherous Subjects: Gender, Culture, and Trans-Vietnamese Feminism* (Philadelphia: Temple University Press, 2012).

17. Olga Dror, "Introduction to *Mourning Headband for Hue*," in *Mourning Headband for Hue* (Bloomington: Indiana University Press, 2014), xxvii.

18. Ibid., xxii–xxiii.

19. The following website promotes the film in order to sell it online: "*Land of Sorrows* on Create Space," accessed May 1, 2015, https://www.createspace.com/225161.

20. George Washnis, personal correspondence, April 15, 2015.

21. Information regarding this film has been culled from *imdb.com*, accessed May 15, 2015.

22. "Politburo's Resolution on Viet Kieu." *Embassy of the Socialist Republic of Vietnam*, accessed March 3, 2004, http://www.vietnamembassy-usa.org/news/story.php?d=2004051170158.

23. *Khát Vọng Thăng Long* [The Prince and the Pagoda Boy], dir. Lưu Trọng Ninh, Film, Ky Nguyen Sang Studio, 2010.

24. *Âm Mưu Giày Gót Nhọn* [How to Fight in Six Inch Heels], dir. Ham Tran, DVD, Galaxy Film Studios, 2013.

25. *Đoạt Hồn* [Hollow], dir. Ham Tran, Film, BHD and Old Photo Films, 2014.

26. Martin Gainsborough, "State, Party, and Political Change in Vietnam," in *Rethinking Vietnam*, ed. Duncan McCargo (New York: RoutledgeCurzon, 2004), 51.

27. "Remittances to Developing Countries to Stay Robust This Year, Despite Increased Deportations of Migrant Workers, Says WB," World Bank Group, accessed July 11, 2014, http://www.worldbank.org/en/news/press-release/2014/04/11/remittances-developing-countries-deportations-migrant-workers-wb.

5

Liberal Humanitarianism and Post–Cold War Cultural Politics

The Case of Le Ly Hayslip

JEEHYUN LIM

When they were first published, Le Ly Hayslip's memoirs, *When Heaven and Earth Changed Places* (1989) and *Child of War, Woman of Peace* (1993), offered a unique perspective on the much written about Vietnam War.¹ In the words of a *New York Times* reviewer of Hayslip's first memoir, the late 1980s was a time when the sentiment that "we Americans have been too intent on nursing our own wounds from the Vietnam War to take much notice of those suffered by the Vietnamese" was slowly rearing its head, and narratives on the Vietnam War from the perspective of a Vietnamese woman of peasant background filled a cultural lacuna in the U.S. discourse of the Vietnam War.² In the criticism of Hayslip's memoirs, the writer's subject position as a Vietnamese peasant woman who survived the war, became an American citizen, and subsequently joined the first group of returning Vietnamese, or Viet Kieu, has also been at the center of critical interest. Taking into consideration the political and cultural climate of *When Heaven*'s publication, which was marked by a move toward reconciliation between the United States and Viet Nam, critic Viet Thanh Nguyen reads Le Ly as an "emblematic victim" for U.S. readers who simultaneously performs the function of witness to the collective suffering of the Vietnamese and has the power of forgiveness as a victim.³ Bringing into high relief the rhetorical workings of "an essential feminine pacifism" in *When Heaven*, Leslie Bow shows how the narrative (unwittingly) authorizes a politics of neutrality that "justifies American interests."⁴

In this chapter, I revisit Hayslip's widely read memoirs with an eye to how the idea of agency in these narratives intervenes in a post–Cold War cultural politics. Arguably, the sense that Hayslip's memoirs engage in a cultural politics of the post–Cold War era underwrites both Nguyen's and Bow's analysis. The trope of reconciliation that Nguyen traces in *When Heaven* presages the normalization of U.S. foreign relations with its former enemy, and the concern over "American imperial dominance" in "the economic arena enabled by opening Vietnam to Western investment" is clear in Bow's interpretation of *When Heaven*.[5] Yet little attention has been paid to the exigencies of the liberal person that Hayslip creates in her memoirs or the kinds of cultural and political agency that stem from this idea of personhood. Attending to the contours of agency that is based on the rhetoric and ideas of liberalism in Hayslip's memoirs first and foremost allows one to think about the possibilities of imagining political subjectivities in the post–Cold War landscape. Additionally, it enables an extended look at Hayslip's humanitarianism, which features prominently in her second memoir, *Child of War, Woman of Peace*, but has been overlooked due to the concentration of popular and academic interest in *When Heaven* in which she chronicles her experience of the Vietnam War.

My interest in the rhetorical construction of agency in Hayslip's memoirs is most strongly subtended by the critical discourse on political agency in the age of neoliberalism.[6] Nebulous as it still remains outside the few political and economic policies described through the modifier neoliberal, the term "neoliberal" requires careful attention, especially in relation to what it shares with and where it departs from liberalism. From the U.S. side, the decade when Oliver Stone's film adaptation of Hayslip's memoirs was released and then-president Bill Clinton announced the normalization of U.S. relations with Viet Nam was also a decade that saw the continuing erosion of the welfare state, increasing privatization of public resources, and ongoing U.S. military ventures around the world. The 1990s was the "twilight of equality," according to Lisa Duggan.[7] From the side of the Socialist Republic of Vietnam, the 1990s was the decade that started seeing the effects of *doi moi*, or economic reform largely characterized by the socialist state's adoption of what is called market-style socialism. Heonik Kwon's chapter in this volume shows some of the freedoms regarding mourning that resulted from *doi moi*. The loosening of state regulations in certain sectors of society in Viet Nam, however, was accompanied by a rise of national debt to such transnational institutions as the International Monetary Fund and the World Bank, as Gabriel Kolko shows in his analysis of postwar Viet Nam.[8] My critical objective in this chapter, then, is to examine subject formation in Hayslip's memoirs with the advantage of the historical hindsight of the neoliberal—or, rather, neoliberalizing—policies of the 1990s in both the United States and Viet Nam. It should be made clear that my aim is not to suggest that Hayslip espouses neoliberalism or that her memoirs evince a neoliberal turn. Rather, I am interested in how and when the all-too-familiar liberal subject and its accompanying political agency lend themselves to neoliberal logic.

Recent critical conversations on human rights in the fields of history and cultural criticism, particularly the critical attempts to trace and understand the rise and predominance of human rights as something whose moral imperative can be taken for granted—what Joseph Slaughter aptly calls "the legibility of human rights"—also underwrite my attention to Hayslip's humanitarianism in this chapter.[9] While Hayslip relies on the vocabulary of humanitarianism, rather than human rights, to show and discuss her desire to contribute to rebuilding Viet Nam, there are several reasons that compel an examination of her memoirs through recent critical insights on the cultural and narrative work of human rights.[10] First, the circulation and consumption of her memoirs take place in the context of the popularity of "life narratives in the field of human rights" surveyed by Kay Schaffer and Sidonie Smith.[11] Wide-ranging as they are, these are typically life narratives that convey experiences of trauma, violence, and loss. They at once bear the historical weight of "global transformations [that] have spurred developments in the field of human rights" and are subject to "global forces of commodification that convert narratives into the property of publishing and media houses."[12] But, more importantly, bringing to bear on Hayslip's idea of liberal personhood the insights gleaned from recent scholarship on human rights enables a deliberation of the conditions under which a foreign other is read as similar to the self or as deserving of the same as the self. Slaughter perceptively points out that there is a "tropological gamble" in human rights laws' conceptualization of the human. While it employs the "rhetoric of obviousness" in declaring human rights as self-evident, these laws "can only pretend to know the yet unfamiliar properties of the international human that it aspires to effect."[13] If a crucial rhetorical element of Vietnam War propaganda was to create an image of the Vietnamese as the alien enemy—and if Cold War culture relied on the binary of the free world versus communism, with the two terms being incommensurable—the post–Cold War era embraces the sameness of humans. Whether such an embrace of sameness does not mask or erase structural inequalities or gloss over political differences that need to be accounted for in the realization of democracy is an abiding question.

Choice and Contract in the Making of the Liberal Person

> I cannot remember the exact moment when I decided to leave Vietnam. But one day I became aware that everything I had done for the past few months had been a preparation for departure—a ritual leave-taking that meant little when those acts were considered by themselves but, when viewed together, were much like my father's own preparations in anticipation of his death.
>
> —Le Ly Hayslip, *When Heaven and Earth Changed Places*

In this passage, Hayslip includes a commentary on autobiographical memory. She claims that once she decided to leave Vietnam, her actions of the recent past fell into place in a narrative of departure. As scholars of autobiography have repeatedly pointed out, autobiographical memory is unreliable when viewed in terms of its veracity to what actually happened.[14] What is more important for autobiography is how the subject of memory makes sense of the passage of time and events in the narrative. Passages like this show Hayslip's awareness of the power of the narrative in textual self-representation. I rely on the retrospective insight Hayslip draws attention to in creating a narrative of the experiences of a Vietnamese American woman to show not only that a demonstration of liberal personhood is central to Hayslip's narrative of agency but that this liberal personhood is also presented as natural. On the one hand, Hayslip's memoirs evince a developmental narrative where the passage of time is accompanied by growth, be it psychological and political maturation or economic mobility. On the other hand, this developmentalism is undermined by a persistent rhetoric of choice as the foundation of agency. Here I look at three pivotal moments in *When Heaven* where Le Ly recounts her struggles through the vocabulary of choice—being raped by Viet Cong soldiers, having sex for money with American soldiers, and marrying a much older American man—to illustrate this incongruous liberal personhood that is at once attained and that always was. The narrative momentum in all three instances hinges on Le Ly's assertion of herself as someone whose agency depends on the ability to choose. These narrative moments form the plot of a liberal subject formation in that, as I show later, it is as a person with choice that Le Ly is able to seamlessly enter the modern world of the social contract.

Early on in her first memoir, Le Ly's rape by two Viet Cong soldiers is a moment when Le Ly assumes recognizable victimhood and refutes this through self-blame. In her childhood, Le Ly is a Viet Cong sympathizer, like most of her fellow villagers in the agrarian village of Ky La. To the peasants of Ky La, the Viet Cong represent familiar values and morals as well as the imperative of national liberation, whereas the Republicans (the Army of the Republic of Vietnam) and the Americans are associated with foreign values and colonial domination. The moral failings of the Viet Cong are starkly displayed when Loi and Mau, the two Viet Cong soldiers who have been assigned to kill Le Ly after she is tried at a kangaroo court based on dubious charges of consorting with the enemy, end up raping her in exchange for her life. Both her age—she is fifteen—and the circumstances of her persecution make it almost impossible to assign blame on Le Ly. Going against this narrative direction of judgment, however, Le Ly seemingly asserts accountability. "Both sides in this terrible, endless, stupid war had finally found the perfect enemy," she declares, "a terrified peasant girl who would endlessly and stupidly consent to be their victim—as all Vietnam's peasants had consented to be victims from creation to the end of time!"[15] The word "consent" in this sentence is jarring because Le Ly's rape is the exact opposite of consensual sex. By willfully employing the term, Hayslip seems to want to draw attention to the possible agency that can emerge from the victim's recognition of victimization.

The resulting agency in this narrative account of rape, however, is somewhat contradictory. On the surface, Le Ly disavows any kind of political allegiance. Her new credo is self-preservation. "I promised myself," she claims, "I would only flow with the strongest current and drift with the steadiest wind—and not resist. To resist, you had to believe in something."[16] Self-preservation is presented as a moral imperative separate from and above politics in this instance. Yet her calling into being a Vietnamese collective of peasants who could possibly have wrested political power from the two sides of the war by recognizing their victimization is a gesture with clear political implications.

Such contradiction notwithstanding, the narrative account of rape proves a turning point in Le Ly's engagement with the world. Not only does she completely lose faith in the Viet Cong but she is also forced to leave her village as her family is branded as traitors. Furthermore, Le Ly also comes to realize that she needs to revise her future prospects as her rape leaves her unfit for marriage according to the customs of the village. Le Ly decides to befriend American men in Saigon as a means of gaining security and later of leaving the war-torn country, and it is in this process that, as Leslie Bow observes, "sex literally becomes a commodity bartered for survival" in *When Heaven*.[17] No other temporary relationship that she has with American men shows Le Ly's thoughts on the commodification of sex as well as her one-time exchange of sex for money with U.S. soldiers. As a black marketer, Le Ly is already familiar with the army base and the kinds of economic transactions that take place on the campground between Vietnamese peddlers and American soldiers when she is approached by a military police officer, Big Mike. Much to the moral turmoil of Le Ly, Big Mike presents her with the unexpected proposition that she could have sex with two young marines who are at the end of their tour and looking for "souvenir" sex for four hundred dollars—a sum that she immediately realizes would support her and her family for a month.[18]

Despite her previous resolution to "flow with the strongest current and drift with the steadiest wind," Big Mike's proposition leads to a lengthy deliberation on Le Ly's part. The taxonomy of womanhood she employs to first resist and then to justify having sex for money shows Le Ly's renegotiation of a sense of self before she accepts the proposition. The "*good* girl" she refers to herself in her initial strong refusal shows her defining herself against female sex workers, "the *Hoa Phat* or *Nui Phuoc Tuong* bar girls" who are known for being "the best for miles around" but who are presumably considered to be bad girls in terms of conventional morality.[19] When she answers that she is "no cherry girl" to Big Mike's inquiry about her virginity, the decreasing volume of her voice simultaneously suggests Le Ly's wavering over her decision and her hesitation about herself as a "*good* girl."[20] She is, in the eyes of others, not only not a virgin but an unwed mother. Her social value, Le Ly comes to understand in this process, is determined within the parameters of a patriarchy within which her history of rape and her romantic affair with Anh—the biological father of Le Ly's first child and the master of the house where Le Ly and her mother seek work as live-in housemaids—already tarnishes her. Against the moral standards of good and bad girls, in the indeterminate space of not being a "cherry girl" and not being a "whore," Le Ly accepts the economic standard of self-commodification, of placing a monetary value on the act of sexual service.[21]

Hayslip is very clear about the wartime conditions that pressure Vietnamese women to resort to prostitution. When she asks "what else were we to do," actively identifying with the women whose moral status may be questionable according to social conventions, no reader can really answer the question or pass judgment on her.[22] The last of the three narrative instances of choice can also be read in the same vein. Yet Le Ly's choice to marry Ed Munro is also a little different from the previous choices in that it entails a recognizable legal contract. While Le Ly's previous relationships with American men, including the exchange of sex for money, all involve an implicit contract between the parties engaged, her deliberation over Ed's marriage proposal explicitly evokes the idea of the social contract. The contractual nature of Ed's proposal is apparent in the language of his proposal. "I've got another year in my contract and then I'm going home to San Diego," he says to Le Ly. "I've got a nice house there and I've decided I want a wife to share it with me—a good oriental wife who knows how to take care of her man."[23] Le Ly also mulls over what Ed offers "in return for marrying him and coming to America and taking care of him as a wife."[24] Explicit references to the terms of exchange such as these elucidate the parallel between marriage as a contract and the employment contract in the narrative. Just as Ed is on an employment contract in which he exchanges his labor and services for monetary compensation, Le Ly's marriage to him is also a contract that bears an agreement between her and Ed on what they will exchange.

In Hayslip's memoirs, war and displacement lay bare the conditions of the modern social contract. In her groundbreaking feminist critique of the social contract, political theorist Carole Pateman says that "individuals recognize each other as property owners by making mutual use of, or *exchanging*, their property. Exchange is at the heart of contract."[25] "The contracts that have a prominent place in classic social contract theory," Pateman goes on to say, "are not only about material goods, but property in the peculiar sense of property in the person, and they involve an exchange of obedience for protection."[26] Since property in the common sense of tangible goods or liquid assets is something that Le Ly does not have, her bargaining chips are concentrated in her person. In order to become a proper subject of what C. B. Macpherson calls "possessive individualism," the backbone of Western liberalism, Le Ly has to first capitalize on what John Locke defines as the first meaning of property: property in the person.[27]

It is at this point in the narrative that Hayslip's persistent employment of the rhetoric of choice, even in situations when it seems to overburden the individual, can be viewed as an effect of the retrospective scripting of her past self into the liberal person of the social contract that Hayslip embraces. On the one hand, there is a developmental arc in the subject formation Hayslip limns as Le Ly moves away from the rural village of her origin first to urban Viet Nam and later to suburban America. To some extent the macrohistorical narrative of modern liberalism's development can be mapped onto the microhistory of Le Ly's young womanhood in Viet Nam. The macrohistorical narrative of the modern social contract is about moving away from the rule of brute force to a rule of law through the political fiction of the social contract. If Le Ly's rape is her experience of sexual violence by brute force and her exchange of sex for money is her voluntary subordination to power for benefits, then her marriage may well mark her entry into the realm of exchanges governed by the social contract. On the other hand, Hayslip also presents the notion of choice that undergirds the democratic applications and implications of the social contract as an inherent human condition when she attributes the rhetoric to the various iterations of her past selves, thereby naturalizing the social contract as what intuitively makes sense.

The incongruity in Hayslip's portrayal of Le Ly as a liberal person bears out the critiques of the social contract by scholars such as Pateman and Charles Mills who show that the social contract is a historical and social construct based on a white patriarchal power. In *The Sexual Contract* Pateman, for example, suggests that the individual person is "a patriarchal category" and that to argue for civil and political freedom while maintaining the ideas of the social contract and of the individual who partakes in the contract leaves women "with no alternative to (try to) become replicas of men."[28] With his concept of the "Racial Contract," Mills argues that the men referred to in the social contract as a universal and abstract category are in fact only white men and that such racial terms "set the parameters for Lockean and Kantian contractarian theories of natural rights and duties."[29]

This incongruity in the portrayal of liberal personhood, however, is less visible in the second memoir, *Child of War, Woman of Peace*, which prominently features Hayslip's story of settling in the United States, where she becomes increasingly adroit in mastering the game of the contract. First with Ed and later with Dennis, Le Ly holds up her end of the bargain as she conforms to the

Orientalist expectations of her husbands as an obedient and sexually available wife, bears the racism of her husbands' relatives, and performs the emotional and material labor of a housewife. By the time Dennis commits suicide, Le Ly is ready to view her widowhood as a liberation of sorts. "My dreams, for once, were my own," declares Le Ly, "no Ed, no Dennis, no nattering relatives, no war ghosts—nobody but the entity called Phung Thi Le Ly. I enjoyed it immensely."[30] By working outside the house at factories and working inside the house as foster mother to Vietnamese refugee children and youths, Le Ly also acquires economic means sufficient to guarantee her independence. It is at this point when Le Ly arrives at the end of her marriage contracts that she feels like she is in "the America we had dreamed about in Vietnam . . . the America I yearned for when I arrived with Ed."[31]

The disappearance of the contradictions of liberal personhood, I suggest, brings Hayslip's second memoir close to a narrative of immigrant assimilation with an emphasis on economic mobility. Juxtaposing the model minority discourse—which became popular in the media since the late 1960s to explain the high level of (primarily economic) assimilation by Asian Americans—to the narrative of mobility in Hayslip's second memoir, then, may bring into high relief some of the problems resulting from Hayslip's reliance on a liberal subjectivity in narrating her experiences. Several scholars in Asian American studies have recently pointed out the application of the model minority discourse to Vietnamese Americans.[32] Like other examples of the model minoritization of Asian Americans before, these model minority stories of Vietnamese Americans emphasize the work ethic and individual perseverance of Vietnamese Americans as the engine behind their socioeconomic success. While there are many narrative strands in Hayslip's memoirs that resist the discourse of the model minority, the emphasis on liberal personhood combined with the narrative of economic mobility possibly lends itself to neoliberal appropriations that emphasize individual hard work and responsibilities over structural inequalities or institutional racism in accounting for success. This, of course, is not to suggest that Hayslip should not have adopted the terms of liberalism or that liberalism at large is always collapsible into neoliberal ideas or rhetoric. Rather, I am interested in showing that the productiveness of engaging with Hayslip's account of agency lies in the tension between economic and political liberalism she shows through her experiences. Viewing her narrative of liberal humanitarianism as the counterpoint to the liberal individualism of the narrative of economic mobility, in the rest of the chapter I turn to Hayslip's account of her humanitarian work in her memoirs and in personal communications to show where I think her liberal humanitarianism produces political agency that is imbricated in, but not consumed by, the transnational politics of nongovernmental organizations (NGOs).

The Challenges of Liberal Humanitarianism
in the Post–Cold War Era

Our creed of choice—freedom and independence, responsibility and compassion—is the core of our humanity.

—Le Ly Hayslip, *Child of War, Woman of Peace*

You see, Bon Nghe, *they* [Americans] have a choice about what they do. The people here do not. I will simply tell them: Our brothers and sisters under the Communist roof are in a dark age and need a little light. We in the U.S. can give them the light they need—at least a little more than they have right now. Why do you think the Statue of Liberty holds up a torch and not a moneybag or a pistol?

—Le Ly Hayslip, *When Heaven and Earth Changed Places*

With statements like these, in her memoirs Hayslip presents a buoyant humanitarianism as the future of U.S.–Vietnam relations and as her mission as a Viet Kieu. Hayslip places her humanitarianism firmly against what she views as the Cold War politics of paranoia, something that she insinuates is the culture of establishment institutions in both the Socialist Republic of Vietnam and the United States. In *When Heaven*, Hayslip exposes the Vietnamese government's practice of closely watching the Viet Kieu and limiting their mobility. In *Child of War*, one can see the FBI repeatedly harassing and intimidating Le Ly after she visits Viet Nam. In this context of residual Cold War politics, Hayslip's humanitarianism appears to chart a new internationalism with its independence from state institutions and state-sponsored organizations. Le Ly turns to nonprofit organizations that engage in forms of "citizen diplomacy," such as Youth Ambassadors of America or the Vietnam Veterans of America, for models of humanitarian work that are not bound to U.S. policies toward Viet Nam in the late 1980s.[33] With its abnegation of overt politics and its valorization of personal freedom and peace for all, Hayslip's brand of humanitarianism embodies what seems to be a quintessential post–Cold War aspiration.

Here I first examine Hayslip's textual representation of liberal humanitarianism before moving on to her accounts of her lived experience of NGO work in the past twenty-five years or so. In 1988, one year before the publication of *When Heaven*, Hayslip established an NGO, East Meets West Foundation (EMWF), as the institutional base for carrying out the humanitarian work she planned in Viet Nam. Since the publication of her second memoir in 1993, Hayslip has parted with EMWF, which is now Thrive Networks Global Inc., and established another NGO, the Global Village Foundation (GVF).[34] In her personal communications with me, when asked the question of whether her view of humanitarianism in her memoirs was too optimistic, Hayslip said that "yes,

I was very optimistic about the prospects of my humanitarian work and made many mistakes on the way."[35] Her insightful account of what she has learned about the politics of NGOs subsequent to the publication of her memoirs, I think, offers a unique look at what is not fully captured in her view of liberal humanitarianism conveyed in the memoirs.

In *When Heaven* Le Ly most succinctly outlines a rationale for the Vietnamese acceptance of humanitarian aid in an exchange with her brother, Bon Nghe, whom she calls "a dedicated party man."[36] Trying to repudiate the distinction the brother draws between himself as a communist and the American sister as a capitalist, Le Ly presents a metaphor of the nation-state as a house and the "labels" of capitalism and communism as "the roof under which [Americans and Vietnamese] live."[37] The important thing, Le Ly asserts, is that the people have the freedom to choose their roofs, just like "a person can leave one house and live in or visit another without cursing either the old house or the new one."[38] Freedom of choice and personhood are viewed as concepts that exist independently of a political system in this metaphor. In Le Ly's spatial metaphor, the state serves a purely utilitarian function of protecting the individual against harm that can incur from a state of nature. Systems of political beliefs, such as capitalism or communism, are "roofs," a main element of the house's function to shelter, and no different from the house itself from a functionalist point of view. In reality, however, a political system often plays a significant role in the formation of a citizen-subject. The definition and parameters of personhood acquire meaning within a web of cultural, historical, social, and political factors. Hayslip acknowledges as much when she discusses her becoming American in terms of an education in rights. She says that when she first arrived in the United States she had to "learn about my right to live, to act, to have anything and everything I desire to have for my sons, my friends, my partners and myself as a business woman I want to become."[39] In other words, the idea that there is an a priori "person" who can move from the roof of one political system to another is a political fiction that Hayslip needs to extricate her humanitarian aspirations from what she sees as the quagmire of Cold War politics.

In addition to the metaphor of the nation-state as a house, the trope of Enlightenment also stands out in Hayslip's textual representation of humanitarian values. When her brother cannot shake off his suspicion of the professed altruism in Le Ly's humanitarianism, Hayslip suggests that the more enlightened a society is, the more given it is to the spirit of giving without asking for something in return. To her brother who asks why Americans will give to Hayslip's humanitarian cause, she answers "I will simply tell them: Our brothers and sisters under the Communist roof are in a dark age and need a little light. We in the U.S. can give them light they need—at least a little more than they have right now."⁴⁰ While the metaphor of nation-states as houses initially seems to imply a formal equality between the houses, here it is suggested that not all the houses are equal. Some are better lit than others, and those who live in houses that are not as well lit are in need of help from those who live in better-lit houses. In *Child of War*, Hayslip further dispels the idea that all nation-states are equal by hinting at an association between capitalism and humanitarianism. As she is discovering her interest in humanitarian aid work, Le Ly observes that "people [in Vietnam] are always suspicious of 'humanitarians'" and that "the capitalist West seemed the only place where charitable works were accepted at face value."⁴¹ At the same time that she presents humanitarianism as a supranational principle of action in her memoirs, Hayslip also makes palpable the discrepancy between humanitarianism as an ideal and the political and social conditions for humanitarian practices.⁴²

Hayslip's lived experience in NGO work after the publication of the memoirs, then, may well serve as a repository of knowledge gained from humanitarian praxis, as opposed to theory, which complicates her view of humanitarianism as a universal and ideal value in the memoirs. Her recent account of the Vietnamese suspicion over U.S. humanitarian work, for example, is more nuanced. Hayslip mentions that "some humanitarian agencies that work in Third World countries are funded by the U.S. government, and these funds sometimes go to creating front programs for the CIA. Therefore, the governments of the Third World countries have the right to be suspicious."⁴³ Especially when it comes to communist states, Hayslip emphasizes that the legacy of the CIA's work during the Cold War still haunts these states' responses to humanitarian agencies based in the United States.⁴⁴

Likewise, her experience in NGO work since the publication of her memoirs revises her disavowal of the politics of humanitarianism in significant ways. In the present, Thrive Networks is a well-established NGO. It has a number of subsidiaries, including Reach Vietnam, East Meets West Dental Center, East Meets West Foundation, Ghana, and Thrive Networks Foundation, Limited, Hong Kong.⁴⁵ Thrive Networks' website states that the NGO "has invested more than $120 million in serving disadvantaged people around the globe" and its tax reports and independent auditor's statements list the NGO's total assets in years 2013 and 2014 as slightly above $14 million.⁴⁶ According to Hayslip, however, the foundation was not always in such good financial state or had as many donors. In her account, in the early years the foundation was pretty much a one-woman operation. "To learn how to support my foundation and to raise funds," she says, "I took classes, read books, did a lot of volunteering, wrote a number of grant proposals, met with people, made phone calls, collected donations, received supplies, equipments, and funds to take to Viet Nam. I worked so hard from A–Z, 24/7 on my kitchen table with some help from volunteers who were veterans of the Vietnam War."[47] In retrospect, Hayslip views the growth of EMWF as a part of the historical evolution of U.S.–Vietnam relations. Noting that it was "a very special time in the history of Vietnam and the U.S." when she founded the NGO, Hayslip says that "because of the U.S. embargo against Vietnam, not many people were open-minded or had enough heart to help our people who live there. Every time I gave a speech or tried to raise funds for the foundation, the right-wing Vietnamese in the U.S. protested and boycotted my foundation and my name. People who wanted to help our organization were afraid for their lives. For that the foundation really suffered through the first ten years, until my baby grew and became a mature woman, then married a rich man. Then everybody from both countries shut up."[48]

Her account of EMWF's growth may contain a suggestion of personal vindication. Yet this growth of the organization is also what prompted Hayslip to part ways with it. In another interview Hayslip refers to the foundation as a daughter who not only grew up and married a rich man but subsequently went her own way.[49] At one point during the interview, she says that the way she did things met with criticism by other board members of EMWF for not being the "right way, which is the American way, the professional way."[50] Hayslip suggests that she and the other members of the board did not see eye to eye on the political implications of a private donor's funds and on how to disburse the growing funds.[51] To put it in Hayslip's words, "with so much money from rich man, she [EMWF] was able to do much more, but I don't think she was about to do much for the poor in Viet Nam."[52] Her continued commitment to helping the poor in Viet Nam is what prompted her to depart from EMWF as it was gaining visibility and to start another, smaller NGO, the Global Village Foundation.

In her refusal to simply accept the professionalization of NGOs as a natural course of events and in her renewed commitment to the Vietnamese poor, I think Hayslip adumbrates a political agency that is located in the interstices of political and economic liberalism and holds the two in productive tension. While her narrative of economic mobility conforms to the tenets of economic liberalism, the way Hayslip steers her political liberalism clear of business interests and directed at a downward redistribution of material resources reins in the possible excesses of economic liberalism. In response to the question of how the conditions of NGO work in Viet Nam has changed over the years, Hayslip says she feels that the group dynamics of NGO work today is different from that of the past. Whereas previously the social conflict was mainly between the socialist state and CIA, now, she claims, there is a more complex dynamic involving a number of nonstate actors, including local governments, domestic Vietnamese organizations, and overseas Vietnamese NGOs, some of which are professedly anticommunist. The diversification of political actors in aid work in postwar Viet Nam points to new conditions and possibilities of imagining political agency. Rereading the liberal person in Le Ly Hayslip's memoirs may be a preliminary step to engaging with such a task.

NOTES

1. Le Ly Hayslip with Jay Wurts, *When Heaven and Earth Changed Places: A Vietnamese Woman's Journey from War to Peace* (New York: Plume, 1989); and Le Ly Hayslip with James Hayslip, *Child of War, Woman of Peace* (New York: Doubleday, 1993).

2. David K. Shipler, "A Child's Tour of Duty," *New York Times*, June 25, 1989, accessed September 7, 2014. http://www.nytimes.com/1989/06/25/books/a-child-s-tour-of-duty.html.

3. Viet Thanh Nguyen, "Representing Reconciliation: Le Ly Hayslip and the Emblematic Victim," in *Race and Resistance: Literature and Politics in Asian America* (Oxford: Oxford University Press, 2002), 108.

4. Leslie Bow, "Le Ly Hayslip's Bad (Girl) Karma: Sexuality, National Allegory, and the Politics of Neutrality," *Prose Studies: History, Theory, Criticism* 17, no. 1 (1994): 148, 143.

5. Ibid., 152.

6. See Michael Hardt and Antonio Negri, *Empire* (Cambridge, Mass.: Harvard University Press, 2001); Michael Hardt and Antonio Negri, *Multitude: War and Democracy in the Age of Empire* (New York: Penguin, 2004); David Harvey, *A Brief History of Neoliberalism* (New York: Oxford University Press, 2004); and Aihwa Ong, *Neoliberalism as Exception: Mutations in Sovereignty and Citizenship* (Durham, N.C.: Duke University Press, 2006).

7. Lisa Duggan, *The Twilight of Equality: Neoliberalism, Cultural Politics, and the Attack on Democracy* (Boston: Beacon Press, 2003).

8. Gabriel Kolko, *Vietnam: Anatomy of a Peace* (New York: Routledge, 1997), 46–47. Kolko's analysis in many ways foreshadows the application of the term "neoliberal" to certain sectors of Vietnamese society by scholars of contemporary Viet Nam. See *positions: asia critique* 20, no. 2 (2012) for a special issue on neoliberalism in Vietnam.

9. See Joseph Slaughter, *Human Rights, Inc.: The World Novel, Narrative Form, and International Law* (New York: Fordham University Press, 2007), 3; Kay Schaffer and Sidonie Smith, *Human Rights and Narrated Lives: The Ethics of Recognition* (New York: Palgrave Macmillan, 2004); and Samuel Moyn, *The Last Utopia: Human Rights In History* (Cambridge, Mass.: Harvard University Press, 2010).

10. Some scholars, such as Samuel Moyn, suggest that despite their different origins and developments, human rights and humanitarianism have pretty much converged in the present. See Moyn, *The Last Utopia*, 221.

11. Schaffer and Smith, *Human Rights and Narrated Lives*, 13. Bow also reads *When Heaven and Earth* as an example of "Third World women's *testimonia*." See Bow, "Le Ly Hayslip's Bad (Girl) Karma," 142.

12. Schaffer and Smith, *Human Rights and Narrated Lives*, 14, 23.

13. Slaughter, *Human Rights, Inc.*, 23.

14. As longtime scholars of the autobiography, Sidonie Smith and Julia Watson suggest it is "autobiographical acts" that matter rather than facts in autobiography. See Sidonie Smith and Julia Watson, *Reading Autobiography: A Guide for Interpreting Life Narratives*, 2nd ed. (Minneapolis: University of Minnesota Press, 2010), 64.

15. Hayslip, *When Heaven*, 97.

16. Ibid.

17. Bow, "Le Ly Hayslip's Bad (Girl) Karma," 155.

18. Hayslip, *When Heaven*, 257.

19. Ibid.

20. Ibid., 258.

21. Ibid.

22. Ibid., 256.

23. Ibid., 333.

24. Ibid., 343.

25. Carole Pateman, *The Sexual Contract* (Stanford, Calif.: Stanford University Press, 1988), 57.

26. Ibid, 58.

27. C. B. Macpherson, *The Political Theory of Possessive Individualism: Hobbes to Locke* (Oxford: Oxford University Press, 1962), 263.

28. Pateman, *The Sexual Contract*, 187.

29. Charles W. Mills, *The Racial Contract* (Ithaca, N.Y.: Cornell University Press, 1997), 17.

30. Hayslip, *Child of War*, 204.

31. Ibid., 205.

32. See Sylvia Shin Huey Chong, *The Oriental Obscene: Violence and Racial Fantasies in the Vietnam Era* (Durham, N.C.: Duke University Press, 2012), 162–171, for Chong's analysis of the temporary model minoritization of Nguyen Ngoc Loan, the infamous South Vietnamese general of Eddie Adams's Pulitzer-winning photograph. See Cathy J. Schlund-Vials, *Modeling Citizenship: Jewish and Asian American Writing* (Philadelphia: Temple University Press, 2011), 154–157, for a discussion of former assistant attorney general Viet D. Dinh in a twenty-first-century variation of the model minoritization of Vietnamese Americans.

33. Hayslip, *Child of War*, 301, 306.

34. I use East Meets West Foundation when I refer to the NGO prior to its name change in 2014, which is consistent with how Hayslip referred to the organization in her e-mail correspondences and phone conversation with me. East Meets West Foundation's petition for changing its name to Thrive Networks Global was filed with the California Secretary of State on August 26, 2014. Moss-Adams LLP, "Report of Independent Auditors and Consolidated Financial Statements," April 28, 2015, accessed August 31, 2015. http://thrivenetworks.org/uploads/downloads/Thrive-Networks-FS-2014.pdf, 7.

35. Le Ly Hayslip, e-mail communication with author, January 1, 2015.

36. Hayslip, *When Heaven*, 228.

37. Ibid., 342.

38. Ibid.

39. Hayslip, e-mail communication with author, January 1, 2015.

40. Hayslip, *When Heaven*, 342.

41. Hayslip, *Child of War*, 330.

42. Le Ly's observation about a tradition of charity or philanthropy in the West accords with the scholarly view that "modern humanitarianism's origins are located in

Western history and Christian thought." Yet it is also because of this origin in Western expansionism and imperialism that modern humanitarianism has a checkered record. See Michael Barnett and Thomas G. Weiss, "Humanitarianism: A Brief History of the Present," in *Humanitarianism in Question: Politics, Power, Ethics*, ed. Michael Barnett and Thomas G. Weiss (Ithaca, N.Y.: Cornell University Press, 2008), 7.

43. Hayslip, e-mail communication with author, January 1, 2015.

44. Ibid.

45. Moss-Adams LLP, "Report of Independent Auditors," 7.

46. "Thrive Networks: Financials," accessed August 31, 2015, http://thrivenetworks.org/about-us/financials.

47. Hayslip, e-mail communication with author, January 1, 2015.

48. Ibid.

49. See "Le Ly Hayslip Interview March 21, 2008," *Vietnam Anonymous Unlimited* blog, accessed September 7, 2014, http://vietnamanon.blogspot.kr/2008/04/le-ly-hayslip-interview.html, for the interview a group of anonymous bloggers engaged in aid work in Viet Nam conducted with Hayslip on March 21, 2008. Part of the same interview can also be seen on Global Village Foundation's wordpress.com page: "Le Ly Hayslip Interview," *Global Village Foundation* blog, accessed September 7, 2014, http://global villagefoundation.wordpress.com/our-founder/.

50. "Le Ly Hayslip Interview March 21, 2008," accessed September 7, 2014, http://vietnam anon.blogspot.kr/2008/04/le-ly-hayslip-interview.html.

51. Le Ly Hayslip, phone conversation with author, January 2, 2015. The private donor Hayslip refers to here is Charles Frances Feeney, a successful businessman and philanthropist. An account of Feeney's interest and involvement with EMWF as well as some of EMWF members' embrace of Feeney's approach to the running of the foundation can be found in the following biography of Feeney, especially chapter 27. See Conor O'Cleary, *The Billionaire Who Wasn't: How Chuck Feeney Secretly Made and Gave Away a Fortune* (New York: Public Affairs, 2007).

52. Hayslip, e-mail communication with author, January 1, 2015.

6

Ann Hui's *Boat People*

Documenting Vietnamese Refugees in Hong Kong

VINH NGUYEN

At the eve of the fortieth anniversary of the Fall of Saigon, and the fiftieth anniversary of official American military involvement in Vietnam, to (re)collect Vietnam is to remember and assemble histories of imperialism, war, and migration not only from a variety of different perspectives but also from different *places*—places that reveal the conflict's global reach; political, social, and epistemological multiplicity; and what Jodi Kim calls the Cold War's "protracted afterlife."[1] This chapter argues that one of the most important cultural documents of the war in Vietnam emerged not from the usual "sites" of production—the United States, the Socialist Republic of Vietnam, the now defunct Republic of Vietnam (South Vietnam), or the Vietnamese diaspora—but from the Hong Kong film industry of the 1980s. Produced during Hong Kong's "New Wave" of cinematic innovation and the "second wave" of Vietnamese boat refugees in the wake of the war, Ann Hui's *Boat People* (1982) is an early and, as I will demonstrate, rare visual text that represents the plight of Vietnamese refuge seekers. As the movement of Vietnamese bodies gained global attention in the late 1970s and early 1980s, Hui's film depicted *why* so many people braved the open seas—where they experienced storms, starvation, disease, pirate attacks, and death, among other hardships—in search of a different life. In doing so, I suggest, it stands as a seminal "documentary" text in the history of the late twentieth-century Vietnamese diaspora.

I employ the term "documentary" to describe *Boat People*, even though it is a narrative film, in order to register the impulse to document, to record, and to chronicle the lives of the Vietnamese. Perhaps it is instructive to examine the film through the form of the docudrama, or dramatized documentary. According to Alan Rosenthal, docudramas are broadly understood as "*based on or inspired by* reality, by the lives of real people, or by events that have happened in the recent or not too distant past."[2] As a hybrid blending of documentary and melodrama, the docudrama uses what Marita Sturken identifies as "the dual role of cinema as a representation of the real and a source of fantasy and identification" to, in the words of Leslie Woodhead, "tell to a mass audience a real and relevant story involving real people."[3] While the plot of *Boat People* is fictionalized, the details of the narrative are based on hundreds of interviews Hui conducted with Vietnamese refugees and on other source materials, including a written memoir, about real persons and events.[4] This incorporation of historical testimony and stylistic realism into the process of dramatization is an aesthetic strategy that helps to bolster the film's political argument. In Hui's film, the desire to document is thus both an aesthetic and a politics, functioning to illuminate individual lives against a dire situation of forced migration and asylum seeking.

My discussion aims to reposition *Boat People* within the larger archive of "Vietnam"—the historical narratives, memorializations, cultural and popular representations, and political debates on and about the war in Vietnam and its aftermath that have proliferated in the decades following its end. Although Hui's film diegetically focuses on the lives of a group of ordinary Vietnamese individuals as they attempt to survive in and escape from reunified Vietnam under communist rule, no sustained critical analysis of it has elaborated on the historical frame of postwar Vietnam and refugee migrations that structure what the director calls the film's particular "human story."[5] Moreover, despite the considerable amount of critical attention the film has received—as one of the masterpieces of Chinese cinema—it has yet to be read in relation to the sociopolitical context, the refugee "problem," that prompted its production. That is to say, Vietnamese refuge seekers—who occupy the central positions narratively—have remained in the margins of scholarly analysis, displaced in critical narratives of a foundational film in Hong Kong cinema.[6] My chapter thus shifts the analytical lens to consider the film apropos the very people it depicts and within a framework that privileges a history of Vietnamese migration. In turn, it becomes possible to examine not only the film's politics but also how it circulated as a political document within a specific sociohistorical moment.

The general neglect of Vietnamese subjects in discussions of *Boat People* is a direct result of what critics have termed the "1997 factor"—the predominant interpretive lens whereby films made before British withdrawal from Hong Kong were read as allegories for the grim future of the colony under Chinese communism. Such dominant and overdetermined interpretations have resulted in restrictive, and oftentimes reductive, understandings of highly complex films such as *Boat People*. While the 1997 phenomenon is undoubtedly an interesting manifestation of inter-Asian Cold War politics—that is, the mapping of anti-Chinese-communism onto the Vietnamese refugee crisis speaks to the imbrication of political ideologies that have shaped and continue to shape global Asia—that deserves further attention, my purpose here is to step outside of its frame in order to open up other interpretive possibilities. My point is not that an allegorical reading of Hui's film is without value or merit but rather that the controversies regarding the film's anti-China "message" that arose from them have at times overshadowed the film's narrative and the literal, as opposed to symbolic or allegorical, politics of that narrative. My approach here departs from critical tradition by considering a perspective centered on Vietnamese refugees and the issues that surround their presence in diaspora. I suggest that Hui's main intervention lies in her attention to the (extra)ordinary, lived experiences unfolding against a backdrop of social and historical forces. This detailing—in fact, the very occasion of telling itself—of the lives of Vietnamese refugees (or would-be refugees) importantly provides dimensionality to a category of people who are often understood without identity—because they are without citizenship, rights, nation—and who exist through affective fear and helplessness, treated as undifferentiated "masses" of people suspended in a state of precarity. Put otherwise, *Boat People* offered *context* to the hundreds of thousands of Vietnamese boat refugees arriving in Hong Kong in the wake of war.

It must be remembered that when Hui's film was made, Vietnamese asylum seekers were washing ashore not only in Hong Kong but also in Southeast Asian countries such as Malaysia, Thailand, Indonesia, and the Philippines every week, if not daily. Although Hong Kong never turned them away like other countries, there existed a general lack of understanding as to why Vietnamese refugees were in, and allowed to be in, Hong Kong, and eventually a sense of "compassion fatigue" set in, as it did elsewhere in the region. *Boat People* addressed this social situation, and because of its political orientation—and I do not mean its "anticommunism" but rather its desire to empathize and sympathize with the refugees, to tell a "refugee" story—the film is an important and precursory text that speaks with a host of "boat people" and refugee narratives that have emerged in the past forty years.

Boat People was not Hui's first foray into the topic of Vietnamese refugees. In 1978 she directed "The Boy from Vietnam," a sixty-minute segment for Radio Television Hong Kong's highly rated television series *Below the Lion Rock*. In the short fictional piece, a young teenager (Ah Man) arrives in Hong Kong by himself after having escaped Vietnam on a boat. The film details his struggle to learn Cantonese, find work, and adapt to life in the city as he reunites with a cousin. By the film's end, Ah Man's cousin (Johnny), a gigolo, is murdered by one of his clients, and a close confidant (Chan Zhang) is deported, leaving him alone yet again. The most striking aspect of the short film is its depiction of the interior psychology of the main character. Through techniques such as flashbacks and voiceovers, viewers get a sense of the alienation and precarity that mark refugee lives in Hong Kong. "A Boy from Vietnam" would later become the first installment in what critics call Hui's "Vietnam Trilogy."

The second part of the trilogy, and Hui's third feature, is 1981's *The Story of Woo Viet*, starring a then unknown Chow Yun-Fat as an ex-South Vietnamese soldier (Woo Viet) who flees to Hong Kong en route to America. Violent encounters in the refugee camp—connected to Viet Cong agents—force the protagonist, along with a female love interest (Shum Ching), to illegally enter the United States via the Philippines. In the Philippines, Shum Ching is trafficked into prostitution and Woo Viet turns to the criminal underworld to save her. While the film can be seen primarily as a crime drama that is only incidentally about Vietnam, Patricia Brett Erens reminds us that it also "chronicles the various problems and brutalities to which the Vietnam refugees (boat people) were subjected: dismal refugee camps, physical abuse, robbery, bribery, attack by guards and other inmates, forced prostitution, and drug addiction, all of which led many to turn to crime as a means of survival."[7]

Boat People is in many ways a culmination of the themes explored in "A Boy from Vietnam" and *The Story of Woo Viet*. The film takes the "refugee narrative" back spatially and temporally to consider Vietnamese refuge seekers *before* their escape, chronicling the social and political conditions that created their exile. Set in Danang three years after the communist takeover, the film follows a Japanese photojournalist (Shiomi Akutagawa) as he travels to document postwar Vietnam. Initially, Akutagawa, guided by government officials, tours prearranged new economic zones (NEZ) that display happy and healthy children. When he returns to Danang, however, Akutagawa gains permission to move about the city unaccompanied. He then befriends a fourteen-year-old girl, Cam Nuong, on the streets and through her sees a country filled with poverty, brutality, and tyranny, including scenes of political repression, hunger, children foraging dumping grounds, forced relocations, imprisonments, and executions that occur in an atmosphere of fear and hopelessness. After a series of tragedies, Akutagawa sacrifices himself to help Cam Nuong gain passage out of Vietnam. The film ends with a close-up, freeze-frame of Cam Nuong and her little brother on a boat, facing an uncertain future.[8]

Upon completion, *Boat People* was screened in the *film surprise* sidebar at the 36th Cannes Film Festival. Originally slated for the official main competition, the socialist government of France, concerned about diplomatic relations with Vietnam, had requested the film's removal and thus limited its public profile at the event. Even with little publicity, the film was highly anticipated and stirred controversial debates over its "anticommunist" message. Subsequently, many reviewers found the film moving, but others criticized it for being "naïve, opportunistic, deficient in matters of historical perspective and melodramatic or sentimental."[9] Despite these initial mixed reactions, Poshek Fu and David Desser point out that the film "showed the world that there was more to Hong Kong cinema than stylish mayhem and that it had a politically engaged and deeply humanistic sensibility as well."[10]

Internationally, *Boat People* received a significant amount of attention, both as a distinct, socially conscious kind of Hong Kong cinema and as a charged political "condemnation" of communism. In Hong Kong, the film was an unmitigated box office success, earning over $HK15,500,000 and winning five prizes at the second annual Hong Kong Film Awards, including best picture and best director. Scholars have attributed this mainstream commercial success to the "1997 factor," citing moviegoers' and critics' adept ability to perform double readings of the film and thereby project the upcoming Chinese handover that preoccupied Hong Kong society onto the film's narrative. Li Cheuk-To, for example, states that, "when the film was released in Hong Kong, the local audience had no trouble in equating the Vietnamese Communist characters with their Chinese counterparts. Postliberation Vietnam was tantamount to post-1997 Hong Kong."[11] Yet, even with this early public presence and recognition, the film was eventually pulled from distribution in its home city and at one point banned in both Taiwan—because it was filmed in mainland China—and China—because of negative interpretations associated with the "1997 factor."[12]

From this cursory summary of how the film was initially received, it is evident that external political forces weighed heavily on the film, forces that at times displaced and obscured its narrative content as well as compromised its accessibility. Various political actors and interests shaped how *Boat People* circulated and how it was engaged as a cultural text in ways that diverted emphasis away from the plight of Vietnamese refugees. Now, over thirty years after its release, the film is often hailed as Hui's masterpiece and as one of the best Chinese films ever made, helping to define the career of one of Hong Kong's most prominent auteurs and its new wave movement. Li writes that the film was "a work that represented the climax of the new wave movement in Hong Kong."[13] However, the film is rarely screened either within or outside of Hong Kong. Julian Stringer argues that, while *Boat People* generated considerable political controversy, it "subsequently failed to achieve widespread international distribution," thus rendering it difficult to access, which has in turn limited opportunities for critical reconsideration.[14] He goes on to claim that the film text thus occupies the metaphoric position of a "refugee," uncannily mirroring its subject matter. *Boat People*'s complicated reception history—its "refugee life," if you will—reveals that it has been a difficult film to place. Though it stands firmly in the Chinese canon, it has also, as Stringer puts it, "remained stuck in a 'no-man's land,' waiting to arrive."[15] Thus, it is "hard for international film culture to 'remember' much about *Boat People* outside the '1997 factor.'"[16]

My discussion begins the work of critical reconsideration by highlighting the film's (as well as the Vietnam Trilogy's) uniqueness as a cultural document. First, in the context of Hong Kong cinema, *Boat People* is exemplary of the new wave movement that combined social realism with stylistic experimentation to tackle the "social problems" that concerned Hong Kong and its peoples. As such, it is one of the few films that, at a time when action and martial arts films dominated the mainstream market, attempted to direct filmic and public attention to important social issues, such as the boat refugees, through a delicate blending of art and entertainment.[17] Second, the focus on Vietnamese refugees was both timely and expedient—Hui has been criticized for being "opportunistic"—but was also not an obvious or standard production choice within the industry. To my knowledge, Hui remains the only prominent Hong Kong film director to have taken up the issue of the Vietnamese "boat people." It is safe to say that Hui's film played a formative role in the development of Hong Kong cinema, but pre-cisely because of that, it was also an anomaly when it first appeared on the scene.

Additionally, it is also instructive to position *Boat People* in relation to Hollywood in the late 1970s and early to mid-1980s, when an "explosion" of films about the war in Vietnam and its aftermath occurred on the big screen. As many scholars have pointed out, these movies tended to focus on the return-ing veteran and his experience of posttraumatic stress disorder.[18] That is, Hollywood was predominately interested in exploring how the war injured and damaged the (white) men—and, by extension, the American nation—who fought in it. As hundreds upon hundreds of thousands of Vietnamese refugees fled their homeland and immigrated to the United States, the filmic narratives being produced emphasized American losses. This is in line with American cultural memory of the war as a period of national injury, in which the only grievable, and thus valuable, lives were American ones.[19] In such a context, a film like *Boat People* could not have been—indeed, was not—made. At a time when Hollywood was building an industry on, and rewriting history through, filmic representations of "Vietnam," Hui's film focused on those pushed to the margins and background of American cinema. As David Desser notes, "in virtu-ally all these [American] films about the war except as targets, the Vietnamese scarcely exist; they are absent as people . . . few films deal with, or even acknowledge, the Vietnamese as subject."[20] Cross-read with classics such as *The Deer Hunter* (1978), *Apocalypse Now* (1979), *Platoon* (1986), and *Full Metal Jacket* (1987), Hui's film can be interpreted as a text that humanizes and makes griev-able the "targets" of American violence—the screaming and cowering villagers, the Viet Cong in black pajamas, the bodies in the ditches, the street prostitutes—that litter the backdrop of American action, both military and filmic.

The work of humanizing Vietnamese refuge seekers on film addresses a material referent and pressing social situation that preoccupied both Hong Kong and the world in the late 1970s. I turn now to the historical context of Vietnamese refugees in Hong Kong in order to explore the circumstances in which Hui's film emerged. Doing so sheds some light on what it attempted to *do* as a cultural object. In the years preceding the release of *Boat People*, the number of Vietnamese boat refugees arriving in Hong Kong surged to reach its highest levels. From 1978, when the "second wave" of refugee migration began, to 1981, one year before the film's premier, there were a total of 92,363 arrivals.[21] By the end of 1979 alone, over 55,000 refugees were housed in camps across the territory. These figures attest to the deepening "refugee crisis" developing in Hong Kong during the late 1970s and early 1980s. In reciting these statistics, I want to stress that Hui's film appeared at a crucial moment in the history of Vietnamese migration to Hong Kong, and examining *Boat People* within this historical frame allows us to focus in on the very people it depicts.

While the 1978 "second wave" was not the first group of Vietnamese refugees to come to Hong Kong (close to 4,000 refuge seekers landed in 1975 and were subsequently resettled in third countries within three years), they arrived at a time when the city was experiencing a period of rapid development and transition. The then-British crown colony was beginning to transform economically into a global city. Moreover, the 1997 handover, where the British, who had administered the city as a colony for over 150 years, would return Hong Kong to Chinese sovereign rule, lay on the not-so-distant horizon. Anxieties surrounding the future of the colony under communism abounded. As Yuk Wah Chan notes, "news about the influx of the Vietnamese boat people and the outflow of Hong Kong people ran parallel in the columns of Hong Kong newspapers."[22] Yet, despite, or perhaps because of, emerging and already existing concerns about the city's stability, it was perceived that the presence of Vietnamese refugees in Hong Kong threatened an established way of life: they were a potential disruption to the delicate social structure that the local people had worked hard to build.[23] Thus, while they were received at the ports, their presence in the city was not generally met with welcome.

Hui's film was made during a time in which initially sympathetic attitudes of the local society toward the boat refugees began to waver. The mass influx of refugees in the late seventies and steadily increasing numbers every year sparked fears of limited resources and lack of available space to accommodate them. Furthermore, this change in public opinion was fueled by reports that many of those arriving were part of the "refugee trade," in which the Vietnamese government itself facilitated the "smuggling" of these individuals out of the country, thus rendering them not refugees but opportunistic economic migrants in the eyes of many countries of first asylum. The largest source of

resentment, however, came from what many Hong Kong locals (of predomi-
nantly Chinese descent) perceived as the differential treatment that Vietnamese
refugees received in comparison to refuge seekers from mainland China.
In 1974 the Legislative Council passed a law declaring that illegal immigrants
or would-be refugees crossing the border from China would be summarily
returned. Hong Kong's borders were heavily policed, and those caught entering
from China were deported without leniency. In light of such hardline treatment
of people from China, the comparatively open and welcoming policy toward
Vietnamese asylum seekers was deemed "two-faced" or "double-standard."

It is within this larger climate of resentment, fear, and competing politics
that *Boat People* exists as a piece of cultural activism. That is, Hui's film is an
artistic intervention that aims to redirect political conversations, to affect social
change. Navigating criticism of the film's politics, Hui clearly explains her guid-
ing motivation: "It's just that I am trying to explain this particular phenomenon
of the boat people and their fleeing from the country, and to make people
understand why they flee. And that has the immediate effect of making the
Hong Kong people much more sympathetic."[24] While it is difficult to gauge
whether the film made individual or groups of filmgoers more sympathetic
toward the boat refugees, it was a categorical failure in terms of influence on
public opinion and official policy. Although it provoked controversy and debate,
as we have seen, the political discussion was directed away from the Vietnamese
refugees. As I have noted, the contemporary viewing public and reviewers of the
film saw it simply as an occasion to reflect on the fate of Hong Kong.

Moreover, treatment of the boat people worsened as the decade went on.
In 1982 a "closed camp" policy was initiated: where previously the refugees
could move about freely in the daytime, find employment, and enroll their
children in schools, they were now restricted to the confines of the camps,
which were run in a similar fashion to prisons. In the late eighties a strict status
determination procedure was set up to screen and differentiate "legitimate"
political refugees from "economic migrants." Those who did not fulfill the cri-
teria outlined for refugee status were streamlined for repatriation, which
quickly became the preferred "solution" to the crisis. The distinction between
refugee and economic migrant became pertinent as numbers of arrivals rose
amid compassion fatigue and pushback from western resettlement countries,
leaving ports of first asylum like Hong Kong to absorb the pressure and responsibility. Economic migrants, it was argued, abused the resettlement program,
turning it into an immigration system. Besides, they were not ideologically useful for many Western countries, particularly the United States, which built its
refugee policies around what Gil Loescher and John A. Scanlan call a "calculated
kindness"—an anticommunist ideology that privileged asylum seekers fleeing
("voting with their feet") communist regimes.[25]

Alex Cunliffe argues that the transformation of Hong Kong's refugee policies, from liberal humanitarianism in the late seventies to "humane deterrence" in the eighties, reflects the "changing character of the international refugee environment."[26] He writes, "In a post–Cold War environment when claims for refugee status spring mainly from third world crises, western policies towards asylum seekers appear to be more illiberal, and the capacity of the UNHCR to continue to promote durable solutions other than repatriation becomes more circumspect."[27] The developments of the global Cold War and the West's increasing reluctance to admit asylum seekers had direct effects on how a small city like Hong Kong administered its refugee populations. In the late eighties and early nineties repatriation was the clear plan of action at all levels in the international response. After some high-profile forced deportations resulted in riots and hunger strikes in the camps and detention centers, Vietnamese refugees in Hong Kong subsequently gained a reputation for being violent and unscrupulous. The outright maltreatment of the boat people and the hardening of Hong Kong's attitude toward refugees are indicative of how Hui's film did little to impact the government's handling of the "boat people" crisis, or of society's perception of them.

How the film gets taken up by the media and the public may determine its effectiveness as an activist piece and shed light on the society at large, but it does not negate the narrative that was captured on celluloid, the finished product that Hui delivered. To be clear, I am not making an argument based on the intention of the artist but rather on how successfully that intention was achieved or realized in the finished piece of art. And in that respect, Hui can be said to have rendered a complex and powerful story in which a crucial fragment in the Vietnamese migration narrative is told. Through what Mirana M. Szeto calls her "cinematics of everyday life," "an exploration of ordinary qualitative time and affective space," Hui offered a "human story" that provided much needed perspective and visualized a dimension of the refugee narrative that seldom gets considered.[28] From this angle, it is possible to view *Boat People* as an attempt to join public discourse on Vietnamese refugees in Hong Kong, one that was becoming increasingly hostile to the boat people. I maintain that even if the film failed as an activist piece, it was nonetheless an intervention and, crucially, one that narrates an important tale that resonates deeply with the Vietnamese diaspora, then and now.

The opening sequence of *Boat People* visually declares Hui's commitment to the ordinary people who bear the brunt of war on their bodies. In a medium long shot, the film's first image introduces Akutagawa as he photographs soldiers and tanks parading triumphantly in the street. The camera then pans out to give a bird's-eye view of the military procession and the civilians who have come to witness the liberation of Danang. As the scene proceeds, Akutagawa continues to intently snap pictures of the spectacle. Then both Hui's cinematic camera and Akutagawa's photographic lens rest on a boy with a maimed leg, using crutches as he begins to limp away from the crowd. Akutagawa follows the boy and takes a photo of his silhouette moving slowly down an empty alleyway. A burst of cheer is heard and the scene cuts back to a long shot of the parade. This first scene is a powerful commentary on storytelling and representation central to the film's politics: the disjuncture between appearance and reality, the official story against the lived one. With this opening, Hui emphatically establishes her perspective and her project—that of depicting the stories rarely seen or heard by the global community, the images not endorsed by governments, the people scarcely understood by asylum host societies.

The image of the maimed boy becomes a haunting symbol of the condition of life for ordinary people in postwar Vietnam—a society broken by war, individuals and families struggling to survive, wounds that have not yet healed. Three years after this image was taken, Akutagawa returns to Vietnam to document the country's reconstruction. The guides who oversee his visit are aware that the photos he captures will become important mediations between Vietnam and the rest of the world and thus arrange for a group of school children in an NEZ to perform "happiness" through song for his camera, as if to supersede the earlier image of the crippled boy. After this sanitized visit, Akutagawa meets Cam Nuong on the streets of Da Nang. Their first encounter involves hunger, a powerful sign of the deprivation and desperation the people endure: when rice noodles spill on the ground at a street stall, Cam Nuong and some other children scramble to gather them up. Akutagawa, standing nearby, takes their picture—one of his first "real" photographs in the country. He then follows Cam Nuong to the house she shares with her family, telling them, "I'm here to see how you live."

This desire to "see" what life in Vietnam is actually like becomes the driving thrust for Hui and her stand-in protagonist, who provides the central point of view and identification for audiences. To "see" how Vietnamese people live, or are unable to live, is to see the reasons they seek life elsewhere. When Cam Nuong agrees to have her picture taken, even though it is against the law to do so, Akutagawa gains "vision," a small opening into the lives of individuals who will at a future point in time become "boat people." As Akutagawa follows Cam Nuong on her daily routines, he begins to understand her desires, dreams, and struggles, and she becomes, for viewers, not only a sympathetic character but also one through whom a sense of identification is possible because the devastation of the surroundings are seen through her experience. She reveals how the war has destroyed her family: a dead father, a sick mother who resorts to prostitution to provide for her children, a hustling younger brother, and a toddler brother continually hungry. She takes Akutagawa to the "Chicken Farm," a bloody execution ground in which people gather to strip those executed of any remaining valuables for their own survival. She brings him to a landfill to watch people forage for scrap metal, where they both witness her brother's gruesome death from an unexploded ordnance. For Akutagawa, this "vision" is terrifying in its brutal revelation; the economic, social, and physical precarity in postrevolutionary Vietnam complicates the outsider's innocent desire to look and see.

In addition, Akutagawa becomes involved with a host of other characters whose lives one by one facilitate a deeper, more complex, and troubling understanding of postwar Vietnamese society. He encounters To Minh, who desperately tries to steal Akutagawa's camera in order to secure "exit money" and gain passage out of Vietnam. His subsequent arrest and deportation to an NEZ, where men are forced to remove unexploded landmines, provides a glimpse into the labor camps and prisons that were a mainstay of postwar life. In the camp, To Minh bribes an official to arrange for his escape. Having taken the gold, the official, who operates a "refugee trade," traps To Minh in a deadly scheme. In one of the film's most grueling scenes, To Minh clandestinely boards a boat full with passengers in the dark of night. As the boat drifts out onto the water, a flare is shot into the sky, illuminating the boat, and another boat carrying unidentified men (most probably guards) approaches with machine guns spraying bullets and murders the escapees. The men then board the boat to gather valuable possessions from the bloody corpses. This violent scene of desperation, corruption, and deceit articulates, in an extreme but utterly real way, the social climate in which many people weighed their chances at life and death. And while in this instance the guards and officials, those with power, are the enactors of violence, the film also shows us that no one is safe in such a system. Officer Nguyen, a nostalgic, French-educated government official with whom Akutagawa forms a brief friendship in the beginning of the film, is quickly and without much explanation, save a cadre's cryptic utterance that true comrades are without "petty bourgeoisie emotions," removed from power and mysteriously sent to a different NEZ. Read together, To Minh's death and Officer Nguyen's removal—different fates for two men in different social positions—are both part of the same unstable, capricious, and unforgiving society in which Vietnamese people existed in the wake of war. The attempted escape that To Minh undertakes, while dangerous and ultimately fatal, makes sense in absence of the rights, guarantees, and necessities for life.

It is this politically repressive and socially broken society that Akutagawa witnesses and that, through him, the film visually relays to audiences. The docudrama effectively uses this outsider character to describe the realities of postrevolutionary Vietnam. Yet, as a Japanese national, a foreigner, Akutagawa's function as the central point of reference in a movie about Vietnamese people might problematize their subjectivity by displacing them. However, even as Akutagawa is positioned as our eyes or interpretive lens, Hui undermines his role as protagonist. According to Stringer, Akutagawa "comes across as a severely compromised figure—a loner, ineffectual, a walking funeral pyre."[29] This is due to the director's decision to devote "screen time to a variety of secondary characters," which "works to deny the subjectivity and narrative stability of the . . . protagonist."[30] But rather than being a fault, as Stringer sees it, the destabilization of the main character in order to give glimpses of subjectivity to the people around him is precisely the kind of sensitivity that imprints itself on all of Hui's films and is undoubtedly the brilliance of her humanist sensibility. The forsaking of a consistent, central hero to accommodate multiple stories and perspectives is a choice that reveals the film's politics, one that emphasizes the Vietnamese people; Akutagawa here becomes a means through which to depict the main subjects of Hui's film.

To add to his conflicting positionality, Akutagawa's nationality—as a sign—complicates a simple reading in which the film is a straightforward critique of communism. Akutagawa can be read as an inscription of the complicated history of colonialism in Vietnam, of the spread of Japanese imperialism in Asia in the early and mid-part of the century. His presence in Vietnam suggests that in addition to French and American imperialism, the Japanese occupation of Vietnam is complicit in bringing about the contemporary conditions that force escape. Here Hui is not displaying historical naiveté but historical depth by linking the layered circuits of empire that shaped postcolonial Vietnam. In his seminal study *Vietnam at War*, Mark Philip Bradley writes, "Japan occupied Vietnam for most of the Second World War, creating an ever larger political and military vacuum in the country. . . . In fostering a potentially radical environment, Japanese occupation of Vietnam created critical preconditions for the communist rise to power in the August Revolution of 1945."[31] In no small part, for better or for worse, Japanese imperialism laid the groundwork for the political struggles and military conflicts that would entangle Vietnam in a long hot war during the latter part of the twentieth century. I contend that Akutagawa's insertion in the narrative as a Japanese national in Vietnam, however seemingly arbitrary, is a subtle critique of imperialism and, by extension, the capitalist order that both supports and is supported by it. His supposed role as "rescuer," as the foreigner who intervenes and saves the lives of the local people—itself a colonial trope—is disrupted when he finds himself overwhelmed by the dire postrevolutionary situation. Part of the reason he is "compromised" is that his character does not play out a familiar cultural script. His sense of inadequacy in the face of the complexity and immediacy of the events unfolding around him dislodges his unequivocal characterization as *the* foreign savior.

After witnessing hopelessness in the city and the harsh conditions of the NEZs, Akutagawa comes to the realization that postwar Vietnam is, for many, materially unlivable. In a scene late in the film he forgoes his photo project and tells a colleague, pointing to Cam Nuong and her brother: "they are the reality." Thus, when Cam Nuong's mother is publicly denounced by comrades for engaging in sex work and commits suicide, Akutagawa's transformation from observer to participant in the story is complete. He resolves to find passage for Cam Nuong and her brother out of Vietnam on a boat. To fund the escape, he sells his camera, his source of livelihood and agency, a symbol of his very vision. His earlier wish to "see" turns into a desire to help. Here vision demands action, an underlying motivation of the film as it sought to elicit sympathy from the people of Hong Kong and the international community. Yet it is precisely this vision that destroys Akutagawa as he loses his life in his efforts to physically get Cam Nuong on the boat. In the final moments of the film, while carrying a can of diesel fuel heading for the boat, he is shot by police patrols and combusts into flames. Again, while it might be tempting here to interpret Akutagawa as the self-sacrificing savior, his death at this crucial moment does not emphasize his heroism so much as the perils of life in, and escaping from, Vietnam. Akutagawa's dramatic and climatic immolation as the boat speeds away into the dark of night casts these journeys as a pressing matter of life and death. His burning body—death—is the ultimate reason the boat must carry its passengers to a place elsewhere.

The final image of the film, a close-up freeze-frame of Cam Nuong and her brother in a boat moving across the expanse of the blue sea, relays the incompletion of the refugee narrative. If the country left behind contains many dangers, the migration journey holds its own perils, and the place of arrival is never a guarantee for the boat people. The image is a plea in the form of an ethical question: how will the international community come to the aid of these desperate people? The end of the film suggests that the continuation and conclusion of the narrative, the resolution, must occur off-screen, in how governments and the local people, like Hong Kong and its residents, respond to the immediate plight of Vietnamese asylum seekers. As the credits roll against the frozen image, the docudrama asks audiences to consider social conditions and issues beyond the cinema's ultimately limited frame.

In the way that *Boat People* narrates and "documents" the material conditions in postwar Vietnam that led many to flee, the film joins many prominent Vietnamese American / diasporic texts that Michele Janette has categorized as "Tales of Witness."[32] Like Hui's film, memoirs such as Nguyen Ngoc Ngan's *The Will of Heaven* (1982), Le Ly Hayslip's *When Heaven and Earth Changed Places* (1989), and Duong Van Mai Elliot's *The Sacred Willow* (1999) provide insight into the motivations, both subjective and social, that propelled migration, many through perilous boat journeys. It is as a visual narrative, however, that the film becomes an important precursor, anticipating a variety of filmic texts that chronicle the boat refugees such as *The Beautiful Country* (2004) and *Journey from the Fall* (2006). Hui's film emerged at a crucial moment when many Vietnamese people were on the move, scattering outside their homeland in the wake of war. The story of the late-twentieth-century Vietnamese diaspora was forming, but the majority of those who experienced it did not have access to the means of self-representation. *Boat People* visualized moments of their lives, attempting to present a story from the perspective of the refuge seekers and, in doing so, remains an important cultural-historical artifact in the history of the war in Vietnam and its long-lasting aftermath.

NOTES

1. Jodi Kim, *Ends of Empire: Asian American Critique and the Cold War* (Minneapolis: University of Minnesota Press, 2010), 4.

2. Alan Rosenthal, "Introduction," in *Why Docudramas? Fact-Fiction on Film and TV*, ed. Alan Rosenthal (Carbondale: Southern Illinois University Press, 1999), xv. Emphasis in original.

3. Marita Sturken, "Reenactment, Fantasy, and the Paranoia of History: Oliver Stone's Docudramas," *History and Theory* 36.4 (1997): 74; and Leslie Woodward, "The Guardian Lecture: Dramatized Documentary," in *Why Docudramas? Fact-Fiction on Film and TV*, ed. Alan Rosenthal (Carbondale: Southern Illinois University Press, 1999), 104.

4. See Harlan Kennedy, "Ann Hui's *Boat People*—Cannes 1983," *American Cinema Papers*, October 2013, accessed September 2, 2013, http://americancinemapapers.homestead .com/files/BOAT_PEOPLE.htm.

5. Ibid.

6. Seminal analyses of *Boat People* that do not take into account, in a sustained manner, the Vietnamese refugee situation include Li Cheuk-To, "The Return of the Father: Hong Kong New Wave and Its Chinese Context in the 1980s," in *New Chinese Cinemas: Forms, Identities, Politics*, ed. Nick Browne et al., 160–179 (Cambridge: Cambridge University Press, 1994); Stephen Teo, *Hong Kong Cinema: The Extra Dimensions* (London: BFI, 1997); and Patricia Brett Erens, "The Film Work of Ann Hui," in *The Cinema of Hong Kong: History, Arts, Identity*, ed. Poshek Fu and David Desser, 176–196 (Cambridge: Cambridge University Press, 2000).

7. Erens, "The Film Work of Ann Hui," 182.

8. While my focus in this chapter is on *Boat People*, my overarching arguments about Ann Hui's project of representing Vietnamese refugees could be extended to the "Vietnam Trilogy" as a whole. I elaborate on *Boat People* because, out of the three, it has garnered the most critical and commercial success, and because it is, in my opinion and that of many others, a more fully developed film.

9. Summary of criticism quoted in Julian Stringer, "*Boat People*: Second Thoughts and Text and Context," in *Chinese Films in Focus: 25 New Takes*, ed. Chris Berry (London: British Film Institute, 2004), 18.

10. Poshek Fu and David Desser, introduction to *The Cinema of Hong Kong: History, Arts, Identity* (Cambridge: Cambridge University Press, 2000), 4.

11. Li Cheuk-To, "The Return of the Father," 167.

12. Audrey Yue, *Ann Hui's Song of the Exile* (Hong Kong: Hong Kong University Press, 2010).

13. Li Cheuk-To, "The Return of the Father," 167.

14. Stringer, *"Boat People,"* 17.

15. Ibid.

16. Ibid.

17. Teo, *Hong Kong Cinema.*

18. See, for example, Marita Sturken, *Tangled Memories: The Vietnam War, the AIDS Epidemic, and the Politics of Remembering* (Berkeley: University of California Press, 1997); Michael Klein, "Historical Memory, Film, and the Vietnam Era," in *From Hanoi to Hollywood: The Vietnam War in American Film*, ed. Linda Dittmar and Gene Michaud (New Brunswick, N.J.: Rutgers University Press, 1990), 19–40; and Tony Williams, "Narrative Patterns and Mythic Trajectories in Mid-1980s Vietnam Movies," in *Inventing Vietnam: The War in Film and Television*, ed. Michael Anderegg (Philadelphia: Temple University Press, 1991), 115–139.

19. I am drawing on the work of Judith Butler on the notion of "grievability" here. For more, see Judith Butler, *Frames of War: When Is Life Grievable?* (London: Verso, 2010).

20. David Desser, "Charlie Don't Surf: Race and Culture in Vietnam War Films," in *Inventing Vietnam: The War in Film and Television*, ed. Michael Anderegg (Philadelphia: Temple University Press, 1991), 86–87.

21. Yuk Wah Chan, "Revisiting the Vietnamese Refugee Era: An Asian Perspective from Hong Kong," in *The Chinese/Vietnamese Diaspora: Revisiting the Boat People*, ed. Yuk Wah Chan (New York: Routledge, 2011), 3–19.

22. Ibid., 9.

23. Sir Murray MacLehose, then governor of Hong Kong, remarked: "By hard work, social adaptation and realism based on the acceptance of the fact that resources are limited, the people have made for themselves a structure of life enormously better than 10 years ago. It is the benefits of this structure that they fear may be eroded by this influx of boat refugees over which they have no control." Qtd. in Sophia Suk-Mun Law, "Vietnamese Boat People in Hong Kong: Visual Images and Stories," in *The Chinese/Vietnamese Diaspora: Revisiting the Boat People*, ed. Yuk Wah Chan (New York: Routledge, 2011), 121–22.

24. Kennedy, "Ann Hui's *Boat People.*"

25. Gil Loescher and John A. Scanlan, *Calculated Kindness: Refugees and America's Half Open Door, 1945 to the Present* (New York: The Free Press, 1986).

26. Alex Cunliffe, "Hong Kong and the Indo-Chinese Refugees: Reflections on the International Refugee Environment," *Refuge* 16, no. 5 (1997): 39.

27. Ibid., 39–40.

28. Mirana M. Szeto, "Ann Hui at the Margins of Mainstream Hong Kong Cinema," in *Hong Kong Screenscapes: From the New Wave to the Digital Frontier*, ed. Esther M. K. Cheung et al. (Hong Kong: Hong Kong University Press, 2011), 53.

29. Stringer, "*Boat People*," 19.
30. Ibid., 18.
31. Mark Philip Bradley, *Vietnam at War* (New York: Oxford University Press, 2009).
32. Michele Janette, "Vietnamese American Literature in English, 1963–1994," *Amerasia* 29, no. 1 (2003): 267–286.

7

"The Deep Black Hole"

Vietnam in the Memories of Australian Veterans and Refugees

ROBERT MASON AND LEONIE JONES

The war in Vietnam was the first time that conscripted Australian civilians had been sent to fight outside Australian territory, and sixty thousand Australian troops were eventually deployed. The conflict became bitterly divisive over time, and many former service personnel found themselves socially ostracized on their return. The influx of Vietnamese refugees from 1976, following the communist victory, constituted the first significant number of nonwhite migrants to enter Australia since Federation in 1901. They too were viewed askance by the general population, and their experiences of pain and displacement were marginalized in a protracted debate about Australia's connectivity with Asia.

This chapter explores how memories of Vietnam influence both Australian veterans and Vietnamese refugees of the conflict in that country. It does not seek to suggest that the two sets of experiences are equivalent or consistently comparable; bringing together these two narratives highlights separate yet complimentary tensions between each groups' "conscious and unconscious meanings of experience as lived and remembered" and powerful cultural memories that inform an emerging national consciousness regarding the Vietnam conflict.[1] The significance lies in the relationship between memory and history, past and present, and its value in the possibility of new interpretations. This chapter derives from an extensive body of two hundred original interviews with Australian veterans of Vietnam. The interviews were conducted over a two-year period by Leonie Jones as part of a project seeking to give voice to veterans of the Battle of Fire Support Base Coral, Bien Hoa Province, in 1968. This chapter focuses on five key case studies in which veterans recall the Vietnam conflict, their return, and subsequent memories of that country. It juxtaposes these interviews with oral histories from former Vietnamese refugees who arrived in Australia after 1975. These oral histories were conducted as part of digital story-telling projects by the National Library of Australia and the State Library of Queensland. Here too, five key case studies were selected for comparative analysis.

The chapter questions how memories of Vietnam are constructed differently by Australian veterans and refugees. The racialized and militarized mythologies at the heart of Australian nationalism marginalized both groups in different ways. While veterans were unexpectedly denied the status of returned hero, refugees did not fit the paradigm of nation-building European migrant. Both disrupted the accepted categories of Australian citizenship, operating as forms of potential contagion at the heart of the national community. It is only recently that their stories have become publicly tellable.

Australian Experiences in Vietnam

In 1968 John, a willing twenty-two-year-old Australian soldier with 102 Battery, 12 Field Regiment, was on patrol as forward observer in Phuoc Tuy Province, Vietnam. It was a standard harass-and-interdict patrol when A Company came in contact with a Viet Cong patrol. The contact became intense; John called in artillery support, then took his AK47 and engaged with the enemy. He remains unsure if he killed anyone, but he is equally unsure if he did not. The enemy faded into the jungle under artillery and gunfire, leaving the Australians to follow protocol of searching the dead enemy for intelligence and burying the bodies.

John found himself searching a dead Viet Cong situated near him, one he might have killed. He was surprised the soldier was a young woman. John found identity papers on the woman that told him her name was Hieu and that she was nineteen years old. She carried party commendation certificates, a small amount of money, and family photos. John is not sure why he kept her personal effects: perhaps because he considered they were of no value to intelligence; perhaps, like many young soldiers at the time, as a souvenir of war; perhaps because he realized he may have killed this soldier, and this soldier was a woman.[2]

John went on to enjoy a nine-year career with the Australian Defence Force and, as a career soldier, is not sure why this particular memory still haunts him. He is now retired and is a father and grandfather in his late sixties. He infrequently attends Vietnam veteran reunions but takes part in ANZAC Day parades. John somewhat reluctantly revisited these disturbing memories during an oral history interview and later reconciled himself enough with the memory to hand Hieu's personal effects to another Vietnam veteran who

FIGURE 7.1 Ms. Hieu's belongings. Personal collection of Leonie Jones.

regularly travels to Vietnam. This second veteran intends to find Hieu's family and return her personal effects, to tell them their relative died a soldier and was buried with dignity.

John's process of coming to terms with memories of conflict is far from isolated. Over the past forty years, Australian public memory of the Vietnam War has undergone significant shifts. This is due to various factors such as the return of service personnel, public debates over the health of veterans, commemorative practices, and the portrayal of war in popular culture. It is also closely connected to changing conceptions of Australian national identity as the nation adjusts to the multicultural reality of a diverse population with a large number of Asian Australians. Forty years previously such groups had been viewed as anathema by large sections of the Australian population.

Australia has a longstanding historical sense of vulnerability to the Asian north, deriving from its geographical and cultural isolation as a British outpost. Following the Second World War, however, the sense of threat was countered by an increasing cultural and political affinity with the United States. The Australia New Zealand United States Alliance of 1951 helped cement this solidarity and "color line" between the white Pacific powers.[3] The United States' increasing paranoia regarding the spread of communism in Asia found resonance in Australia's own sense of racialized and geographic vulnerability.

It was in the context of escalating American involvement in Vietnam that Australia was called upon to provide thirty army advisors to the South Vietnamese government in 1962. The years following the Korean War had seen a precipitous decline in the size of the Australian Army and, as a consequence, in 1964 the Australian government introduced the National Service Act. The scheme required all twenty-year-old Australian males to register for a random ballot, which selected men by birth date. If selected, men were conscripted for two years of continuous full-time military service in the regular army. In May 1965 the Defence Act was amended to provide that these conscripts could also be required to serve overseas. From 1965 to Australia's withdrawal in 1972, almost 60,000 Australian regular army and national serviceman served in Vietnam. In total, 521 men died as a result of the war and over 3,000 were wounded.[4]

The social divisions caused by the Vietnam War took decades to heal. Australian soldiers had been returning home since the first military advisors went to Vietnam in 1962. However, from 1968 to 1969, Australian soldiers were returning home from active service to a society undergoing rapid transition. During 1968–1969, protests became increasingly violent. As in the United States, university students were at the forefront of these demonstrations, with broadcasters flashing images of protesting students clashing with police during street marches. Detractors called this type of behavior "un-Australian" and treasonous, but the traditional lines between right and wrong had become blurred. The Vietnam War was not the singular point of discontent in Australian society at this time but rather the center stage for a wide range of cultural and political shifts.

Soldiers were largely insulated from the growing discontent on the home front while in-country. However, soldiers arriving back home from 1969 onward found themselves thrust into a situation that surprised and bewildered them. The returned soldier has been an important part of Australian culture, invoking qualities imparted by the legacies of the World War I soldier. Over the ensuing decades Australian society had continued to develop this ethos. Its persistent elaboration put a soldierly masculinity at the center of the national ethos. Going away to fight became the apotheosis of citizenship and manhood, popularly termed "the ANZAC legend."[5] As national serviceman Robert Costello, who returned in 1969, recalls, "we were brought up in the Anzac tradition . . . we went away . . . did what we were asked to do . . . like our fathers before us . . . [but we] came back to a completely different world . . . they didn't want to know us . . . it was pretty rough."[6]

The collapse of Saigon in 1975 and the subsequent expulsion of ethnic Chinese Vietnamese saw the first arrival of Vietnamese refugees to Australia.

Prior to 1975 Australia had not experienced large numbers of Vietnamese or Chinese immigration or refugee entrants. Indeed, the country's immigration policy had been predicated on the exclusion of nonwhite migrants. Known as the White Australia policy, it had mitigated Australian anxiety regarding the country's proximity to Asia by placing white European identity at the heart of national identity. While the policy had been progressively dismantled from the mid-1960s, the country had no substantial Asian population.

Prior to the fall of Saigon, Australia had accepted fewer than one hundred Vietnamese adults. The Australian government's initially "miserly" response stands in sharp contrast to the large number of Vietnamese refugees resettled in the United States.[7] From early 1976, however, Vietnamese asylum seekers began to arrive in Australia by boat regardless of government wishes. While ministers had initially used the language of military invasion, the initial arrival refugees caused relatively little public angst.[8] Over the next five years, however, over two thousand Vietnamese arrived by boat, causing increased public concern and a return of earlier rhetoric of "invasion" and a "flood" of Asian immigrants.[9] From 1975 Prime Minister Malcolm Fraser sought to lead public opinion, increasing the number of Vietnamese refugees that Australia accepted and making significant efforts to limit the risk of a journey by boat. In total, fifty-four thousand refugees were resettled by 1982.[10] The following years would see rapid changes to the country's immigration and settlement policies as the multicultural framework sought to integrate new arrivals into an Australian nation predicated on ethnic diversity. Yet many in the broader Australian community remained profoundly concerned at the new arrivals' possible impact on national identity and culture.[11]

Life-Changing Journeys

The journey to Australia was understandably remembered with great clarity as a moment of central importance to refugees' life narratives. For some this was a moment of great vulnerability, which continues to resonate with contemporary Australian debates about irregular asylum-seeker arrivals by sea. For instance, after failed attempts to pay people to build a boat, Van Huynh eventually secured a passage on a boat bound for Malaysia.[12] With five hundred people crammed on a boat designed for one hundred, they eventually set sail by night. Recalling the extreme insecurity of the leaking vessel, Van recounted the "Thai pirates who did the check on our boat and took all the things, they searching for gold. Because they knew us, when we escape we took our, all the gold, and jewelry, and everything valuable to us. . . . They didn't kill anyone, [but] they all have knife." Terrified, the passengers acquiesced for fear that a struggle would destabilize the overloaded boat and "all the people will die in the sea." Not every stage of the journey was so fraught, and it was also remembered as the start of a new chapter of life in Australia. Van, for example, remembered the intensity of her feelings upon boarding the airplane for Australia in a marked juxtaposition to the insecurity that had gone before. She recalled that they felt "relieved! Wonderful! And, so happy and we just think all our lives in now on, we're going to have wonderful life. Together we all come out in one piece, all four of us."[13]

In contrast to the almost euphoric relief experienced by refugees leaving Vietnam, Australian military personnel experienced departure in a very different manner, and many were hesitant at leaving the army. Les Wilkinson was typical when he spoke of the appeal of the army's "discipline" and its redemptive capacity to "keep me on the straight and narrow."[14] The sense of camaraderie was strong and the return to Australia tinged with a sense of loss. Les said, "I only told one mate of my return date back to Oz as I felt kind of scared I think. As by now I was in a kind of comfort zone as the bond with all your mates was so strong. They were your family, your security blanket. You felt safe and now you were leaving that environment."[15] The journey back home on "the freedom bird" was still welcomed, although the arrival in Sydney was the first in a series of difficult transitions for the servicemen.[16]

The veterans' shock at leaving a combat zone was exacerbated by the maelstrom of feelings generated by the antiwar movement in Australia. While the men had been aware of the protests regarding Australian involvement in Vietnam, they had not been aware of their scale or intensity. One man, echoing similar sentiments expressed by the refugees, felt that "you just came home to a different world."[17] Others struggled to negotiate the sudden change in status. They could not comprehend the lack of the traditional respect afforded to them as returned servicemen and began to make strategies for hiding their time in Vietnam.[18] On his return, Alan Loxton was walking home on the side of a busy road without a sidewalk when he was pelted with fruit. The men's sense of disorientation and bewilderment on their return was marked with "people leaning out their cars yelling and . . . there's people abusing you and shaking their fists and all this sort of stuff." Loxton remembers thinking, "what have you come back to here?"[19]

The initial shock of arrival in Australia and how it was remembered by the war's participants was strongly connected to tangible factors such as the possible presence of family. Remembering the period as adults, the former refugees recall the sense of loss and disconnection. Almost every participant foregrounded the powerful sense of guilt and concern for elderly family members who remained in Vietnam and who would not have wanted to leave family homes even if it had been possible. Communication was at a minimum given the censorship of letters and photographs. The situation differed for those children who had been flown to Australia to be adopted as part of a series of "Babylift" evacuations, but who nonetheless experienced difficult transitions.

The challenge all refugees faced to their sense of self and family identity was profound. Those in Vietnam were simultaneously both physically absent and psychologically present. Family lives remained entangled with Vietnam long after veterans and refugees had left the country. For such war participants, the memories of family continued to resonate in the present, but the concept of family members in Vietnam was imbued with conflict and rupture across time and space.[20]

Landscapes of Loss

Memories of Vietnam understandably focused on conflict and contestation, but veterans' and refugees' sense of the trauma connected with the memories differed. For the refugees, whose entire way of life was altered by the war, concepts of cultural trauma offer a useful means to engage with their remembered experiences. Rather than describe impersonal structures and grand historical narratives of war, participants focused on reaffirming and situating individuals and human individuality in their personal life histories. Veterans, whose trauma was less cultural than individual, were reluctant to speak of the self and struggled to locate the individual in events of great brutality. For these men, Vietnam was the site of historic struggles that demanded recognition and respect.

In their oral history accounts, relatively few of the refugee participants spent extended periods of time describing abstract notions of war and its impact on landscape. Van recalled the Tet Offensive and recalled that "cities were very bad in war. The communist attack everywhere, the fighting all over the city." Yet the personal testimony remains at the heart of the narrative as she continued: "I can see the smoke and the rocket fire from the helicopter, and the people carry their belonging and run around and yelling and crying. The whole town was very scared, we didn't know what happened at all."[21] Personal testimonial was less common for the veterans, although the experience of being in a war zone was nonetheless one of "ducking and weaving, having to wear green uniforms, sling our rifles on our shoulders, worry about the next rosters, and were we on duty that night, and for how long, were we going to be under attack, you know."[22]

Both cohorts departed from a sense of personal testimonial to bear witness to friends and their strength and suffering within the landscape of Vietnam. As Ian McCartney commented about his return to Australia, "In a way we were glad to be away from it, but your mates are still out there and they're gonna cop some more . . . you knew that was going to happen."[23] Such narratives are embedded at the center of the Australian ANZAC legend, which celebrates

FIGURE 7.2 Australian mateship. Personal collection of Leonie Jones.

"mateship" as the central attribute of Australian citizenship. One veteran recalled the time spent relaxing when "you got to meet new faces. In talking to them you found that in civvy street, before they became Nashos [conscripted National Servicemen], the different jobs they had. In my case from the boot trade to sport stars, mechanics, school teachers. There was no discrimination as to who got called up."[24] For Les, this experience was a strong reaffirmation of the traditional egalitarianism at the center of Australian national identity.

Friendship would also become central to integration into Australian society. Refugees and veterans alike drew on remembered friendship to create a sense of stability amid social hostility to them as outsiders. Few of the former refugees described friends lost in the conflict. Instead, in a hierarchy of emotional proximity, they described the loss of close family members during the war. My Linh recalled that the "fall of Saigon in 1975 led to the separation from my family. I was separated from Dad because he was taken as a prisoner of war [when I was] at the age of six."[25] Similarly, Van recalls the earlier Tet Offensive as part of her family history: "The second day it was the third day of the Tet and my father wounded, and we found the way to take him to the hospital to give him some medicine, he came back and got a heart attack and died in that night."[26] These memories provided a sense of personal narrative in the midst of bewildering social, cultural, and personal change for refugees and soldiers alike.

Memories tended to occlude the destruction caused by the war to homes and property from the listener. This may have been partly a response to the refugees' status as people who, as one refugee said, "owe the government and its people for accepting my family and giving us the opportunity to rebuild our lives."[27] It was undoubtedly also a consequence of the awkward positioning of Vietnam in the national imagination. On occasion the destruction caused by troops was voiced as part of the personal narrative, but culpability was obscured. Van recalled that "at that time the war still happened, and at night we had to sleep underneath the very big wooden bed so that could protect us from the bullets and the rocket from the both sides fighting. I was very sad, very worried, if the war happened we didn't have any savings, we didn't have anything to live on."[28] Veterans similarly tended to be silent on the topic of destruction experienced by civilians, partly because of the difficult identification of who were members of the Viet Cong. The men did occasionally allude to the conditions but tended to distance themselves as third-party observers, stating that "you got to travel through villages and to see the houses and what they made them out of. It was very interesting; even old Coke and beer cans flattened out to make walls."[29]

The difficult position of the war in Australian culture intersected with historical fears of Asians to make everyday life difficult for the refugees. Children struggled to blend into an Australian culture that focused on visible difference as a marker of community exclusion. Jen remembered "living in a country town when I was confronted with stereotypes, cruelty, racism and ignorance. I was reminded constantly of not belonging." Confusingly, for the intercountry adoptee, however, "I didn't speak Vietnamese, and I had little knowledge of Vietnam. . . . My parents tried to encourage me to accept my Vietnamese heritage but I was too scared and refused to learn. I was angry; confused about my identity."[30] This was compounded by the ongoing racism in Australian society toward people from an Asian background during the 1980s and 1990s.[31] The intercountry adoptees developed hybrid forms of identity that derived from "having to deal with growing up as an Australian in a Vietnamese body."[32]

Just as refugees struggled with how to integrate their dual identities as Australian and Vietnamese, the veterans similarly struggled with reconciling their role in Vietnam with community norms. Many sought to hide their involvement in the conflict. The accusation that they were "child killers" haunted them in public spaces when their identity was revealed.[33] The public opprobrium "left a sour taste in my mouth as the protest was starting to come real to me. I even threw away my active service badge when it arrived in disgust. So I had nothing to do with the RSL [Returned and Services League] . . . with all the protests that were going on we were made to feel outcasts or something. So we hid the fact of being to Vietnam."[34] This shame was to be a central legacy of the conflict for decades.

The sense of nostalgia for lost heritage present in the refugee narratives was absent for the veterans. Instead, and parallel with the close camaraderie with mates, there was an angry sense of betrayal by broader Australian society. Whereas the refugees were aware of the expectation that they would defer to community norms, veterans expected that the high status of ANZAC heroes would be accorded to them. Instead, social attitudes accentuated their sense of alienation. As a result, Alan felt he "had just changed too much," saying, "I just become less tolerate [sic] of people and so on, and unfortunately I became more bad tempered I guess." Consequently, he said, "I just buried my head in work for many years and that kept me sane. I'd just changed so much . . . you think it won't change you much . . . I'll just get out and it won't change you too much . . . but I had just changed too much."[35] There was disappointment among refugees at community racism, but it was carefully couched. For veterans, society's failure to recognize their service inflicted a double wound on the men, denying them recognition and silencing their voices.

The sense of social ostracism was profound for the veterans. Partly, this drew on their earlier expectation that they would be accorded the usual respect due to returned service personnel. Ian's testimony is typical in this regard, when he commented that "the hard part was we weren't accepted. And my grandfather was in the First World War and my father in the Second and we had respect for them. When we got back, we sort of didn't get that respect."[36] This break from the past was tangible, with social networks and friendships broken in the ensuing debates. Other veterans were bemused at the rapid change in society that suddenly placed them outside parameters of social acceptability. As Alan felt, "if they [the antiwar protesters] were so unhappy about involvement, well that's fine . . . but it wasn't my idea . . . you just came home to a different world. How quickly things change."[37]

One of the main points of similarity between the refugees and the veterans was their inability to speak of the pain that had occurred in Vietnam and that continued to be experienced in Australia. Their time in Vietnam structured much of veterans' personal identity and subsequent social experiences not only in the memory of the violence but also in the lack of social recognition subsequently afforded to their experiences. Speaking for his mates, Ian felt that "they've all been affected and they're still affected and nothing will change that. . . . You're only there for twelve months but that twelve months has affected your whole life."[38] The experience of returned national servicemen differed from enlisted soldiers in that the latter were able to self-counsel during their ongoing careers in the armed services. National servicemen, in contrast, returned home and in so doing were geographically isolated and dispersed from the support their mates offered through shared experience.

Family and friendships were put under immense strain by the inability to speak about experiences that came to haunt everyday life. Many veterans came to recognize the need for medical assistance, but the process took decades of isolation and pain. Ian described the events in Vietnam as a "deep black hole somewhere and you just can't talk about it." His evocative description captures not only the profundity of the memory but also that its presence was defined by absence and an ability to articulate something of great importance. As Lars Frers suggests, the power of absence derives from a personal implication in the events: "Those who experience something as absent have to fill the void that they experience with their own emotions, they have to bridge the emptiness that threatens their established expectations and practices."39 Only when the men met together could they "talk to each other, because we all know. We are all the same."40 The sense of having a shared incommunicable loss, with little individual capacity to resolve it alone, resonated throughout the interviews with Jones. As Les discussed about his mates, "it was good to talk to them as you could get a lot of your hidden memories off your chest."41 These so-called hidden memories are common among those who have experienced loss associated with a trauma that cannot be easily articulated in a society that denies them their legitimacy.

For the refugees, too, there was an inability to articulate the sense of rupture they experienced from their former homes and family networks. Yet they lacked the veterans' sense of collective identity. The Australian community had little interest or capacity to understand the loss caused by the decision to leave homes in Vietnam, given the social emphasis placed on migrant integration and the privilege of Australian residency. They were also deeply suspicious of any possible political views held by the new arrivals, drawing on longstanding national hostility to any risk of foreign influence in the body politic. Such sentiment severely restrained the refugees' capacity to speak outside their families. Similarly to the veterans, the refugees' inability to speak of the mental injuries experienced in Vietnam caused great suffering. My Linh remembers that early "life was struggling. I went through lots of obstacles, even thinking of suicide."42 Anh recalled that "those years proved very difficult for all of us. On my part I experienced a profound sense of inadequacy as I tried to be a mother, daughter, wife, and an aunt all at the same time. Work came a very distant last."43 Faced with the frequent racism of Australian society, it has only been relatively recently that the former refugees found the capacity to articulate their loss and memories in community fora. For both refugees and veterans, the unspeakable nature of the experiences fractured families across generations as parents and children were unable to break the deep silences enforced upon them.

The fraught question of whether to return to the physical landscape of Vietnam is indicative of deep emotional and psychological memories of the country. Refugees were often torn at what return would involve personally and what it would challenge mnemonically.44 Many had returned on a number of occasions, prompted by a desire to see family members before their deaths.

Others sought to maintain their children's connection with cultural heritage. There was a residual fear of return, however, and of their continued emotional implication in the landscape. Jen "always knew that [she] needed to make the journey back to Vietnam, [but] due to fear . . . had always resisted taking that step."[45] Those refugees who did return spoke in general terms about the impression of increased wealth and economic opportunity compared to when they had left. Their tendency to focus on changed cityscapes and familiar smells is consistent with other explorations of how Vietnamese Australians reconnect with their pasts in discussions of return.[46] Interviews with veterans revealed a comparable awareness of change, but Vietnam was an exoticized landscape that remained colored by guilt.

Australian veterans have increasingly returned to visit Vietnam since the Vietnamese government relaxed restrictions in the late 1980s. Veterans return for a variety of reasons, including associated post-traumatic stress disorder illnesses, a sense of pilgrimage, lingering guilt, and the desire to close old war wounds. Many, in common with American veterans, have become involved in rebuilding schools, orphanages, hospitals, and community centers. Yet veterans overwhelmingly return in order to commemorate and remember. Most Australian veterans haunt familiar sites in Ho Chi Minh City and former military sites. These include the remains of former American and Australian servicemen's "R and R" resort at Vung Tau, the former Australian task force base at Nui Dat and the site of the Battle of Long Tan (1966). The latter is the site of a commemorative cross erected by Australian soldiers three years after the battle in 1969 and is now the site for memorial services held by veterans on the battle's anniversary. Similar services are also held at the site of the Battle of Fire Support Base Coral, where the Vietnamese government erected a memorial over the mass grave dug by Australian soldiers. This site, although erected to honor the North Vietnamese dead, has over the years become a site for Australian veterans to gather and commemorate.

In 2007, to coincide with the forty-year anniversary of the Battle of Fire Support Base Coral (1968), a group of 1RAR (Royal Australian Regiment) veterans traveled to Vietnam to the battle site in Bien Hoa Province. This particular group of Australian veterans was, for the first time, accompanied by North Vietnamese Army veterans. Garry Prendergast, on his second visit to the site, found himself "a little more comfortable this time; the first time was quite upsetting . . . but to come back a second time answers a couple of little questions. It's still emotional, but a little bit more in check now."[47] Garry found himself sharing an emotional, on-site commemorative service with Col. Tran Xuan Ban. According to Garry, to come back and to meet this veteran was one of the best things he had done in his life, and his attitude was understandably both emotional and circumspect: "I remembered my comrades and Vietnamese soldiers in the battle. I feel sad because both sides suffered loss. I have wanted to come back for quite a long time to this place and pay my respect to the soldiers of both sides. I feel so much pain released."[48]

Both Peter Burquest and Alan Loxton, first-time returnees to Vietnam, shared Garry's sentiments and, although initially experiencing apprehension at the thought of being in the physical landscape of the battle, also found the experience to be cathartic and a sense of emotional release and intellectual rationalization aided by the security of being surrounded by mates. Loxton shared, "It's emotional, a bit queasy in the stomach, a bit knotted up. But, it feels rewarding . . . it feels rewarding. It's almost as if I've come out of a cloudy hazy period that's been there for many many years and I'm just sort of coming out into the light."[49] Burquest recalled, "This is a pretty emotional site for me to be hanging around. And I find that now that I'm here it's not as bad. I thought it was going to be something that was going to be ripping my heart out, because good fellas lost their lives here. . . . You know from the interview before that I was personally responsible for killing some people here and that has played on my mind. . . . No . . . I'm coping with it pretty well I think."[50]

Tran Xuan Ban, a twenty-five-year-old North Vietnamese Army tactical consultant at the time of the battle, alluded to the deep psychological and emotional wounds suffered by veterans on both sides when he said that it was time to reconcile the past: "This time is also an opportunity for us to put aside the past, that we feel closer and remember of the dead, that we encourage each other. When we were young, we met in a not so nice circumstance. Now it is time we close the past and look forward to a better future. Today is a special day."[51] Robert Costello shared Tran Xuan Ban's sense of satisfaction regarding reconciliation between opposing soldiers, if not for him personally: "I'm very emotional . . . this made me very, very emotional, particularly laying the poppies. I got very upset. I got upset for our fellows and I got upset for the enemy as well. I believe in the end they got a better country now than what they had before. . . . I don't think I'll be ever able to [reconcile feelings of his personal experience as a soldier in Vietnam]. I do feel very strongly for our soldiers and for the enemy soldiers and now I hope that's been reconciled. I think it has."[52]

Conclusion

The experiences of former refugees and veterans in Vietnam had lasting implications for their integration into Australian society. Testimonials from refugees are characterized by cultural trauma where the collective memory, defined by a perceived loss of a whole way of life, "threaten this society's existence and cultural presuppositions."[53] At an individual level, as collectively, the result is to mar forever their memories and future identities in fundamental and irrevocable ways.[54] In contrast, the struggle with individual and personal trauma haunts the veterans. Both groups have been publicly silenced in their ability to speak and gain recognition of their pain. Society remains unsure of the period historically and of how it should speak of historical justice, legitimate violence, and victimhood for all concerned. The legacies of the conflict in Vietnam continue to resonate throughout Australian society. This is part of global changes in how Vietnam is memorialized and remembered in Vietnam, the Global North, and wherever the Indochinese diaspora is located.

The legacies also reflect the changes in Australian society as the egalitarian and militarized aspects of the ANZAC legend regain a central position in the national imagination, having been challenged in the decades following the Vietnam War. Concurrent to this process, visibly different migrants from Asia are no longer viewed as community outsiders. Just as the refugees are now recognized to have brought complex memories of difficult pasts with them, those memories are memorialized as part of the social and historical connections that bind Australians to the world. The ethical imperative felt by John at the start of this chapter to return Hieu's personal effects to her family reflects these changes. The contested past remains present, but the trauma is beginning to be reevaluated as part of the global story of dispersal, loss, and re-creation of community.

NOTES

1. Robert Perks and Alistair Thompson, eds., *The Oral History Reader*, 2nd ed. (London: Routledge, 2006), 3.

2. John Harmes, Interview with Leonie Jones, 2007, The Battle of Fire Support Base Coral 1968: Oral History Collection (hereafter BFSBC-OHC).

3. Marilyn Lake and Henry Reynolds, *Drawing the Global Color Line: White Men's Countries and the International Challenge of Racial Equality* (New York: Cambridge University Press, 2008).

4. Ian McNeill and Ashley Ekins, *On the Offensive: The Official History of Australia's Involvement in Southeast Asian Conflicts, 1948–1975* (Crow's Nest, NSW: Allen and Unwin, 2003), 477–478.

5. Peter Cochrane, "At War at Home: Australian Attitudes during the Vietnam Years," in *Vietnam Remembered*, ed. Greg Pemberton (Sydney: Weldon Publishing, 1990), 176.

6. Robert Costello, Interview with Leonie Jones, 2007, BFSBC-OHC.

7. Klaus Neumann, "Oblivious to the Obvious? Australian Asylum-Seeker Policies and the Use of the Past," in *Does History Matter? Making and Debating Citizenship, Immigration and Refugee Policy in Australia and New Zealand*, ed. Klaus Neumann and Gwenda Tavan, 47–64 (Canberra: Australian National University Press, 2009), 50.

8. Department of Immigration and Citizenship, *Seeking Asylum within Australia: Fact Sheet 61*, accessed January 23, 2013, http://www.immi.gov.au/media/fact-sheets/61asylum.htm.

9. Janet Phillips and Harriet Spinks, *Boat Arrivals in Australia since 1976: Background Notes* (Canberra: Australian Parliamentary Library, 2011).

10. Rachel Stevens, "Political Debates on Asylum Seekers during the Fraser Government, 1977–1982," *Australian Journal of Politics and History* 58, no. 4 (2012): 526.

11. Zoe Anderson, "Borders, Babies, and 'Good Refugees': Australian Representations of 'Illegal' Immigration, 1979," *Journal of Australian Studies* 36, no. 4 (2012): 501.

12. Van Huynh, Interview with Ann-Mari Jordens, 2007, National Library of Australia Oral History Collection (hereafter NLA-OHC), accessed December 1, 2011, http://nla.gov.au/nla.oh-vn3998338.

13. Ibid.

14. Les Wilkinson, Letter to Leonie Jones, 2007, BFSBC-OHC.

15. Ibid.

16. John Dalton, Interview with Leonie Jones, 2007, BFSBC-OHC.

17. Alan Loxton, Interview with Leonie Jones, 2007, BFSBC-OHC.

18. Wilkinson, Letter.

19. Loxton, Interview.

20. Robert Mason, "Remembering the Family Home: Emotions, Belonging, and Migrant Men in Multicultural Australia," *Journal of Australian Studies* 37, no. 3 (2013): 380.

21. Huynh, Interview.

22. Dalton, Interview.

23. Ian McCartney, Interview with Leonie Jones, 2007, BFSBC-OHC.

24. Wilkinson, Letter.

25. Qtd. in Nathalie Nguyen, "My-Linh's Story," in Nathalie Nguyen, *Memory Is Another Country: Women of the Vietnamese Diaspora* (Santa Barbara, Calif.: Praeger, 2009).

26. Huynh, Interview.

27. Tung Tran, "Rebuilding Our Lives," *Queensland Stories*, accessed December 1, 2011, https://www.youtube.com/watch?v=ei4SzzOlVjw.

28. Huynh, Interview.

29. Wilkinson, Letter.

30. Jen Thu Ha Fitzpatrick, "Jen's Story," *Queensland Stories*, accessed December 1, 2011, http://hdl.handle.net/10462/deriv/194343.

31. David Mellor, "The Experiences of Vietnamese in Australia: The Racist Tradition Continues," *Journal of Ethnic and Migration Studies* 30.4 (2006): 631.

32. Fitzpatrick, "Jen's Story."

33. McCartney, Interview; and Wilkinson, Letter.

34. McCartney, Interview.

35. Loxton, Interview.

36. McCartney, Interview.

37. Loxton, Interview.

38. McCartney, Interview.

39. Lars Frers, "The Matter of Absence," *Cultural Geographies* 20, no. 4 (2013): 431.

40. McCartney, Interview.

41. Wilkinson, Letter.

42. Nguyen, "My-Linh's Story."

43. Anh Donald, "Two Wars, Three Cities, Four Generations," *Queensland Stories*, accessed December 1, 2011, http://hdl.handle.net/10462/deriv/194344.

44. For additional exploration of how memories of return operate, see Nguyen, "My-Linh's Story."

45. Fitzpatrick, "Jen's Story."

46. Mandy Thomas, "Vietnamese in Australia," in *Encyclopaedia of Diasporas: Immigrant and Refugee Cultures Around the World*, Vol. 1–2: *Overviews and Topics and Diaspora Communities*, ed. I. Skoggard, C. Ember, and M. Ember (New York: Springer, 2005), 1143.

47. Garry Prendergast, Interview with Leonie Jones, 2007, BFSBC-OHC.

48. Garry Prendergast, Interview with Loan Khong, "Poppy and White Rubber," *Tuoi Tre Newspaper*, 2007.

49. Loxton, Interview.

50. Peter Burquest, Interview with Leonie Jones, 2007, BFSBC-OHC.

51. Tran Xuan Ban, Interview with Loan Khong, "Poppy and White Rubber," *Tuoi Tre Newspaper*, 2007.

52. Costello, Interview.

53. For additional explanation of how cultural trauma is defined within a collective memory context, see "Cultural Trauma and Collective Memory" in Ron Eyerman, *Cultural Trauma: Slavery and the Formation of African American Identity* (London: Cambridge University Press, 2002).

54. A more recent (and somewhat controversial) notion of cultural trauma (events not inherently traumatic) and the nature of collective identity is explained in Jeffrey C. Alexander, *Cultural Trauma and Collective Identity* (Berkeley: University of California Press, 2004).

8

Missing Bodies and Homecoming Spirits

HEONIK KWON

In his celebrated novel *The Sorrow of War*, Bao Ninh presents an unsettling view of the physical and human landscape of Vietnam after the war. His moving narrative centers on Kien, a war veteran who struggles with memories of the dead and lost. The novel opens with Kien in the Jungle of Screaming Souls, a remote location in the central highlands, on a mission to recover the bodies of the missing war dead. Kien feels that "for every unknown soldier, for every collection of MIA [missing in action] remains, there was a story."[1] He strikes up a conversation with a comrade, the driver of the body-collecting vehicle, on the meaning of the war for the dead. "If we found a way to tell them news of a victory, would they be happier?" Kien asks. His comrade replies, "Even if we could, what would be the point? People in hell don't give a damn about wars. They don't remember killing. Killing is a career for the living, not for the dead."[2] Later in the story Kien is troubled by memories of dead comrades and friends as well as of the enemies whose lives he took, and he attempts to confront these haunting memories by writing about their lives. After spending a few nights without sleep, writing furiously, Kien finds himself wandering aimlessly in the street and later notices that the street is named after Nguyen Du, an eminent eighteenth-century Vietnamese scholar and author of a powerful poem that is widely used in Vietnamese rituals today as an incantation for the wandering souls of the dead.

Kien's story illustrates that the recovery of the missing bodies of war dead was one of the main priorities of the military and political authorities of revolutionary Vietnam after the fall of Saigon in 1975. Many soldiers volunteered for body-finding missions, and civilians were urged to report to the authorities any known sites of hastily buried combatants. The missing bodies were not only a concern for the state, however. After the war ended, numerous families in

Vietnam continued searching for their missing children and siblings, or their remains.

The Vietnam War was an astonishingly violent, painfully chaotic war that resulted in countless missing persons and deaths away from home villages. When the war was over, the physically and spiritually exhausted survivors returned to begin a new life with what little remained, only to encounter a situation that greatly challenged their ability to start over. Their homeland was now dotted with both deadly weaponry and the remains of the unknown dead buried in shallow graves. The intrusion of foreign dead, Vietnamese and non-Vietnamese, on the village lands was paralleled with another, different crisis in the villages' moral landscape: the bodies of numerous close kin were missing and unable to be buried in their home villages. This war-induced displacement of human lives long haunted postwar Vietnamese villages (particularly in the south), which were never the same as before, despite the appearance of recovery and normality encouraged by the postwar national reconstruction efforts. The surviving families faced the reality of missing persons and missing bodies with immense anxiety, guilt, and pain—despite the continual efforts of the postwar state authority to motivate the people to look forward with hope rather than back toward the ruins of history.

The postwar Vietnamese state took over the role of funeral host from the families. At the center of every village a cemetery was built for the village's fallen war heroes to be laid to rest according to the disciplinary and geometrically ordered burial tradition of European war cemeteries. The state taught the villagers to treat the cemetery as the most sacred place within the village and, moreover, to distinguish the sacredness of this place from their traditional notions of the sacred customarily associated with their ancestral graves and altars.

The state also undertook the laborious work of locating and recovering the still-missing war heroes. The postwar state bureaucracy allocated immense administrative resources to the search for the MIA heroes of the war against America, sending joint army and party search teams to the remote highlands and ruined cemeteries. Within their communal and domestic lives, however, the citizens of postwar Vietnam were discouraged from dwelling on the missing members of the society, especially when these amputated members of the family fought and died on the opposite side of the revolutionary war. The state of Vietnam was a single, monopolistic undertaker in the postwar era, and Vietnamese families were not allowed to challenge its authority to regulate life as the "objective afterlife."[3] However, much of this situation has changed since.

After the *doi moi* reform in the late 1980s, Vietnamese families became increasingly free to commemorate their dead in ways they felt appropriate, often in less secular ways than previously allowed. Today the commemoration of the dead is also more inclusive than before in that it has become increasingly open to the memory of the dead who fell on the "wrong" side of the civil war. However, still today—a generation after the war has ended—the recovery of missing bodies remains a vital element in the story of the American War told and experienced in Vietnam.

In postwar Vietnamese society, there was initially a turbulent relationship between the political authority and the family and community with regard to the question of body recovery. Similar disputes have existed in the history of modern warfare.[4] These disputes between the state and the family can barely be heard on the street while the drum of war is being beaten; however, the loud drumbeats never entirely silence the family's voices or quiet its anxious nerves. In modern warfare, the clash between the family and the state may continue after the war has ended in the controversy over burial. A well-known example is the controversy in post–World War I France between the families of the fallen soldiers, who hoped to bury the bodies in their home regions, and the state, which insisted on keeping the bodies in the battlefields where the soldiers had fallen. Who should determine the destiny of the bodies of the fallen? Who has the right to decide the home of their afterlife? These questions have been central not only to many postwar societies in modern times but also to the theory of politics since the time of G.W.F. Hegel, who understood that the question of a soldier's burial can complicate a family's political life and that an inappropriate burial can shake the family's moral ties to the sovereign order. Although postwar Vietnamese society had much in common with other postwar societies, there are distinct features in the Vietnamese culture of commemoration that should be considered in order to understand the significance of missing bodies and of the efforts to account for them in the postwar social and political development of Vietnam. The concept of *xác*, one of the Vietnamese terms for body, is particularly relevant in the consideration of commemorative efforts at the family and community level.

The Concept of *Xác*

The concept of *xác* is special among the several Vietnamese terms that refer to the human body. It means "corpse" (as in *xác chết*); however, its meaning incorporates not only the material condition of a body that is lifeless and immobile but also the related but opposite condition of a soul that is free and full of life. When the body dies, a common popular Vietnamese belief is that the soul becomes free and can move between the place of death and the place of burial as well as among other places with historical attachment and where its historical identity is remembered, such as the family's domestic ancestral altar. The mobile soul of the dead may also appear in different places simultaneously, and this is recognized as a sign of its vigor and power, which the Vietnamese express with the concept of *linh*, meaning "efficacious," "vital," or "powerful." When a spirit intrudes directly into someone's body in what is commonly referred to elsewhere as spirit possession, the mode of communication is called *xác* or *nhập xác*, which in this context means "the spirit enters the body." In central Vietnamese regions, these two terms are also colloquial references to spirit mediums, that is, "people whose bodies are capable of receiving spirits."

Just as there are two opposite conditions of *xác*, Vietnamese mortuary culture demonstrates two different ways to relate to death. One is an elaborate and complex system of dealing with the lifeless body. Here the corporeal integrity of the deceased is of great importance, and proper ritual preparation of the body for internment is considered essential for the welfare of the deceased person and a precondition for a harmonious relationship between the dead and the living. The place of burial should be well ordered and permanent, and it should be marked by clearly identifiable structures and borders. It is believed that unless the bodies are buried in a proper place, following an appropriate rite, the commemoration of death remains incomplete. Vietnamese mortuary tradition has developed a long, elaborate sequence of rites to separate the soul from the body. In this process, popularly called *hồn bạch*, which refers to the white cloth or paper object used to capture the freed soul of the deceased, it is necessary for the living to undertake the public lamentations called *khóc*. The process is also necessary to help the dead realize that they have undergone the radical transition of death and to start relating to the environment accordingly. This process of helping the dead find a different, nonphysical existence requires the presence of the dead person's body, which is why people missing in action became the object of great pity and concern and why different institutions in Vietnam, from the family to the state, made determined efforts to find their remains after the war.

At the other end of the spectrum, the idea of *xác* indicates that the presence of the dead can be permeable, unmarked, and unspecified, and that it may be widely diffused within the place of the living. It is believed that the spirits of the dead may wander freely about the village—among the ditches, footpaths, school buildings, police stations, sand dunes, and household kitchen areas— particularly at dusk. On the fifteenth day of each lunar month, the number and intensity of traveling spirits is thought to increase radically, according to a village spirit medium in Quang Ngai. When a family holds an important funerary or commemorative event, the entire population of wandering spirits in the area may hurry to the site of the ceremony, making it look like a crowded early-morning marketplace. This is how a ritual specialist in Quang Nam Province described his experience of such ceremonies. In the popular conceptualization, the dead who are properly entombed at an appropriate site according to ritual

propriety are less inclined to roam about the streets than those who are improperly buried and who did not benefit from remembrance rites. These hungry,
thirsty, unclothed, and unmourned spirits of the dead make up the majority of
the lost and wandering ghosts believed to exist in contemporary Vietnamese
communities.

Thus, the concept of *xác* denotes both a particular condition of the body,
which is characterized by immobility and lifelessness, and, more implicitly, a
related specific condition of soul, which is mobile and vital. Following Emile
Durkheim, we may think of the dual referential reality of *xác* as the freedom
of the soul from the prison of the body.[5] Furthermore, it should be mentioned
that *xác* interacts with a further dual conception of soul. In traditional
Vietnamese understanding, the human soul consists of the spiritual soul of
hồn and the material soul of *vía*. Because of this duality, the spirit of a deceased
person is believed to be able to feel cold or hunger through its material soul
and to transform this sensation into self-pity or anger through its spiritual
counterpart. Therefore, in the context of violent war death, the experience of
bodily pain may remain in the material soul of the dead, and its spiritual
counterpart may try to relieve the pain. These pains are conceptually real
irrespective of the spiritual soul's awareness of whether the death the body
experienced was for a good and just cause. The concept of the spiritual soul is
similar to that of "pure reason" in the Platonic philosophical tradition; the
spiritual soul can think and imagine independently from sentiments and
bodily desires. Although it is coupled with its material counterpart, it is superior and guides its lower material partner to sensible ways. For the living, the
spiritual soul is universal and, thus, a facet of humanity rather than personality. In contrast, the material soul is specific to an individual's moral character
and unique personality. It is the material soul that can feel hunger or thirst
and anger or fear, and through which the human soul can be gentle (*vía lành*)
or wicked (*vía dữ*).

The eminent French scholar of Vietnamese religion and culture Léopold
Cadière calls *hồn* and *vía* the superior and the inferior principles of vitality. He
explains that neither of these vital life principles entirely disappears upon
death in the Vietnamese conception. Some vital forces are situated and settled
through appropriate rituals; others are let loose without a place to anchor.
Some are treated well and honored; others are unwanted and feared. According
to Cadière, learning to relate to these multiple spirits that are recognized in
various forms and modes of afterlife is central to Vietnamese religious practices
and moral life.[6] The concept of *xác* is useful in considering these forms of afterlife, the metaphoric fusion of life and death, and vitality versus lifelessness. In
certain contexts, the concept can signify the condition of the human body in its
fullest and most radical commemorative act—spirit possession.

The Homecoming Spirit

An episode of a homecoming spirit illustrates war-caused complications in the moral life of postwar Vietnamese families. A journalist working for the official newspaper of a central Vietnamese town recently set out to investigate a rumor of a spirit possession. He was swiftly reprimanded by his superiors, and the rumor subsequently grew in popularity among the townspeople. There was nothing extraordinary about the rumor, which was about a man encountering the spirit of his late brother; such incidents are commonly discussed in Vietnamese towns. In this particular incident, however, the man was an acting official in the provincial Communist party, and the spirit happened to be that of his elder brother who was killed in action as a soldier of the former South Vietnam. The following is a summary of what the townspeople said about the official's family.[7]

The official became mysteriously ill, and the family, after failing to receive a satisfactory explanation for the illness, decided to consult with a local spirit medium. In a séance, the spirit of the missing soldier demanded a formal apology from his younger brother in front of the entire family. The spirit was furious and pointed out that the official had been unsympathetic to their mother's wishes. For years after the liberation, the official's mother had been preoccupied with finding her missing son, which had provoked a series of conflicts within the family, in particular with the official, the missing man's younger brother. It was known among the locals that the younger brother, obsessed with the postwar economic reconstruction, had argued with his mother that the family, like the nation, should look forward rather than dwell on the past. Against his wishes and those of her other children, his mother had continued her search privately. She had also wanted to build a family altar upon which she could lay the photograph of her dead son and, thus, clashed with her other children, who disapproved. (In the house of an acting official of the Communist party, her wish for an altar was unacceptable in the immediate postwar period, particularly because it concerned a politically impure death.) Against this public accusation from his elder brother, the official had to admit his misdeed in the presence of his younger siblings.

These instances of extraordinary encounters, which people in the town called "the spirit enters the body" (nhập xác), contributed to breaking the political barriers to remembering the dead. When people experienced what they understood to be a face-to-face encounter with the spirit of a missing person, it became practically impossible to ignore its existence, even if the spirit were a politically undesirable one. The intrusion of a spirit—in the form of an apparition, in a dream, or as a result of a spirit-related illness—was typically interpreted to be the spirit claiming the right to be properly remembered.

In this situation, there was a shared cultural understanding that people were justified in accommodating the intrusive spirits, regardless of the latter's political backgrounds during their historical lives, because the initiative to do so was not necessarily their own but originated from the grievous missing dead.

Social dramas involving intrusive ghosts of war were by no means unusual in Vietnamese communities, and they occasionally led to efforts to seek out and repatriate physical remains. This was the case in the official's family, who later succeeded in finding the remains of the missing soldier in a remote region of the central highlands with help from a local religious specialist in such tasks. The spirit's intrusion also developed into a change in the domestic ritual space. This change typically involved the incorporation of the missing or forgotten dead into the household's ancestral shrine and ritual commemoration.

Stories of this kind are familiar to the people in southern and central Vietnam. The experience of the Vietnam War made the improperly buried bodies and their displaced, lost souls a generalized phenomenon rather than an isolated event. Death away from home was as common for civilians as for combatants in this total war, and so it was common to find many shallow graves of unknown dead when people returned home. These unknown dead represented people missing in action from elsewhere. As previously mentioned, postwar Vietnamese families and communities faced radical challenges to their communal integrity by not having the bodies of their kinsmen buried near their villages. The Vietnam War resulted in a generalized situation of displacement in death and thus posed a crisis to the traditional culture of commemoration. The postwar revolutionary politics of the unified Vietnam added even further to the crisis of afterlife displacement.

For people in central and southern Vietnam (what was South Vietnam during the war), the Vietnam War was not a single war. It was a revolutionary struggle against foreign aggressors but also a vicious civil war and domestic confrontation. People in these regions were forced to fight against the revolutionary war as well as in support of it. Against this backdrop of political bipolarization, family genealogical histories in southern and central Vietnam typically keep memories of political disunity related to the bifurcated mobilization on both sides of the American War. When the war was over and the nation was reunited under the revolutionary state, the memories of the dead from "that side" (bên kia, meaning "the American side," against bên ta, "the revolutionary side") were banned from the new political community of the nation and, by extension, presented difficulties to the moral community of family ancestral worship. As a result, after the war a large number of the war dead became politically engendered ghosts, who, according to Hue-Tam Ho Tai, "dying unmourned, constantly haunt the living in an attempt to force their way into the consciousness of the community, to be acknowledged as worthy of being remembered if only because they once walked the earth."[8]

The memories of war dead excluded from the postwar institutions of commemoration were not merely those of the fallen soldiers on "that side." There were also difficulties involving the huge civilian sacrifice to the war in the postwar politics of memory. The Vietnamese revolutionary state made serious administrative efforts to battle against what it considered to be feudal and backward customs. This policy resulted in the wide-scale closure of traditional ancestral temples and other sacred places of the village world as well as the conversion of the traditional familial and communal institutions of ancestral death remembrance to political shrines meant exclusively for the commemoration of the heroic revolutionary war dead.[9] This postwar politics of memory meant that for the local communities in the southern and central regions, a large number of family ancestors, except the chosen few endorsed by the state, were stripped of a home (a place where they are remembered according to the appropriate rituals) and thus relegated to the category of ghosts. These politically engendered ghosts were not antithetical to ancestors but rather constituted a crowd of ancestors uprooted and displaced from their homes. This displacement, for many ancestral spirits, was caused by the politics of national memory, but for others it was related to the total destruction of homes in a violent war, which resulted in the termination of family lines and the consequent loss of the social basis of death commemoration.

Rituals for Displaced Spirits

The condition of having a displaced afterlife, missing from one place and unknown in another, relates to another important concept in Vietnamese mortuary culture, chết đường ("death in the street"). This concept coexists with the antithetical concept of "death in the house" or "death at home" (chết nhà). The conceptual scheme broadly relates to the contrast between "good death" and "bad death" presented in the sociological literature of death and death ritual. "To die a good death," it is argued, is "to die in the house and home," implying that the event of death takes place in the presence of kindred who will ritually appropriate the death to a benevolent ancestor.[10] In contrast, a "bad death" is a sudden, violent death in a distant and unknown place away from home, which destroys the possibility of ritual appropriation and transformation of the deceased into an ancestral entity.

This house-centered dual conception of death in the tradition of central Vietnam places the ritual practice of commemoration between two different surfaces of memory—between the ancestral shrine placed in the interior of the house and the milieu of street-wandering, displaced spirits of the dead.

The typical manner in which people in this region conduct their regular domestic ancestral rites is to kowtow in the house to the ancestors and then to walk outside and repeat the action toward the imaginary world of wandering ghosts. This two-sided commemorative practice is also found in wider community affairs, such as the opening ceremony of a village communal house or a lineage ancestral temple. The street-side worship is formally on behalf of the unknown and unrelated souls of the dead who exist in the neighborhood or who are assumed to have gathered for the occasion from more distant locations, and it is structurally similar to the act of distributing small offerings to the unknown graves found in the vicinity of the ancestral tombs after giving offerings of incense and flowers to the ancestors. Offerings to ancestors acknowledge the exclusive ties of kinship between the donor and the recipient; the distribution of offerings to other graves recognizes the inclusive ties of residence between the ancestral identities and the non-ancestral beings.

In this system of dual structure and two-way practice, there emerge two distinctive ways to imagine social solidarity. On the house side, we may say, following Durkheim, that the commemorative act affirms the given solidary relations between the living and the dead, thereby generating the sense of mutual belonging and that of a coherent social wholeness—whether we call it genealogical unity or the lineage paradigm.[11] This affirmation is particularly evident in the regular ceremonies held at the communal house (dinh), which is dedicated to the founding ancestors of the village and is its most important site of worship. All family and lineage groups of the village are expected to take part in these occasions or to at least make contributions to them, including people from the village who have relocated to faraway places. The participants listen to speeches about the founding ancestors' legendary history of migration and settlement and make gestures and offerings of tribute to their memory according to the order of seniority and lineage statuses. The organization of this village-wide ancestral rite also includes ritualized interactions with wandering ghosts. After the house-side worship is finished, the participants turn to the opposite direction and make prayers and offerings on behalf of the displaced spirits. These spirits, unlike ancestors who are believed to be settled within the temple, do not have the privilege of having a home. The street-side worship does not follow a strict order of seniority such as that in the house-side worship and, hence, has a chaotic appearance. On certain occasions the prayer activity for ghosts may also be accompanied by a traditional prayer of spirit invitation and consolation, calling in all tragic or displaced deaths and urging the spirits to receive the villagers' gestures of sympathy and hospitality. The prayers are often improvised versions of the famous classical poem *Văn chiêu hồn* or *Văn tế cô hồn* ("Calling the Wandering Souls") composed by Nguyen Du, the eminent Mandarin scholar of the eighteenth century.[12]

The revival of these rituals took place in a time of momentous socioeconomic change in Vietnam. The 1990s was a time of formidable change for the country. During this relatively short period of time, in the view of the outside world, Vietnam was transformed from a poor, isolated country ravaged by successive wars to a politically stable, vibrant economic society. In the 1980s, in the midst of a deep economic crisis of high inflation and low productivity, Vietnam's political leaders embraced a program of general economic renovation, shifting toward a regulated market economy. The shift in economic ideology involved a growing political tolerance for communal activities, including religious worship. As a result, one of the most remarkable changes in Vietnamese society during the 1990s was "a nationwide resurgence of religion and ritual,"[13] most notably the revival of ancestral worship. In the central region, as previously mentioned, the revival of ancestral rituals took place in parallel with the reinvigoration of ritual activity intended for wandering spirits. When the renovation of domestic ancestral shrines and communal ancestral temples began, in many communities of this region, people expanded the renovations to include shrines for unknown and displaced spirits, popularly called *khom* in the local language.[14]

This communal development arose in central and southern Vietnam against the enduring wounds of a war still felt in community life as well as against the background of the postwar politics of memory, which focused on the legacy of heroic war death. These persistent wounds have found powerful expression in the stories of grievous ghosts of war popular in rural Vietnam. In the part of Quang Ngai Province that came to be known by the international community as My Lai during the Vietnam War, after a tragic mass killing of civilians in March 1968, the residents told many stories of the spirits of the dead in pain.[15] Some of the villagers vividly recalled the lamentations of ghosts in the villages, cries that they had heard coming from the killing sites. Residents in one particular settlement claimed that they had seen old women ghosts licking and sucking the arms and legs of small child ghosts; they interpreted this scene as an effort by the elderly victims to ease the wounded children's pain. Some people in another settlement graphically described young women ghosts, each walking with a small child in her arms and lamenting over the child's lifeless body. The mother ghosts were grieving for their dead children, the villagers explained. According to the old village undertaker, the village's "invisible neighbors," as he referred to them, could lament their own physical pain or feel pain when their loved ones suffered pain; they might have grievous feelings about their own tragic, unjust death or cry over their children's deaths as if they, themselves, were not yet dead. Their moods and sentiments—and even their forms—fluctuated with the circumstances. The child ghosts appeared dead in their grieving mothers' arms on a moonless night during a rainy season, and yet these same children could be seen playfully running after their mothers on a pleasant evening before the anniversary day. The My Lai villagers regularly held modest rituals at home and outside their homes on behalf of their "invisible neighbors"—offering them incense, food, and sometimes votive money notes to the *khom*, the sites of apparitions, or elsewhere—and they explained the condition of these invisible neighbors' lives using the concept of "grievous death" or "unjust death" (*chết oan*, in Vietnamese). In this concept, the agony of a violent, unjust death and the memory of its terror entrap the soul in negative afterlife conditions. The human soul in this condition of postmortem incarceration does not remember the terror as we, the living, would; rather, the soul is believed to relive the violent event, perpetually reexperiencing the agony of violent death. The memory of death for the tragically dead, in other words, is a living memory in its most brutal sense.

The idea that the dead can feel physical pain has a long history in Vietnamese mortuary and religious tradition, and it relates to the notion that the human soul is a duplex entity, as mentioned earlier, consisting of the spiritual part of *hồn* and the bodily, material part of *via*. The material soul senses and feels; the spiritual soul thinks and imagines. In a "death at home" (as opposed to "death in the street") under peaceful circumstances, surrounded by loved ones, after enjoying longevity, the material soul eventually perishes with the decomposing body. Only the spiritual soul survives a good death (although if the deceased's body is buried in an inappropriate place for entombment, the material soul is reawakened and may feel the discomfort and pain of improper burial). It is believed that the ritually appropriated pure spirit travels across the imaginary threshold between the world of the living and the world of the dead to eventually join the pure domain of ancestry and ancestor worship. In contrast, the soul of one who experienced a violent death away from home remains largely intact and keeps its pre-death dual formation because of the absence of ritual separation. The material soul is believed to linger near the place of death and the place where its decomposing body is buried. It feels the discomfort of improper burial and awakens the spiritual soul to the embodied memory of its violent death. The material soul's bodily pain and the spiritual soul's painful memory communicate, and this communication between the two kinds of souls can generate the undesirable condition of "grievous death."

The story of the elder brother introduced earlier involved a soul of grievous death; he had a history of violent death, and his body was missing; therefore, he did not receive a proper burial, and his memory was unaccounted for in the ritual milieu of kinship. The mass deaths such as those suffered at My Lai, though they took place "at home" (and thus, may not be "death in the street," strictly speaking), nevertheless constitute *chết đường* and *chết oan*. In this case, the intensity of violence changed the notion of home, turning it inside out.

It also resulted in mass graves in which people unrelated in ties of kinship were buried together, which violates the organizing principle of the kinship-based, traditional Vietnamese culture of commemoration.

Beyond Grievous Death

Trapped by the memory of its violent death, the soul experiencing grievous death is unable to depart to the other world until the situation is corrected by the intervention of an external power. This perpetual reexperience is described as "incarceration" (*ngục*), which means that the souls of the dead are trapped in the mortal terror and traumatic experience of violent death. The grievance of *oan* and the self-imprisonment of *ngục* describe the same phenomenon— grievance creates the imaginary prison, whereas the prison captures the grievance and heightens its intensity. The My Lai villagers recalled the names of certain deceased villagers as the most aggrieved victims of the 1968 massacre, and these names belonged to families whose genealogy was decimated by the violence. This decimation provoked the strongest sense of injustice and moral indignation in other Vietnamese communities affected by civilian massacres. A grievous death, in this context, is not only the destruction of innocent lives but also a crisis in the social foundation of commemoration. According to this culturally specific conceptualization of human rights, the right of the dead to be liberated from the violent history of death is inalienable, and the protection of this right depends on the secular institutions of commemoration.

The concept of grievous death signifies a state of imprisonment within the vexing and mortifying memory of a violent, unjust event, but it also has a progressive connotation that points to concrete measures that can be taken to break free of the captivity. In vernacular Vietnamese language, the liberation from the incarceration of grievous memory is referred to as "disentangling the grievance" (*giải oan*) or "breaking the prison" (*vượt ngục*). The work to release a soul from the grievance involves the appropriate intervention of sympathetic individuals: family- or village-based death commemorations and the provision of ritual offerings to the "invisible neighbors" are two prominent forms of this moral intervention. The commitment to this work of memory and its demonstration in communal ritual activities were the most prominent changes in Vietnamese villages in the 1990s.

The work of memory is also a collaborative project that involves not only acts of outside intervention in the form of death commemoration but also the soul's strong will for freedom from history. Apparitions, such as those of the mother and child ghosts, are commonly understood as a sign of the growth of self-consciousness and self-determination on the part of the sufferers of grievous historical memory. That the souls of the dead can suffer from the enduring effects of a traumatic historical experience is an established, legitimate idea in Vietnamese moral and cultural tradition, which is entrenched in the eruption of "commemorative fever" and in the related vigorous ritual revival. The idea is bound up with everyday Vietnamese ritual commemorative practices that characterize the world as a place the living must share with the dead. In this milieu of interaction with the past, the apparitions in My Lai are more than history's ruins or traces of the uncanny. Rather, these ghosts are vital historical witnesses, testifying to the war's unjust destruction of human life with broken lives but unbreakable spirits.

The same idea applies to the incident of the party official's encounter with the spirit of his elder brother. The intrusion of this spirit into the home and body of his younger brother was interpreted by the townspeople as a legitimate action on the part of the intrusive spirit (claiming its right to be remembered) but also as a sign of the spirit being *linh*, that is, vigorous and auspiciously powerful. The ensuing success in the family's mission to recover the missing man's body was likewise understood as an expression of the missing man's spiritual vitality. The story about this man's missing body and lost soul as a result of war embodies the two phenomena of *xác*—the first when the spirit caused an illness in his brother by intruding into the brother's body, and the second when the spirit was invited into the body of a local spirit medium to express his grievances and wishes. The way the townspeople referred to the phenomenon of *xác* in relation to the official's family indicated that this Vietnamese term is indeed full of semantic qualities that are meaningful for vital human actions and the vitalization of the human condition, which relate to its double meaning of a lifeless human body and vitalized human soul.

The political authority of postwar Vietnam sought to come to terms with the destruction of war with a forward-looking spirit and, in turn, by mobilizing the heroism of patriotic and revolutionary sacrifice. In recent years the emphasis on commemoration in Vietnamese society has shifted focus from the centrality of heroic memory to the plurality of historical memory. The latter, and its manifestation in the recent revival of ancestral and other commemorative rituals, is based on the notion that the spirits of the dead can suffer from grievous historical memories as well as the related awareness that the living have an ethical responsibility to help free these spirits from their confinement in historical trauma. The notion that the spirits of the dead can feel historical pain and express their grievances and aspirations is firmly integral, at the grassroots level, to the pluralization and democratization of war memories in contemporary Vietnam. Furthermore, this idea is grounded in the specific conceptualization of the human body as *xác* and *nhập xác*, which projects the continuity of the human spirit beyond the destruction of human lives and which, therefore, enables communication between the spirits of the dead and living humans with regard to the history of destruction.

Acknowledgments

A version of this essay originally appeared in French in *La colonisation des corps: De l'Indochine au Vietnam*, edited by Agathe Larcher-Goscha and François Guillemot (Paris: Vendémiaire, 2014), 393–414.

NOTES

1. Bao Ninh, *The Sorrow of War: A Novel of North Vietnam* (New York: Riverhead Press, 1993), 91.

2. Ibid., 41–42.

3. Jean Baudrillard, *Symbolic Exchange and Death* (London: Sage, 1993), 144.

4. See Jay Winter, *Sites of Memory, Sites of Mourning: The Great War in European Cultural History* (Cambridge: Cambridge University Press, 1995).

5. Emile Durkheim, *The Elementary Forms of Religious Life (1912)*, trans. K. E. Fields (New York: Free Press, 1995), 280.

6. Léopold Cadière, *Croyances et practiques religieuses des viêtamiens*, vol. 2 (Paris: Ecole Française d'Extrême-Orient, 1957), 53–66.

7. This and other related events are described in more detail in Heonik Kwon, *Ghosts of War in Vietnam* (Cambridge: Cambridge University, 2008), 57–62.

8. Hue-Tam Ho Tai, "Commemoration and Community," in *The Country of Memory: Remaking the Past in Late Socialist North Vietnam*, ed. H. H. Tai (Berkeley: University of California Press, 2001), 228.

9. Shaun K. Malarney, *Culture, Ritual, and Revolution in Vietnam* (Surrey, U.K.: Routledge-Curzon, 2002).

10. John Middleton, "Lugbara Death," in *Death and the Regeneration of Life*, ed. M. Bloch and J. Parry (Cambridge: Cambridge University Press, 1982), 145.

11. Durkheim, *The Elementary Forms*.

12. See Tan Viet, *Tap Van Cung Gia Tien* (Prayer book for ancestor worship) (Hanoi: Nha xuat ban van hoa dan toc, 1994), 105–114; and Nguyen Khac Vien, *Vietnam: A Long History* (Hanoi: The Gioi, 1993), 130–132.

13. Shaun K. Malarney, "Return to the Past? The Dynamics of Contemporary Religious and Ritual Transformation," in *Postwar Vietnam: Dynamics of a Transforming Society*, ed. H. V. Luong (Lanham, Md.: Rowman and Littlefield, 2003), 225. See also Hy Van Luong, "Economic Reform and the Intensification of Rituals in Two North Vietnamese Villages, 1980–90," in *The Challenge of Reform in Indochina*, ed. B. Ljunggren (Cambridge, Mass.: Harvard Institute of International Development, 1993), 259–292.

14. Heonik Kwon, *After the Massacre: Commemoration and Consolation in Ha My and My Lai* (Berkeley: University of California Press, 2006), 79–81.

15. For these and other stories like them, see Heonik Kwon, *After the Massacre: Commemoration and Consolation in Ha My and My Lai* (Berkeley: University of California Press, 2006), especially chapter 3, "A Generation Afterward."

9

Agent Orange

Toxic Chemical, Narrative of Suffering, Metaphor for War

DIANE NIBLACK FOX

Like the term "Agent Orange" itself, this chapter can be read in several ways. One way to read it is as an introduction to the intersecting issues signified by the memorable but imprecise polyvalent term "Agent Orange." At times the term serves as a generic for the dioxin-contaminated chemicals the United States used during the wars in Việt Nam, Laos, and Cambodia; at times as an explanation for the experience of people living with the long-term conse- quences of those chemicals; and at still other times as a metaphor for the ramifications of war that extend to people, places, and times far beyond the battle site.

A second way to read the chapter is as a modest step toward addressing a gap in the record of the war that Brenda Boyle discusses elsewhere in this vol- ume: the lack of humanizing depictions of Vietnamese people in American war novels and the general absence of Vietnamese women as well. The person whose experience of Agent Orange is recounted in this chapter is Vietnamese and a woman, Mrs. Nguyễn Thị Hồng, who lived and fought in the south of Việt Nam during the war: her story, my retelling, our interaction.[1]

A third reading of the chapter is suggested by *The Politics of Storytelling: Violence, Transgression, and Intersubjectivity*, in which the anthropologist Michael Jackson argues for the power of collaborative storytelling to rework trauma— not to save the sufferer from the effects of that trauma but to unfreeze the pres- ent from the death grip of the past, to subsume the trauma as one part of life, not to let the trauma subsume the whole of life.[2] Jackson draws heavily on Hannah Arendt's concept of storytelling as "'the subjective in-between,' in which a multiplicity of private and public interests are always problematically in play," and where each person is both a "who" and a "what," both an actor and acted upon, struggling to sustain and synthesize a self in a world that "simultaneously

subjugates one to other ends."3 Mrs. Hồng answers my questions about Agent
Orange, and moves the conversation in directions of her choosing, illustrating,
as she expands the topic, the way a discussion of Agent Orange feeds into a
discussion of war and its legacies. I ask her to help me understand her situation;
she asks me to be a tool for conveying her situation to a larger audience. We
selectively refashion ourselves, in Jackson's paraphrase of Arendt's thought, to
make ourselves real and recognizable to each other, each responding and initi-
ating as we move through our conversation, using the power of the word to
both commemorate and lessen the power of trauma: life is affirmed in the face
of death, the dead are rejoined to the living, and a world is created in which the
past is both remembered and effaced.

The story retold here is a fragment—a fragment of the stories Mrs. Hồng had
to tell, and a fragment of my own work on Agent Orange. "There's a lot more . . .
there's a lot more, and still more," as Mrs. Hồng puts it near the end of our conversation. "Oh! I tell you, you will never be able to bear witness to all the pain
and loss that the Vietnamese people have borne through so many wars."4

As a fragment of my own work on Agent Orange, our conversation is one of
thirty-eight interviews from the center, north, and south of the country, and of
countless stories told to me by friends and in chance encounters, in both Việt
Nam and the United States. By the time I met Mrs. Hồng, I had been living in
Việt Nam for ten years, half of each year from 1991 to 2001, as a teacher, a feature writer, and copy editor. Dr. Lê Cao Đài of the Agent Orange Victims Fund
of the Vietnamese Red Cross, with the support of the International Red Cross
and Red Crescent society, arranged for me to conduct interviews throughout
the country that would contribute to the Red Cross's understanding of people
it labeled "the disabled poor, including those thought to be affected by Agent
Orange"—interviews that served as the basis for my dissertation as well.

Contexts

For the purposes of this book, the most obvious context is war—war and the
legacies of war, and the rebuilding of houses, lives, and social structures in
ruins. For perspective, it is helpful to remember that Việt Nam is roughly the
size of New England—New York, New Jersey, and Delaware combined—or,
for readers more familiar with the West Coast of the United States, is three-
fourths the size of California. During the war, 15–29 million bombs cut large
swathes through towns and fields and forests, leaving craters often fifty feet
across and thirty-six feet deep that still affect life today. Thousands of villages
were razed (one account claims nine thousand) along with several major towns
and much of the infrastructure—roads, railways, bridges, hospitals, schools,
electricity, waterworks—left in shambles. An estimated 2 to 4 million people

were killed or wounded, and 10 million people were internally displaced, seeking safety as refugees.[5] Of the land then known to Americans as South Việt
Nam, 10–15 percent of the total vegetation was denuded by chemicals; in some
provinces that figure was over 50 percent. Some vegetation has regrown, but
large patches have not or have regrown with tough, unusable grasses. The dangers did not end with the end of the war. By 2014 more than one hundred thousand people, a third of them children, had been killed or maimed by unexploded
ordnance.[6] And the health legacy of exposure to toxic chemicals continues to
this day, particularly in areas of most intense spraying: around the perimeter of
former military bases, at storage sites, or in the forty-seven places where a
plane was shot down with its full load of chemicals.

Agent Orange, the topic that brought me into conversation with
Mrs. Hồng, is the generic name loosely given to those chemicals. Agent Orange
proper is the nickname for a 50–50 mixture of 2,4 D and 2,4,5 T. It is the best
known and most widely used of the six "rainbow chemicals" that got their nick-
names not from the color of their liquid or their spray but from the color of
identifying stripes painted on their storage barrels. From 1961 to 1971, some
21 million gallons of these chemicals were sprayed by airplane, helicopter, and
by hand in order to destroy foliage that could conceal opposition forces, and to
damage their food crops. Approximately 24 percent of the inland forests of the
South and 30–50 percent of its coastal mangroves were defoliated by these
chemicals, along with 4 percent of the food crop.[7]

Four of these chemicals—Agents Purple, Pink, Green, and Orange—were
contaminated during the production process by varying degrees of TCDD
dioxin, a persistent, highly toxic substance that has been linked to a long list of
cancers, neural disorders and other conditions in men, and to numerous birth
and developmental anomalies in pregnant and nursing mothers and their
fetuses and infants. A National Institutes of Health "study of studies," initiated
in 1991 by George H. W. Bush and supported by every president since, had by
2012 confirmed the following list of diseases and conditions as being associated
with exposure to Agent Orange: chloracne, Hodgkin's disease, multiple
myeloma, non-Hodgkin's lymphoma, acute and subacute peripheral neuropa-
thy, porphyria cutanea tarda, prostate cancer, respiratory cancers, soft-tissue
sarcomas, type 2 diabetes (diabetes mellitus), chronic lymphocytic leukemia,
B-cell leukemia, AL amyloidosis, Parkinson's disease, ischemic heart disease,
stroke, and the birth defect spina bifida.[8] An updated list is published every two
years and serves as the basis for the U.S. Department of Veterans Affairs (VA)
compensation to American veterans.

In the children of women veterans, the VA recognizes seventeen other birth
defects as linked to the "Việt Nam experience" but not specifically to Agent

Orange. In 2002 the director of the experimental toxicology division of the U.S. Environmental Protection Agency named TCDD as associated with the following effects in children: developmental effects on the thyroid status, immune status, neurobehavior, cognition, and dentition. Exposure to TCDD also correlates to an altered sex ratio.[9]

The use of these chemicals was controversial from the beginning. There were those in the government who argued that it was a more humane form of warfare, with no damage to people, only to plants that would recover. Others called it chemical warfare.[10] These decisions were being made at a time before Rachel Carson's *Silent Spring* did much to awaken the public to the dangers that chemicals pose to health and the environment. At times the conversation on Agent Orange is still clouded by hyperbole or denial that is fueled by a mix of the fear and frustration that accompany the slow unfolding of scientific understanding and political action.

A Conversation in Biên Hòa

Mrs. Hồng's city of Biên Hòa is the capital of Đồng Nai Province, which lies just to the northeast of Hồ Chí Minh City, across the Đồng Nai River. In the days when the city was known as Saigon, Đồng Nai was a site of intense warfare. Biên Hòa was the site of a large U.S. Air Force base engaged in the storage, transfer, and spraying of Agent Orange. During the late 1990s Biên Hòa was reconfiguring as a major hub for international manufacturing.

At the time of my visit in 2001, the particular ward of Biên Hòa where Mrs. Hồng lived, Trung Dồng, was home to eighteen thousand inhabitants. International researchers were testing residents for high levels of dioxin in their blood and fatty tissues; as of that time, sixty-nine families in the ward had been identified as having high levels of dioxin contamination. By 2010 the Hatfield Consultants, a highly respected Canadian environmental remediation group, had identified three people who fished in a lake contaminated by run-off from the base whose body burden of TCDD was thirty-five times higher than the standard set by the World Health Organization.[11]

Trung Dũng is the part of the city closest to that lake, Hồ Biên Hùng (Biên Hùng Lake). There is evidence of a 7,500-gallon spill on the base that researchers theorize may have drained into a canal that feeds the lake, helping to explain the high incidence of cancer in the ward—forty-nine times that of the ward with the least incidence of cancer, the local Red Cross told us. There was a reduction in the number of children born with birth defects once it was understood that the water source was contaminated and uncontaminated water was brought in, they added.

In 2001 the Ministry of Labor, War Invalids and Society gave 88,000 *đồng* (roughly US$6) per month to those thought to be affected by Agent Orange if they were Việt Minh (communists or their allies). Others—the Army of the Republic of Vietnam (ARVN) troops and their supporters—had to rely on charities like the Red Cross, much like their counterparts now living in the United States, who are not eligible for the compensation granted to the U.S. soldiers they fought alongside.

Mrs. Hồng's house lay off one of the busy main arteries of Biên Hòa, down a narrow path that led back between two shops to a row of cement-walled, sheet-metal-roofed houses. We are invited into a small, light colored front room, where we sit on a vinyl couch and folding stools placed beside a simple glass-fronted cabinet that holds neatly arranged dishes. Doubling as the ancestral altar, the cabinet top is adorned with flowers, incense, and pictures of the deceased. A sixteen-stringed zither is suspended in one corner of the room, above a second altar placed on the floor. A small white teapot and set of cups, ornamented with a rose decal, sit on a cloth-covered low table that is the room's other main furnishing. The sitting area is divided from the rest of the house by a curtain of beaded strings of bamboo segments, painted with a bucolic scene of deer in the forest.

Mrs. Hồng is welcoming, energetic, and matter-of-fact.[12] As our conversation begins, we are both rather hesitant and reserved. As our conversation proceeds, we realize that we are both the same age, both with first children, daughters, born the same year—similarities that link us and underscore our differences; my daughter was born in the peace of a city hospital while hers was born in a jungle during war.

"You want to know about my family's situation, about our lives, about the reality—why we are still in this situation," Mrs. Hồng began quietly. "Let me remind you that in Việt Nam, the Vietnamese people have been through so many wars—and so my family. . . ." Here she pauses for a moment, as she does several times at points in our conversation when hard moments are brought to mind. "My family's life is extremely hard. We have struggled and lived on this piece of earth that is our homeland. . . . From my own grandfathers right down to myself, we are all people who participated in . . . we call it . . .." Here Mrs. Hồng hesitates and looks toward the doctor from the Red Cross for help finding the right words.

"Protecting the country," the doctor interjects. The war is often referred to as "a resistance war against the Americans to save the country." Given Mrs. Hồng's later expression of delicacy toward what she imagines may be my sensibilities as an American, it seems likely that her hesitation comes from a reluctance to offend by using this terminology. Her sensitivity to phrasing also demonstrates the difficulty of finding a common language.

"Protecting the country," she picks up the phrase and continues:

> That is . . . from the generation of my father and the generation of my
> mother and then my older brothers and sisters, all of them, the whole
> family participated in protecting the country.
>
> The war to protect the country had some things that were good and
> some that were bad for me myself, and in the end I myself have some
> illnesses and my own family is among those handicapped, and this is
> because of the consequences of war.

Like many of the people I spoke with, Mrs. Hồng speaks of the consequences of
war, not just the consequences of Agent Orange; the terms at times are used
interchangeably.

"For example," she continues, "my father-in-law is in pain and has a weak
appetite and is paralyzed, and all my younger siblings have died of diseases—all.
Only I am still alive, living here . . . and that's thanks to the help, and the concern, and the care of the party and the country and the people . . . if not I would
have been gone long ago." This gratitude is echoed by several, but not all,
families I spoke with. While some families called on both their government and
the U.S. government to offer compensation for Agent Orange–related diseases,
others explained that without the help of the government in the immediate
postwar years, they could not have survived. A farmer in the countryside not far
from Biên Hòa, for instance, told us how the government supplied food until
the land in that region, which had been inundated with salt water when the
mangrove forests that served as a barrier to the sea were destroyed by defoli-
ants, could be desalinated and farming could recommence.

Mrs. Hồng went on to explain the help she received. "In '92 there was a
medical program, and after the check-up I discovered that I had internal illnesses.
Well, the first disease that was discovered was my liver . . . our government took
care of me and then complications set in with my spleen—it was inflamed, contaminated, and it turned out they cut it out." Then she developed stomach ulcers
and myelitis, then troubles with her entire digestive tract, high blood pressure,
and a condition that caused her feet to turn pale from time to time. She had lost
the hearing in one ear due to the explosions of bombs and artillery, and her vision
was now blurry. "As for my physical condition," she concluded,

> that's how it is. Every month I have to go to the hospital for treatment,
> every month, and buy medicine. That's how my health is. As for my eco-
> nomic situation . . . I'll explain it to you like this. In the past I worked for
> the government. Then our disabilities [her husband's as well as her own]
> caused us to retire and live on our pension, at home. I lost my hand, but

I still have to struggle to embroider, and sew, and sell a few sundries. We do whatever we can to earn a living. If we want to live, we have to take care of ourselves.

"Here," she says, turning to her husband, "show her what I make to sell." Stepping through the bamboo curtain, he brings out a basket filled with bright pieces of cloth. "I join these small scraps of cloth together to make into material to make a curtain, or a quilt . . . make decorative things." Some of the pieces are hexagons joined in a pattern I learned in childhood to call Grandmother's Flower Garden.

"And," she continues, "I still don't have a stable place to live, we're still renting. Wherever the rent is lowest, we move to the place where it's lowest. We run from this place to that: wherever a low price shows up, then we go there to live."

After a moment of respectful silence, I ask how many children she has. "It's a lot, if you are talking about the pregnancies," she replies. But only four survived, all girls. The first was born in 1970, in the jungle, in the war zone. Her second, born in 1976, is sickly; she can only work for a time and then suffers exhaustion; each time she goes for a check-up, she has a fever. Her third child, born in 1979, has congenital heart trouble. The fourth, born in 1984, has headaches due to a nervous disorder. "When the sun is hot and bright like this," Mrs. Hồng explains, "she can't do anything at all."

Picking up on her earlier reference to her hand, I use a common Vietnamese way of bringing up difficult subjects and ask, "Forgive me, but how did you lose your hand? Was it the war?"

"This hand was because in 19 . . . 1971 I went out . . ." Mrs. Hồng pauses. "Sorry—can I use the word 'American?'—and I was shot by the Americans . . . yes . . . and was wounded. I'm a wounded soldier of Việt Nam, a veteran and wounded soldier of Việt Nam. . . ."

I nod in recognition. "When you were . . . when you were hurt like this," I ask, "where did you find the strength to overcome?"

"In general, in life you have to have something to believe in . . ." she replies.

That is, I . . . I still have my country, still have my government, still have my homeland, my father and mother, my ancestors, my children, my comrades, my fellow soldiers—I have to push myself, struggle, overcome . . . that means, overcome all the disabilities, try to struggle to overcome by myself in order to create a life for myself, and I can't just depend on others, but I myself must struggle.

Generally speaking, that's what the war gave—in war, I myself had to fight, and for the illnesses, I myself have to have the mental strength, thanks to a belief, a belief in my country. I must try to overcome. . . . I can't say 'Well, I'm this way, because of my illnesses, because of whatever situation, so I must bear it, must resign myself.' No, I'm strong of heart, steadfast. That's more or less it.

For an ordinary person like you, with two hands, then naturally, when you lose a hand then the process is you have to practice. For example, long ago, I couldn't hold a bowl and chopsticks, but now I can lift a bowl like this and eat like everyone else. For another example, when I couldn't hold a needle, I tried to practice to be able to use something to hold it. That is a process of self-transformation.

"And this [Red Cross] program," I ask, "how does this program help?"

"Well . . . in general, if you speak of a need, then I [here the tape is indistinct] many things," Mrs. Hồng begins, "but here I'm talking about the spirit of this program—that there must be responsibility. If the means exist to help me stabilize my life, that is, to support me so I have something for medicine, in order to secure my health, and to raise my life a little higher, so that in the society, in the community, I can be at ease—I mean, happy to live in the community." This is a sentiment I hear phrased often in other conversations as well: the desire to be able to contribute to the community, not to be a burden.

"And so," I say, not certain whether we have already taken too much of her time, "I'd like to thank you very much for all that you . . . you have helped us understand and know. Is there anything else you would like to say?"

"Yes, well . . . there's only this much is all: We Vietnamese, to speak truthfully and frankly. . . ." She hesitates for a moment.

Sometimes it's easy to hurt feelings but it's necessary to tell the truth about how it is. The circumstances of war are like this, so now we have things happen like this. So on the one hand I struggle, and on the other hand—speaking generally about . . . about all the countries that cause war—they must take responsibility, they must give support and help so that our people can, after peace comes, progress with the community to reduce these illnesses and wounds and losses, to share with us. I've been speaking truthfully and frankly, and I hope you will understand . . . And I'm also afraid . . . it's easy to offend.

"I think you must speak frankly so that those who hear can have empathy and understand," I tell her. I thank her for speaking with us, and ask if there is anything that anyone else would like to add.

The doctor from the Red Cross asks about the war. "You were in the jungle, then . . . before, in the jungle . . .?"

Mrs. Hồng answers, "Yes . . . I went to fight with the resistance in the jungle . . . went to join the resistance when I was very young, sixteen. My father also joined the resistance, and my mother also went to fight . . ."

"In addition to the bombs and bullets, was there anything else?" the doctor asks.

"Yes, well," she replies,

> there were the toxic chemicals they sprayed. For example, in that year, in '64, the year of the first round of spraying that fell . . . it was like there was not one leaf left, not one leaf of a tree, every last one had fallen. That's how it was. The first day we were exposed we thought it was mist, but afterward they made it known it was a kind of toxic substance that caused that effect.
>
> That was in War Zone D, it was right . . . I don't know what it is called now. In the past it was called Vĩnh Cửu, Đồng Nai Province. Now it is reforested . . . the coastal forest of Đồng Nai Province, but then it was still a wasteland, not like now. . . . It's in the northeast part of Đồng Nai.
>
> I remember that year was '64. The year '64 was the year we started to have B-52s, to have the biggest storm of them. The first year was from '63, '64, '65, when there were B-52s, masses of B-52s dropping baby bombs and big bombs, and carpet bombing—all those were dumped right on that region, so many that there was not a single leaf left. The vegetation was a mess . . . all the leaves had fallen. And I remember that the animals no longer had any place to stay. There were some monkeys and birds that no longer had any place for shelter. The leaves of the forests were all gone.

Farmers in the region have told us how the land was so stripped of leaves that you could see twenty kilometers at a stretch, with nothing to obstruct your view. A member of the local Red Cross team recalls seeing the heavy pods of durian split open, still hanging on the dead trees.

I ask Mrs. Hồng how long she had lived in that region.

"Well . . . I took part from 1961, when the build-up began, until the day of liberation . . . until 1975. I lived right there the whole time," she recalls. "I lived right there."

She had come there at age sixteen, with her mother and father, from their home in Long An. "A land of rice fields in Long An Province," she calls it, "a land of rice fields. And because of the war I went to the capital, following the revolution, joined the revolution—at sixteen years old!" she marvels, remembering. "Sixteen and I had already gone. . . . The whole family . . . my older and younger siblings, all . . . ."

Again I thank her, and again ask if anyone has any more questions.

This time she asks the Red Cross doctor if I need to know anything about the resistance region. In place of an answer, he asks whether friends of hers from the war now have illnesses like those of her children.

"Well . . . I can count on my fingers many, many people with serious ill-nesses like this, just like this. There are those in each office, this workplace and that workplace here in the city. But in 1975, at the beginning of liberation, everyone just dispersed to different places. How can I know which diseases they still have?"

The Red Cross doctor muses: "During the war you didn't know anything was wrong, but you've only just learned." She replies,

Yes. We didn't know anything at all, just thought it was mist, or fog, and then later, with experience, the Vietnamese government led us to under-stand that that was bitter poison, toxic substances carrying very poison-ous chemicals that the country over in America brought to release in the war in Việt Nam—they let us know what it was so we could protect our-selves. But how could we completely protect ourselves in such rudimen-tary conditions—with pieces of cloth, small handkerchiefs? How could they shield, protect us? Those were poisons! But we still fought, and the more we fought, the less we knew fatigue.

Here Mrs. Hồng turns the conversation in another direction, speaking with such animation and feeling that it is difficult for me to follow. "There was a friend . . . I'll tell you her story," she begins.

I had a friend who was captured by the Americans and taken up in a helicopter and brought back dead. She was captured by the Americans and taken up in a helicopter, and they took turns raping her until she died. I think about it all the time . . . all the time—will always remember. The pain burns in my heart. It increases my strength for the struggle, increases my strength to fight. And afterward, I always remembered . . . remembered her smile, remembered the way she walked, remembered that we had slept together, fought together, lived together, shared sweets with each other. She was so full of love for life, and that young woman was also charming, charming. Her name was Hồng Sinh. She was a reporter working in Quảng Bình. They grabbed her . . . they grabbed her and took her up in the helicopter.

At first I did not understand all that Mrs. Hồng had said, and apologized, knowing my reactions were not commensurate to the emotion of her story. I explained that I could see she was very moved but could not understand every-thing. The Red Cross doctor repeated the story in a simpler fashion, and then we sat silent for a while.

"There's a lot more . . . there's a lot more, and still more," Mrs. Hồng at last continued.

Oh! I tell you, you will never be able to bear witness to all the pain and loss that the Vietnamese people have borne through so many wars. There is still much, much more.

I met you, a person—that is, a woman. Although you are from another country far away but, forgive me, you are still in the same plight. We are both women, the contact between us is easy, and it's easy to talk openly with each other. I want to express and share some sweet and bitter things that we have received from the past. There is the bitter . . . like the hardship. That is how we won the unity of our country for ourselves, won a sweeter future . . . could stand up, could be our own masters of our own land. The country is one country because of the courage, the fearlessness of our women, who are not just weak-legged with soft hands. Weak legs and soft hands still had to fight, still had to stand firm, still had to advance right beside the men.

"Yes . . . well . . ." I begin haltingly, groping for words to ask how to live beyond this legacy of conflict and hardship, "and do you think this is a story that should be told to everyone so they know, or should it be forgotten?"

"You must tell it," Mrs. Hồng replies, "must put it into the pages of history, it must get into the pages of the history of our country, our generation, of the world, to understand that the country of Việt Nam has people—men as well as women, old as well as young—all of them living a life like this. Before, it was like I have told you, and now there are lives of struggle like this. Let them see everything."

She talks about all the burdens Vietnamese women must shoulder, and says that she can't do it anymore—that her strength is all used up, "dried up and turned to ashes."

"So then," she asks us, "Do you all have anything else to ask? Is there anything else?"

"Well," I reply, "there is still more—we could stay many days, many weeks, many months to talk more. But there comes a time when we must say good-bye."

"All right," she says.

But though we say good-bye here, I think that when you are here or when you go back to your country—on your side I think you will certainly remember us Vietnamese women. And I hope that this feeling is a . . . a relationship. We can sympathize with each other. . . . I hope we will always remember and respect each other. Although you are from a far country, a country that caused us much loss—that's not a reason to lose a friendship. Do you agree? The Vietnamese have this saying: "Add a friend, lose an enemy." The time of war has passed, so now we can be friends with each other.

"I think that in America, war is a problem of the government, not the people," I respond. "I think ordinary people can have sympathy and understanding for each other and together build a different future."

"What you are saying," she interprets, "is that the policy of the American government is not the ideal of each individual who lives on American soil, that not everyone shares those ideas. They also love peace, really want there to be peace, don't want war." It is a thought that runs counter to her experience of Americans, and she stops to ponder it.

"Yes," I reply. "When you were in the jungle, I was in the streets, protesting."

The Red Cross doctor mulls it over: "Ah . . . ah . . . protesting the war. . . ."

Mrs. Hồng turns the phrase over and over: "Down into the streets, down in the streets. There were some who took to the streets even in America, took to the streets even . . . protested the war in Việt Nam."

"Everywhere there are ordinary people," the doctor observes.

I explain that I was a student at the time, and that many students protested.

The doctor, who is roughly our same age, muses: "So long. . . . it stretched out so long—from 1954 to 1975—drawn out interminably. Even one day was dangerous enough, but how many years . . . one day was hard enough to bear."

We are again silent for a while. Then I repeat my thank yous, and the doctor makes a presentation on behalf of our small delegation. I think back to his reaction when we were making preparations for our visits, and I had asked how to present the small gifts I had brought. As gifts from the Red Cross, the doctor had replied without hesitation, adding: "People here would never accept gifts from an American."

Mrs. Hồng says she will walk me out. She takes me by the hand, by the stump of her hand, and we walk out. "Don't forget us," she says. "When you are over there, think of the Vietnamese mothers from time to time."

The next day the Red Cross staff, which during my stay there had been intensely busy both with me and with other visitors and meetings, offered to take some time to show me around. When they asked what I would like to do, I said that if they thought it would be possible, would not be a bother, I would like to return to Mrs. Hồng's to see if she had some quilting pieces she would like to sell, some she might be able to sell without causing problems for her work.

They thought it might be possible, but first they wanted to show me a supermarket—a super-supermarket—that had recently been built near the new industrial zone on the outskirts of the city. It occupied the major portion of an enclosed mall that also featured a popcorn vending machine, an ice-cream shop, and an auto display—all in astonishing, scandalous contrast to the simple and sometimes abject and miserable homes we had been visiting over the past week. We wandered like zombies through the heaps of household goods and sterile aisles of shrink-wrapped produce: our souls were elsewhere. At the sight of two donation boxes, both for the Red Cross, our spirits revived. One was marked for general disaster relief, the other for the victims of Agent Orange. Both were about half full of small bills. The head of the provincial Red Cross explained with enthusiasm that this was a new idea. The boxes generally collected enough money to construct one house per month for the homeless, she said.

When we returned to Mrs. Hồng's, she welcomed us enthusiastically and greeted my request for quilt pieces with good-natured laughter and puzzlement. What good could unfinished squares be? But if I wanted them, she was happy to let me have them; no, it wouldn't be any trouble. I explained that I wanted them to give to people as a way of making the stories she had told me more concrete, more tangible to those so far away. At first she insisted on giving them to me, but in the end happily accepted the money I slipped into her hand.

"With your work," I observe, "you keep people warm, and create beauty."

"Yes," she says. "I like to create beautiful things—all women like beauty of course! Sometimes I make *áo dài*. People around here know me, and they come to place their orders. They ask for the woman with the chopped-off hand." She laughs and shakes her head, her eyes twinkling.

She would like to make me a pillowcase, so that when I go to sleep "over there" I will remember my younger sister "over here." Once again she walks me out, swinging my arm and laughing. "Remember your younger sister," she reminds me. "Remember that there is a woman like this, with all these stories, and one hand lopped off in the war. But remember too that she loves people, she loves her country, and she loves life."[13]

Mrs. Hồng's story is not representative; nor is it unique. It is a fragment, a sample, one piece of a mosaic, one patch in a quilt.

Other people told other stories. While a few spoke with Mrs. Hồng's resolute and cheerful spirit, others spoke in tears. I heard many stories about the day-to-day tasks of caring for children, many of whom were then in their late twenties and thirties: stories of prechewing food for children who could only swallow with difficulty, stories of caring for toileting, feminine hygiene, and bathing needs, and of the difficulty of carrying grown children from place to place for these needs. I heard many stories as well about the difficulty of making enough for the family to survive when one of the main income-earners had much of her day absorbed in these tasks. I heard the stories of several women who were the sole support of their families, either because their husband was also disabled or had died. Several people spoke of their attempts to make sense of what had happened to them, of their search for meaning through visits to fortunetellers, geomancers, physiognomists, and mediums. Many people spoke of fatigue and of fear for what would happen to their children when their own strength gave out. There were long silences and torrents of words, thoughtful reflections, quiet fortitude, protests against an unjust fate, and angry outbursts against "the former American government." The word "responsibility" came up often, as did the word "exhausted."

With variations that reflect local circumstances, similar stories are told by veterans of the wars who are now scattered across the globe and by workers and families in the forty places where these chemicals were manufactured, tested, stored, transported, and eventually disposed of and destroyed—from Australia and New Zealand to Korea, Okinawa, and Canada, and in numerous sites across the United States. These stories cross boundaries of nation, political preference, wealth, gender, and generation, creating unexpected collaborations across time and place. People affected by Agent Orange and their supporters share stories and scientific findings as well as approaches to raising public awareness and to seeking compensation from their respective governments and from the corporations that manufactured the chemicals.[14] Currently, six countries—the United States, Australia, Canada, New Zealand, South Korea, and Việt Nam— compensate their veterans for exposure to Agent Orange, and veterans continue to win legal battles that expand the list of those exposed and thus eligible for compensation.[15]

Conclusion

The topic of Agent Orange—whether taken as chemical, experience, metaphor, or a blend of these—spills over boundaries, binaries, received categories, and neat definitions. Some categories are destabilized by a leap of recognition when people see themselves in each other's stories across boundaries that once were taken as defining: ally and enemy, self and other, actor and subject. As a U.S. veteran observed, referring to a family he met in Việt Nam whose child endured the same health problems as his own, which both families attributed to the consequences of Agent Orange: "It was like looking in a mirror."[16]

Other disruptions of received categories have less to do with human perception than with the sad ironies of chemical effect. Chemicals that targeted hormone growth in plants turned out to have related effects on humans. Chemicals that some decision makers had argued would provide a more humane form of warfare by causing only short-term destruction of foliage while sparing human beings turned out to have long-lasting, devastating effects for both the environment and human health. American soldiers who sprayed the chemicals became victims of the spray along with Vietnamese soldiers and civilians who lived beneath that spray. The efforts of the American and ARVN military to deprive northern Democratic Republic of Vietnam and southern National Liberation Front troops of food and protective camouflage exposed perhaps five million or more southern civilians to the poison at the time (and untold numbers in the years following), laid waste to the productive forests and cropland of the very south they were trying to defend, and destroyed the means of subsistence and ways of life of another uncountable number of southerners, in particular those who lived in and on the forests—people they were trying to win to their side.[17]

In the context of a book on looking back on the Vietnam War, reflection on Agent Orange and its ramifications can contribute to breaking apart old configurations so that we can see the past and present with greater nuance and complexity. This, Michael Jackson contends, is our role as intellectuals: to subvert traumatic events by telling stories that rework history to make it bearable, while neither repressing memory nor denying that history.[18]

In the context of this chapter as a collaboration, however, that is only part of the story. The last words go to three people I spoke with in Việt Nam. The first was a pharmacist in Thái Bình, a man whose two older sons were near death from a crippling, wasting disease and whose third son was born with a heart defect. When I apologized for coming with only small gifts to share—a few small cakes, some sugar, a can of condensed milk—he replied, "Your attention, the attention of the American people—is a precious spiritual gift." I treasured his words for a long while.

But later, in looking over my interviews, I found another recurrent theme as well, expressed by another man whose own two sons were crippled: "We don't need your respect. We need help."

In Mrs. Hồng's words: The countries that make war must take responsibility. Add a friend, lose an enemy. Put it into the pages of history.

NOTES

1. Numerous critics have written of the dangers of reproducing colonial relationships through scholarship; much has been said about "the West" turning "the East" into an object of analysis or desire. While appreciating these critiques, I take the position of Aihwa Ong, who has argued that the "greater betrayal" of those we speak with lies in a refusal to recognize "the informant" as active and in a refusal to "help marginal groups intervene in global narratives." Aihwa Ong, "Women Out of China: Traveling Tales and Traveling Theories in Postcolonial Feminism," in *Women Writing Culture*, ed. Ruth Behar and Deborah A. Gordon (Berkeley: University of California Press, 1995), 353–354.

2. Michael Jackson, *The Politics of Storytelling: Violence, Transgression, and Intersubjectivity* (Copenhagen: Museum Tusculanum Press, 2002).

3. Ibid., 11–13.

4. Interview, Nguyễn Thị Hồng, Bien Hoa, April 18, 2001.

5. See Guenter Lewy, *America in Vietnam* (New York: Oxford University Press, 1978); Marilyn Young, *The Vietnam Wars* (New York: HarperCollins, 1991); and Le Cao Dai, *Agent Orange in the Vietnam War: History and Consequences* (Hanoi: Vietnam Red Cross Society, 2000), among many others.

6. "Project Renew," accessed December 15, 2014, http://www.landmines.org.vn/. Unexploded ordinance still contaminates some 20 percent of the land overall and over 80 percent of the land in areas that were part of the former demilitarized zone.

7. Lewy, *America in Vietnam*, 258.

8. Institute of Medicine of the National Academies Press, "Summary," *Veterans and Agent Orange, Update 2012 (2014)*, National Academies Press, http://www.nap.edu/openbook .php?record_id=18395&page=1.

9. Linda S. Birnbaum, "Health and Environmental Effects of Dioxins" (Paper presented to the Yale Vietnam Conference 2002: The Ecological and Health Effects of the Vietnam War, New Haven, Connecticut, September 13–15, 2002).

10. See William A. Buckingham Jr., *Operation Ranch Hand: The Air Force and Herbicides in Southeast Asia 1961–1971* (Washington, D.C.: Office of Air Force History, USAF, 1982), iii.

11. "Environmental and Human Health Assessment of Dioxin Contamination at Bien Hoa Airbase, Viet Nam. August 2011," http://www.hatfieldgroup.com/wp-content/uploads/ AgentOrangeReports/O33_1579/Bien%20Hoa%20Final%20Full%20Report_August%20 2011.pdf.

12. An earlier version of this interview appeared in *Le Viet Nam au Feminin* (Paris: Les Indes Savantes, 2005).

13. Six years later, in New York, Mrs. Hồng presented me with the pillowcase she had promised. After our talk she had been chosen to represent the Việt Nam Association of Victims of Agent Orange at a court hearing, appealing for the right to sue the chemical manufacturers. By then her illnesses were quite advanced; she died three weeks after her return to Việt Nam.

14. There are many such groups and many more small-scale individual efforts. A few examples: In the United States, the War Legacies Project and the Agent Orange Relief and Responsibility Campaign; in France, Les Enfants de la Dioxin; and in England, Len Aldis's work with the Vietnamese Friendship Association. Among the corporations that manufactured the chemicals, Dow and Monsanto are the most recognizable names.

15. In January 2015, for instance, veterans who flew the spray planes after they were repurposed but not decontaminated won a court battle granting them compensation.

16. The veteran was speaking at an open mike to a meeting of dioxin experts convened by the National Institute for Environmental Health Sciences at the Hyatt Regency in Monterey, California, in August of 2000, to help the United States prepare for its first official talks with Việt Nam about conducting joint scientific research on the ongoing consequences of dioxin / Agent Orange. The history of the rocky road from outright denial of U.S. responsibility to halting cooperation still needs to be written.

17. These two paragraphs have been reworked from my essay, "Agent Orange, Viet Nam, and the United States: Blurring the Boundaries," in *Vietnam and the West: New Approaches*, ed. Wynn Wilcox (Ithaca, N.Y.: Cornell University, Southeast Asia Program Publications, 2010), 175–194.

18. Jackson, *The Politics of Storytelling*.

10

Re-seeing Cambodia and Recollecting *The 'Nam*

A Vertiginous Critique of the Military Sublime

CATHY J. SCHLUND-VIALS

ARCLIGHT: B-52 bombers flew so high they were invisible from the ground and the first time you knew they were there was when the sky turned blue-white with the glare of the bombs, hence, ARCLIGHT.

–"'Nam Notes," *The 'Nam* (vol. 3)

[Unidentified Narrator] *Cautious minutes later . . .*
"This must go miles into Cambodia!"
"Yeah. What are the Cambodians going to think about that?"

–Specialist Dennis Daniels and Private First Class "Pig" Meachum
responding to a B-52 attack on the Vietnamese–Cambodian border
(*The 'Nam* 1, no. 33 [August 1989], emphasis in original)

Written by Doug Murray and edited by Larry Hama (both Vietnam War veterans), Marvel Comics' *The 'Nam* (1986–1993) was originally advertised as a "twelve-year limited series" focused in "real time," with a distinct historical span (1966–1972) and told from a "grunt's point of view." As Hama recalled in the 1999 reissue of the series, "Every time a month went by in the real world, a month went by in the comic. . . . It had to be about the guys on the ground who got jungle rot, malaria, and dysentery. It had to be about people, not ideas, and the people had to be real, not cardboard heroes or super-men."[1] Previously known for his work on *GI Joe: A Real American Hero*, based on the Hasbro soldier toy line, Hama's insistence on "people not ideas" who were "real, not cardboard heroes" marked a profound departure and unparalleled endeavor for Marvel Comics, which had built its media empire on the likes of the Fantastic Four, the X-Men,

Spider-Man, Iron Man, and the Incredible Hulk, among others. Admittedly, the series was not the first of its kind with regard to a comic treatment of the conflict, though it was unique in its adherence to the Comics Code Authority, which dictated in conservative fashion the editorial removal of adult language (primarily swearing) and the avoidance of controversial plotlines (involving, for example, extramarital affairs, militarized rape, and illegal drug use).[2] This sanitized version of the war was deliberate given that The 'Nam's editors were invested in creating a work that could suitably transmit and appropriately translate the wartime experience to and for the children of Vietnam War veterans.

True to intended form, The 'Nam's eighty-four issues juxtaposed historical events such as the Tet Offensive and the Robert Kennedy assassination with more personal stories of life on base and in-country military campaigns. Moreover, each issue included a glossary of military terms, as evidenced in this chapter's opening epigraph's delineation of "ARCLIGHT." The accessibility afforded the comic via mass production was matched by its aforementioned negotiation of civilian *and* military audiences. While Jan Scruggs, president of the Vietnam Veterans Memorial fund, critically questioned whether the war should be the subject of a comic book, *Newsweek* editor William Broyles praised the series, highlighting its "certain gritty reality."[3] Without a doubt, The 'Nam's initial success was critical *and* commercial: the inaugural December 1986 issue outsold a concurrent installment of the widely popular *X-Men* series.[4] Perhaps most telling with regard to the comic's cultural resonance was its reception from Bravo Organization, a notable Vietnam veterans group: The 'Nam was recognized by the organization for the "best media portrayal of the Vietnam War," beating out Oliver Stone's Academy Award–winning film *Platoon* (1986).[5]

Notwithstanding market success and veteran praise, it is the comic's nuanced visual/verbal work—particularly its strategic rendering of militarized sites and tactical depiction of collateral damage—that presages this chapter's overall focus on Marvel's The 'Nam. Expressly, the graphic representation of wartime sites and sights—inclusive of multiple Southeast Asian fronts and manifold soldier perspectives—engenders a syncretic interpretation of the Vietnam War as confused endeavor *and* recollected conflict. Such chaotic ways of seeing, observable in The 'Nam's radial portrayal of troop movements and large-scale bombing campaigns, operate in seeming contrast to the comic's serialized emplotments, which occur in "real time" and adhere to a decidedly more linear remembrance narrative. This juxtaposition of perceptual disorder and narrative uniformity foregrounds this chapter's central contention that integral to Marvel's "grunt's point of view" account is a conspicuously *vertiginous* and ultimately cohesive critique of U.S. militarization (which will later be defined under the delineated auspices of the "military sublime"). Such a vertiginous critique, as this chapter subsequently argues, is on a general level fixed to the hybrid visual/verbal idiom of comics. On a more specific level, these critical evaluations coincide with *The 'Nam*'s overt memory-oriented objective as intergenerational, soldier/civilian narrative.

Hence, despite Scruggs's above-mentioned criticism that comics were not suited to the task of translating soldier experience via (belated) wartime remembrance, this chapter opens with and supports an oppositional assertion: as graphic "memory work," *The 'Nam* accommodates both radial and linear perspectives, laying bare the flexible parameters of an inventive visual/verbal medium. In so doing, *The 'Nam* as layered narrative makes clear the comic's narrative suitability vis-à-vis the traumatic and contradictory dimensions of the Vietnam War.[6] As a further theorization of the vertiginous and deeper contemplation of the military sublime accentuates, *The 'Nam*'s use of various sightlines disrupts amnesiac narratives of collateral damage that ignore the very real disorder, chaos, and destruction that were necessarily part of an expansive, imperial conflict. These graphic sightlines—part and parcel of Marvel's *The 'Nam* as a hybrid mode—displace and disrupt the ostensible orderliness of the military sublime as euphemistically comprehended, militarized aesthetic. This multivalent mediation of and critical contemplation on the Vietnam War as *drawn event* coheres with Gillian Whitlock's rightful insistence that comics "are not a mere hybrid of graphic arts and prose fiction but a unique interpretation that transcends both, and emerges through the imaginative work of closure that readers are required to make between the panels on the page."[7]

Vertiginous Sights and the Military Sublime

Suggestive of a medical condition ("vertigo") that, in common parlance, is erroneously linked to a fear of heights ("acrophobia"), "vertiginous" operates as apt and critical adjectival modifier with regard to U.S. war-making. To elucidate, whereas the imperial gaze affords a seeming sense of order from sites above, such readings of orderliness are made more tumultuous from sights on the ground (or below). This contradistinction—dependent on vertical vantage points and horizontal vistas—mimetically reflects the many sites of U.S. militarization that outwardly encompass all points insular, oceanic, continental, and hemispheric and include the base, the camp, and the front. As familiar vertiginous referent, one could turn to Alfred Hitchcock's *Vertigo*, wherein the film's plot pivots on the protagonist's trauma-induced acrophobia and vertigo; both render him unable to see a plot involving murder and an unhealthy romantic obsession. Surprisingly, perhaps, Hitchcock's *Vertigo* proves a useful frame to reconsider the shifting sights of U.S. militarization during the early years of the Cold War.

Expressly, the year *Vertigo* made its cinematic debut—in 1958—the Soviet satellite *Sputnik* was launched (on January 4), signaling the first major milestone in the so-termed Space Race. The United States followed suit twenty-seven days later, with the successful launch of *Explorer* and the soon-after formation of the National Aeronautics and Space Administration. The year 1958 also witnessed a series of significant military accidents involving large-scale munitions. On February 5 a B-47 unintentionally dropped a 7,600-pound Mark 15 nuclear bomb near Savannah, Georgia (by Tybee Island), which to this day remains undetonated and lost.[8] Almost a month later, on March 11, another B-47 accidentally unloaded a 26-kiloton Mark 6 (a more powerful version than the "Fat Man" dropped on Nagasaki).[9] The bomb fell 15,000 feet and landed in Mars Bluff, South Carolina, in Walter Gregg's backyard.[10] While the plutonium core remained intact, 6,000 pounds of conventional high explosives detonated, though miraculously, no deaths were reported.[11]

These "vertical events," indicative of a war waged from air and space, suggestive of a regularity undermined by accident and chaos, are indirectly accessed in *Vertigo*, which pioneered an unsettling in-camera effect known as the "dolly zoom." Intended to shift normative perception, the dolly zoom engaged the following technique: camera dollies move away from the subject while the lens zooms in or out, making less stable a clear field of view. What emerges is a "falling-away-from-oneself feeling" or "feeling of unreality" aimed to indicate that a character is undergoing a profound realization that causes that person to reevaluate everything that was previously believed.

Such accidental drops, muddled objectives, and perspective manipulations undergird this chapter's reading of "vertiginous" as chaotically "sighted" (via ways of seeing) and peculiarly "sited" (in terms of location). Furthermore, this multivalent dizziness coheres with the chapter's concomitant focus on the ways in which en masse militarization—in B-52 campaigns such as the above-mentioned Operation Arclight (1965–1968) that extended beyond the confines of Viet Nam and targeted, from above, nearby Cambodia (along with neighboring Laos)—is grasped and misremembered by what Samina Najmi characterizes as a masculinist "military sublime."[12] Such sublimity, according to Najmi, encompasses a distanced aesthetic/political mode marked by "dramatic, large-scale spectacles of war," which dominate mainstream portrayals of contemporary American war-making: recall, for instance, "shock and awe" footage of cluster bomb conflagrations, wide-angle shots of long-range missile assaults, and aerial perspectives that overlook vast areas of superficially unoccupied land.[13] These associations, symptomatic of the American military sublime as ordered and clean, are productively undermined in Marvel Comics' *The 'Nam*, which engages the vertiginous vis-à-vis its frenzied characterization of Cambodia as tangled Vietnam War–era front and disremembered Cold War bombing sight.

These vertiginous frames—inclusive of confused sightlines and unclear per-spective points—signal a particular hegemonic crisis or rupture within the seemingly well-arranged registers of the American military sublime. As tracta-ble memory medium, comics are, to reiterate and expand, able to simultane-ously accommodate unruly sights and multiple spaces; in sum, the paradoxically clear and confused perspectives afforded by the form vertiginously undercut the ostensibly methodical dimensions of the American military sublime.

As primary text, I turn to a particular issue of *The 'Nam*, published in August 1989, which focuses its narrative attention on protagonist Specialist Daniels's involuntary redeployment back to Southeast Asia, specifically his for-ays along the Viet Nam–Cambodia border. This particular setting foregrounds a brief recapitulation of foreign policy vis-à-vis the aforementioned bombing campaigns over Cambodia; such forgotten campaigns accentuate the ways in which devastating U.S. airpower is problematically obscured by the idealized sublimity and perceived distance of American militarization. As necessary background, I briefly consider the relationship between distant warfare, aero-mobility, and the military sublime; I then provide a short overview of this spe-cific Cambodian campaign in order to further contextualize *The 'Nam* issue, titled, "Back in the Saddle Again," which strategically revises a reading of the war as temporally confined (e.g., limited deployments and campaign timeta-bles) and geographically contained (via front and battlefield). Not coinciden-tally, the issue's title accesses Gene Autry's nostalgic song of the same name, which, reminiscent of Richard Slotkin, recalls a western imaginary marked by ostensibly open expanse and gun violence.[14] Through a close reading of issue, text, and image, I contend that the issue's reiterative use of aerial sights (pri-marily its depictions of B-52 bombings), tactical revelation of multiple milita-rized sites (in the United States, Viet Nam, and Cambodia), and individualized portrayals of North Vietnamese and Khmer Rouge troops confirm and disrupt a sublime reading of the conflict as *distant* and *distanced* war.

Re-seeing Distant Warfare: Aeromobility, Cambodia, and the Military Sublime

To read the United States through frames of continual combat necessarily moves beyond the recent Cold War past (or even the contemporary War on Terror moment); indeed, war and militarization have been part and parcel of what Yến Lê Espiritu characterizes as a multicentury racialized national proj-ect.[15] Correspondingly, as Catherine Lutz reminds, the United States was "birthed not just by the Revolution of 1776 but also by wars against Native Americans and the violence required to capture and enslave millions of people," underscoring the degree to which so-known Manifest Destiny was viciously enabled and aggressively facilitated in the eighteenth and nineteenth centuries by wide-ranging troop deployments (inclusive of continent and ocean), the extensive establishment of strategic camps (particularly military forts and frontier outposts), and the rise of mass transportation (for example, the construction of intercontinental canals and the completion of the transcontinental railroad).[16]

In turn, such militarized nation-building—which in the eighteenth, nineteenth, and twentieth centuries involved the en masse movement of peoples (voluntary and forced), the feverish construction of bases, and the furious development of transport—renders perceptible an all-too-familiar yet still confusing time–space compression wherein various technological innovations (e.g., the telegraph, the train, and the rise of ostensible "free markets") collapse in dense fashion immense spatial and temporal distances.[17] Situated within this compressed temporal–spatial context, it is therefore not surprising that American war-making and U.S. imperialism—on one level—are proximately comprehended through historical citation and past reference (e.g., "another Vietnam"). On another level, the cartographic convergence of war-determined geographical space and conflict-governed historical time is even more apparent not by land and sea but by air. As Caren Kaplan provocatively maintains, the imperial sights afforded by eighteenth-century aerial campaigns, in which distanced vision operated in tandem with distant warfare (e.g., the use of surveillance balloons during the French Revolution), was consistent with contemporaneous projects of exploration and conquest.[18]

Furthermore, when situated within the twentieth-century context of global war and large-scale human loss, such aeromobility, according to Kaplan, authorizes a troublingly euphemistic relationship to distance predicated on the largely unfounded conviction that, in "the aftermath of World War I's previously unimaginable number of civilian as well as military casualties . . . precision bombing would be a more humane practice than previous strategies of ground wars. Intrinsic to the argument for aerial bombardment are the key European Enlightenment precepts of distance, precision, and the truth-value of sight. Each of these concepts itself requires an underlying belief in the mastery of technology and the superiority of information systems that privilege vision."[19] This wide-ranging aeromobility, inclusive of firebombing campaigns over Japan in World War II, munitions runs through Laos during the American War in Viet Nam, and more recent drone strikes in Baghdad (among so many others), privileges a militarized mode of sight that in the end fails to see—as countless missed targets and millions of unintended deaths signify—that with significant distance inevitably comes great imprecision. Alternatively, the conquering of distance through air and space—emblematized by the technological capacity to cover vast areas in the span of minutes and hours—has analogously engendered a discomfiting sense of déjà vu (which, fittingly, translates into "already seen" in French). This "already seen-ness" or, more apropos, the perception that one has previously "been there," is confirmed via intermittent American foreign policy returns to overseas military bases in the Far East, militarized zones in the Southeast, and war-weary fronts in the Middle East.[20]

This distanced war-making, which achieves an uncannily sublime register, is troublingly evident with regard to the covert bombings of the Cambodian countryside. According to Ben Kiernan and Taylor Owen, between October 4, 1965, and August 15, 1973, the United States dropped 2,756,941 tons of munitions on 113,716 Cambodian sites. An estimated 230,516 sorties were flown over Cambodia, which had—through its then-head of state Prince Norodom Sihanouk—declared a neutral position vis-à-vis the Vietnam War.[21] Of these missions, 3,580 involved "unknown targets" and 8,238 failed to list any target whatsoever. While the Lyndon Johnson administration's use of air-based munitions and the Richard Nixon administration's bombing of the Cambodian countryside (under the auspices of the B-52 "Menu" campaign, 1969–1973) are widely recognized (particularly in the aftermath of Pentagon Papers publication and the Kent State shooting), less acknowledged is the extent to which the American War in Viet Nam—from the outset and to restate—time and again involved adjacent Cambodia (along with bordering Thailand, Laos, and Burma).[22] As Kiernan and Owen further synopsize, when President Richard Nixon "telephoned his national security advisor, Henry Kissinger, to discuss the ongoing bombing of Cambodia" on December 9, 1970, the "sideshow to the war in Vietnam, begun in 1965 under the Johnson administration, had already seen 475,515 tons of ordnance on Cambodia."[23]

Denotative of "a small show or stall at an exhibition, fair, or circus" and "a minor or diverting incident or issue, especially one which distracts attention from something more important" (*Oxford English Dictionary*), the use of "sideshow" in conjunction with Cambodia purposely belies—by way of historical juxtaposition and military magnitude—the degree to which U.S. bombings had an impact that far exceeded immediate foreign policy objectives (e.g., the disruption of the so-termed Ho Chi Minh Trail, which extended along the Cambodia–Viet Nam border). As Kiernan and Owens assert, the civilian casualties that resulted from these bombings (which number between 50,000 to 150,000) "drove an enraged populace into the arms of an insurgency that had enjoyed relatively little support until the bombing began, setting in motion the expansion of the Vietnam War deeper into Cambodia, a *coup d'état* in 1970, the rapid rise of the Khmer Rouge, and ultimately the Cambodian genocide."[24]

Such disastrous legacies, which occur notwithstanding Cambodia's geopolitical status as a "sideshow" vis-à-vis the Indochina conflict, agonizingly bring to light the capaciousness of not only U.S. war-making but the Cold War non-containment of the American War in Viet Nam. Measured by hundreds of thousands of air force sorties and millions of tons of munitions, such warfare fulfills by way of mathematical greatness the far-reaching parameters of the military sublime. Encompassing an enormity that is inconsistently calculable (via numerical measurement) *and* incalculable (with respect to collateral human cost), to read the American bombing of Cambodia via the military sublime is to acknowledge the pugnacious capaciousness and distanced vistas of U.S. empire, a project marked not by moderate program but by excessive force.

Comparably, such imperial excesses are affectively evident and sublimely apparent in first-person accounts such as the following given by an anonymous Cambodian survivor: "We heard a terrifying noise which shook the ground; it was as if the earth trembled, rose up and opened beneath our feet. Enormous explosions lit up the sky like huge bolts of lightning; it was the American B-52s."[25] Reminiscent of aforementioned "dramatic, large-scale, spectacles of war," the survivor's concluding revelation of American B-52s follows ominous, sensory-driven recollections (for instance, "a terrifying noise" and the trembling of earth) and descriptions of cataclysmic conflagrations which resemble "huge bolts of lightning." These intensely personal remembrances of American military power on the one hand collapse the geopolitical space between the United States and Cambodia by way of munitions transport (in the case of the former) and natural landscape (with regard to the latter). On the other hand, such non-state-authorized accounts accentuate through sublime characterization and vertiginous categorization the collateral costs of U.S. foreign policy via enormity, confusion, and scale. Accordingly, what is originally "seen" or experienced as natural is subsequently exposed as not only man-made but American. As significant, what is visible from the ground (e.g., conflagration and bomber) is by and large invisible from above.

These militarized magnitudes, which are perceived differentially (based on ground/air position), couched according to an affective language of fear, and understood through a metaphoric allusion to nature, are to varying degrees and divergent ends reminiscent of Romantic characterizations of wartime sublimity; as Immanuel Kant avers in *The Critique of Reason*:

> War itself, provided it is conducted with order and a sacred respect for the rights of civilians, has something sublime about it, and gives nations that carry it on in such a manner a stamp of only the more sublime the more numerous the dangers to which they are exposed, and which they are able to meet with fortitude. On the other hand, a prolonged peace favors the predominance of a mere commercial spirit, and with it a debasing self-interest, cowardice, and effeminacy, and tends to degrade the character of a nation.[26]

Notwithstanding this martial relational, which joins war politics to sublime aesthetics, it is the terribleness of B-52 bombings conveyed in the abovementioned eyewitness account—which uncovers a disregard for civilian life in the face of Cold War objective—that adheres more directly with what Kant's contemporary Edmund Burke maintained was fundamental to the sublime: a connection to devastating pain and tremendous trepidation. As Burke asserts in *Philosophical Enquiry into the Origins of Our Ideas of the Sublime and Beautiful* (1758), "Whatever is fitted in any sort to excite the ideas of pain and danger, that is to say, whatever is in any sort terrible, or is conversant about terrible objects, or operates in a manner analogous to terror, is a source of the sublime; that is, it is productive of the strongest emotion which the mind is capable of feeling."[27] Predicated on "pain," "danger," and "terror," Burke's characterization of the sublime pivots on "whatever is in any sort terrible" or "is conversant about terrible objects."

Likewise significant, these sublime classifications are in the end reliant on what "the mind is capable of feeling," which suggests rational comprehension of the threat (e.g., danger) and an affective reaction to its effect (i.e., pain). When situated adjacent an expansive milieu of the American War in Viet Nam, the question of comprehension in the face of militarized enormity is one that, in *The 'Nam*, is answered via a convergent combination of individual recollection (via individual soldier accounts "on the ground") and collected remembrances (particularly those involving experiences "in the air" and "over there"). Such convergences, which are distinctively made possible by comics as an interdisciplinary and citation-based image/text genre are, as the next section makes clear, at once evident in the conflation of multiple media forms (particularly in terms of news reports, cinematic allusions to Vietnam War films, and widely circulated aerial views of B-52s dropping payloads).

Critiquing the Military Sublime and
Recollecting Cambodia: *The 'Nam*

Initially set roughly 9,700 miles away from Viet Nam and Cambodia, "Back in the Saddle Again" opens in Fort Huachuca, an American military installation located in southeast Arizona. Originally constructed in the late 1870s as a southerly border patrol site and anti-Apache stronghold, Fort Huachuca would at the turn-of-the-twentieth century serve as Army home for African American "Buffalo Soldiers" stationed in the American West.[28] During World War II, Fort Huachuca was a primary training base for African American troops, and it remained in operation until 1953, when the base closed in the aftermath of the Korean War. However, seven months later, in 1954, Fort Huachuca was reactivated and emerged as a significant site for "electronic warfare," which entails the military use of long-range electromagnetic antiradar pulses as a means of distanced conflict.[29] In 1967, as the American War in Viet Nam increased in size, scope, and intensity, Fort Huachuca would serve as the headquarters of the U.S. Army Strategic Communications Command; it is presently home to the U.S. Army Network Enterprise Technology Command.[30]

These base details, which lay bare the local/global dimensions of U.S. militarization (inclusive of history, place, and use), are predictably omitted from the comic's main narrative; instead, this setting is named via a yellow-boxed caption that appears in the left-hand corner of the opening panel. This introductory frame features a white barracks building in the foreground and the shadows of soldiers in the background; a green-clothed Army figure whose face is cut out of the frame occupies the central axis. The following six panels focus on this figure's movement into the barracks, which is initially accompanied by the revelation of last names associated with an Army roll call: in the first, the subject's hand is shown opening a doorknob; in the second, this same figure enters a room marked by a green couch and television set; a hand manipulates a set of blinds (in frames three and four). The previously mentioned black-and-white television occupies the foreground of the fifth panel; on it is news footage from a Southeast Asian war zone. The newscast, which details the following story, is revealed in jagged word balloons that occupy the foreground of the fourth and sixth frames: ". . . convoy from the 25th infantry was ambushed near the Cambodian border. Five soldiers were killed in what officials are claiming was . . ."[31]

The next page incompletely continues the missive (". . . and on the home front, the Pentagon has announced that . . .") and functions as the comic's single-panel title page: "Back in the Saddle" appears in stereotyped, blocky Army script in the bottom right-hand corner, and the comic's main protagonist—Specialist Daniels—sits in front of the television set, confirming by way of concluding the barracks setting that he was in fact the figure featured in each of the preceding frames.[32]

While the opening of "Back in the Saddle Again" is largely quotidian in its focus on the mundane aspects of soldier life, the interruption of domestic existence (in the United States) by foreign news account (in Southeast Asia) replicates the ways in which Americans received news of the war "over there" (on television) and anticipates the primary conflict in the comic: Specialist Daniels's involuntary redeployment to "The 'Nam" as the result of a military policy intended to reduce troop turnover. Both the television account and Daniels's compulsory assignment collapse the distance between U.S. base and Southeast Asian front; such geopolitical compression is further evident on the following page, wherein the first panel features the caption, "Back in the 'Nam, near **Tay Ninh** . . ." (emphasis in original).[33] Whereas the previous frames are marked by the light blue of sky, the olive green of Army uniforms, the whiteness of military barracks, and the orderliness of militarized space, the next section is decidedly more lush and ominous.

FIGURE 10.1 Though marked by a mix of shots, which include close-ups and bridging shots to suggest the passage of time, the prevalence of horizontal lines prefigures an opening reading of the narrative as distinctly ordered. © MARVEL.

FIGURE 10.2 The organization of the panels is much more diffuse. Drawn along diagonals, the embedded shots are reminiscent of a "Dutch tilt," a camera technique, like the dolly zoom, intended to engender a sense of viewer imbalance. Moreover, the frames converge in cyclical fashion, eschewing linearity in favor of simultaneity. © MARVEL.

In the first of four panels, a helicopter occupies the far upper corner of the frame; a convoy of American military tracks occupies the panel's middle portion and extends diagonally to the horizon line. This vehicular formation vertically and horizontally segments the first panel; whereas the upper section features U.S. military technology and the blurred outlines of American military personnel, the lower portion is marked by an overgrowth of green vegetation, dark blues, and five dark purple figures. An editor's note, placed at the bottom of the page outside the panel frame, indicates that the dialogue is "translated from the Vietnamese"; this sense of translation is confirmed via the dotted lines of speech balloons and the use of angle brackets (<and>). This citation occurs in conjunction with one of the statements made by the unnamed figures: "<No! Do not fire!>"[34]

This warning, coupled with the response from one of the figures ("<But why not? Are we not here to slow down enemy supply convoys?>") and in tandem with the next two panels, confirms that the scene depicts North Vietnamese and Khmer Rouge soldiers. While the frames feature U.S. troops (dressed in Army fatigues), North Vietnamese soldiers (who wear identifiable pith helmets), and Khmer Rouge operatives (clothed in black with a red-and-black checkered *krama*), a total reading of the page highlights different perspective points: the first panel offers a panoramic shot of all military actors; the second and third panel offer alternating close-ups of communist soldiers. The final frame—concentrated on U.S. troops on the top of an M2 Bradley infantry fighting vehicle—privileges a North Vietnamese and Khmer Rouge vantage point: the perspective is rendered from above, visually replicating a surveillance position atop a slight incline. Whereas the overall focus of *The 'Nam* is predictably on U.S. troops (given Hama's aforementioned rationale for the comic), the depiction of the communist enemy is ambiguously tempered: the North Vietnamese soldier cautions his Khmer Rouge comrade to exercise moderation because they are outnumbered; he then reminds his companion that "<Soon. Very soon it will be our time again. And soon, my brother, it will be your turn to liberate your own country.>"[35] While the strategy to not fight makes "military sense" (because of numbers), and whereas the notion of liberation was arguably part and parcel of propagandistic depictions of communist ideology, the absence of exclamation marks suggests an even-handed, rational tone. Such intentional characterizations persist in a subsequent image of the enemy that occurs in the comic's middle section, which again highlights military tactics (by way of discussions of strategic positions and the portrayal of North Vietnamese military maps) over emotionally driven outburst and attack.[36]

Notwithstanding these "inimical" portrayals, "Back in the Saddle Again" is largely focused on the experiences of U.S. soldiers; correspondingly, the majority of the comic negotiates Specialist Daniels's incredulousness about his

redeployment and follows American troop movements along the Cambodia–
Viet Nam border. With the exception of two base scenes that occur in the
middle and end of the comic, the emphasis largely settles on the movement of
these troops via various military technologies, particularly tanks and helicopters. Whereas the depictions of the North Vietnamese and Khmer Rouge
soldiers assume an intimate register (via close-up shots and calm dialogue), the
representations of U.S. involvement repeatedly engage spectacles of overwhelming firepower, which involve helicopter machine gunfire, fleets of military transport, and an aerial view of two B-52s dropping their cluster bomb
payload on a vast green expanse. And while Specialist Daniels—as primary
protagonist—functions as an individualized focalizer and central guide via multiple military campaigns to the Cambodia–Viet Nam border, he and his soldier
compatriots are more often than not unclear as to objective. Such confusion is
apparent in an unnamed soldier's disbelief that an Arclight strike is pending;
such incredulousness is replicated in "Pig" Meachum's question following this
strike: "Look at that—how can they fight that kind of power?"[37]

Set against this comic context of military spectacle and spectacular warfare, which involves multiple perspective points and multifaceted sights, what
emerges is a vertiginous characterization of the U.S. presence in Southeast Asia
as military sublime project. The juxtaposition of moderate communist tactics
and prodigious American bombings, along with the confused portrayal of policy
intent and military objective, are revealed via the manipulation of views from
above and experiences from below. Taken together, "Back in the Saddle Again"
presents a critical portrait of the American War in Viet Nam that, in its attention to the confused dimensions of U.S. war-making, makes clear the extent to
which muddled foreign policy necessarily gives rise to "collateral damage"; tell-
ingly, North Vietnamese and Khmer Rouge troops largely fade from view over
the course of the comic's larger narrative arc; yet they still embody an absent
presence even in the closing pages: as Specialist Daniels concludes soon after
the Arclight strike, "They [the North Vietnamese and Khmer Rouge] fight
because they **have** to fight! Just like us!" (emphasis in original).[38] Set against an
imaginary marked by involuntary deployment (for Daniels), compulsory occupation (with regard to the North Vietnamese and Khmer Rouge), and devastating firepower, this analogous characterization militates against a facile "us
versus them" construction by accentuating the purposelessness of American
troops (technologically and militarily) and the purposefulness of Southeast
Asian soldiers (ideologically and politically).

Notwithstanding intricacies of plot, which by and large follows Specialist
Daniels's confused campaigns into Cambodia, it is ultimately the comic's sightlines that provide a clear critique of U.S. war-making through vertiginous
frames. Set against a backdrop of sublime conflagration and seemingly linear

FIGURE 10.3 In these images, aerial shots are intermingled with dolly zoom perspectives. This particular view is evident in the placement of Specialist Daniels, who comes to the realization (mid-page) that both North Vietnamese and Khmer Rouge troops "fight because they **have** to fight . . . just like us." © MARVEL.

storytelling, it is the comic's use of multiple perspectives that makes less stable a contained reading of the Vietnam War as contained conflict. Indeed, as the previously discussed scenes highlight, it is the collapse of multiple temporalities—which involve air force sorties, ground campaigns, and the collective/individualized experiences of soldiers (on both sides)—that renders vertiginously apparent the extent to which "collateral damage" is part and parcel of U.S. militarization. These circuitous perspectives—which emphasize misperception over order, unintended consequence above intentional policy, and Cambodian war more than Vietnam conflict—are evident in characters who consistently and tirelessly look in the "wrong direction" (to reader, away from the sky, or toward the ground).

In conclusion, "Back in the Saddle Again" renders palpable a vertiginous critique of the war that complicates the terrain through which the conflict is recollected as singularly contained (within Viet Nam) or exceptionally possessed (as militarily ordered). Such recollections, which collapse multiple temporalities and encompass conflicting sightlines, assume the registers of a seemingly perpetual "dolly zoom" with regard to the war as sublime military conflict. Indeed, if, as Viet Thanh Nguyen maintains, "All wars are fought twice, the first time on the battlefield, the second time in memory," then the "American War in Viet Nam" occupies a peculiarly vertiginous position within the dominant U.S. imaginary as something historically distanced yet politically "near."[39] The subject of numerous memoirs, novels, and films, the Vietnam War as *remembered* conflict has, as the other essays in this collection accentuate, been indefatigably restaged and rehearsed across decades, diverse genres, and multiple generations. And in a more recent vein, as convoluted U.S. "quagmire" and excessively violent spectacle, the war remains—even with the passage of more than four decades since the fall of Saigon on April 30, 1975—an oft-accessed metaphor for militarized folly, executive-level failure, and miscreant behavior in contemporary wars in Iraq and Afghanistan.

NOTES

1. Larry Hama, "Introduction," *The 'Nam*, vol. 1 (Republished in 1999).

2. Among the more well-known Vietnam War–focused comic series is Don Lomax's *Vietnam Journal*, which was initially published by Apple Comics in 1987. Focused on war correspondent Scott "Journal" Neithammer, the series—which did not adhere to the tenets outline by the Comics Code Authority—was marked by graphic depictions of violence, explicit representations of drug use, and other adult themes. Each issue also included, as printed inserts, newspaper accounts involving those missing in action. Between 1987 and 1991, Apple Comics published sixteen issues of *Vietnam Journal*. Lomax would eventually serve as a writer for *The 'Nam* (1992–1993). In 2004 iBooks published Lomax's *Gulf War Journal*, which featured Neithammer and

concentrated its attention on the Persian Gulf War (1990–1991). It should be noted that *Vietnam Journal* and *Gulf War Journal* are decidedly quite "literal texts" that lack ambiguity, replicating via narrative the comic's black/white color scheme. Indeed, Lomax's work is very much in line with Sylvia Chong's critical assertions about "the Oriental obscene" vis-à-vis hyper-violent war-driven images.

3. Qtd in Paula Span, "Vietnam: The Comic Book War, Marvel Brings Out a Dark, Gritty, and Popular Series," *Washington Post*, September 10, 1986, B1. As the head of the Vietnam Veterans Memorial Fund, Scruggs was heavily involved in fundraising efforts that facilitated the construction of the Vietnam Veterans Memorial in Washington, D.C.

4. While *The 'Nam* was originally successful, as the series continued into the late 1980s and early 1990s, the readership decreased dramatically. In response, Don Lomax introduced antihero "The Punisher" within *The 'Nam*'s larger narrative arc. The appearance of the vigilante signaled a profound departure from Doug Murray and Larry Hama's realistic vision for the comic.

5. Hama, Introduction to *The 'Nam*.

6. This mention of "memory work" accesses James Young's argument about collected remembrance and remembrance-oriented labor.

7. See Gillian Whitlock, "Autographics: The Seeing 'I' of Comics," *Modern Fiction Studies* 52, no. 4 (2006): 967.

8. "For 50 Years Nuclear Bomb Lost in Watery Grave," *NPR News (Weekend Edition)*, February 3, 2008. Accessed January 12, 2015. http://www.npr.org/templates/story/story.php?storyId=18587608.

9. John Thomas Didymus, "Air Force Accidentally Dropped Nuclear Bomb on S. Carolina 1958," *Digital Journal*. April 2012. Accessed December 10, 2014. http://www.digitaljournal.com/article/323778.

10. Ibid.

11. Ibid.

12. See Samini Najmi, "Naomi Shihab Nye's Aesthetic of Smallness and the Military Sublime," *MELUS: Multi-Ethnic Literatures of the United States* 35, no. 2 (Summer 2010): 151–171. Much appreciation is given to Rajini Srikanth, who generously forwarded the article to the author.

13. Ibid.

14. See Richard Slotkin, *Gunfighter Nation: The Myth of the Frontier in Twentieth-Century America.* (Norman: University of Oklahoma Press, 1998).

15. See Yến Lê Espiritu, *Body Counts: The Vietnam War and Militarized Refuge(es)* (Berkeley: University of California Press, 2014).

16. Catherine Lutz, "Making War at Home in the United States: Militarization and the Current Crisis," *American Anthropologist* 104, no. 3 (September 2002): 724.

17. David Harvey, in *The Condition of Postmodernity: An Enquiry into the Origins of Cultural Change* (Malden, Mass.: Blackwell, 1990), critiques postmodernism by focusing his attention on the ways in which late capitalism, which eschews Fordism in favor of flexible accumulation, has given rise to a "time–space compression" that ultimately maintains the exploitative logics of capitalist commodity production and capital accumulation. I draw on the notion of "time–space compression" to attend to the expansive and violent dimensions of U.S. militarization abroad.

18. See Caren Kaplan, "The Balloon Prospect: Aerostatic Observation and the Emergence of Militarised Aeromobility," in *From Above: War, Violence, and Verticality*, ed. Peter Adey, Mark Whitehead, and Alison J. Williams, 19–40 (London: Hurst, 2013).

19. Caren Kaplan, "Precision Targets: GPS and the Militarization of U.S. Consumer Identities" *American Quarterly* 58, no. 3 (September 2006): 699.

20. See Cathy J. Schlund-Vials, "'Finding' Guam: Distant Epistemologies and Cartographic Pedagogies," *Asian American Literature: Discourses & Pedagogies* 5, no. 6 (2014). http://scholarworks.sjsu.edu/aaldp/vol5/iss/6/.

21. Taylor Owen and Ben Kiernan, "Bombs Over Cambodia," *Walrus* (October 2006): 67.

22. See Cathy J. Schlund-Vials, *War, Genocide, and Justice: Cambodian American Memory Work* (Minneapolis: University of Minnesota Press, 2012).

23. Owen and Kiernan, "Bombs Over Cambodia," 66.

24. Ibid., 63. The Khmer Rouge regime began on April 17, 1975, when troops overtook Cambodia's capital, Phnom Penh. Soon after, the Khmer Rouge emptied the nation's cities and relocated its denizens to the countryside, ushering in the so-termed Killing Fields era. Guided by the superseding desire to eliminate all Western influence and create a classless society, the Khmer Rouge prohibited religion, outlawed currency, proscribed education, and strategically targeted those who were most closely allied with the previous regime or deemed "enemies of the people" due to alleged Western affiliations. On January 7, 1979, the Vietnamese ostensibly liberated Cambodia, signaling the end to both regional hostilities and the dissolution of the Khmer Rouge regime. Setting aside the relatively short time period of Khmer Rouge rule, its impact was catastrophic: an estimated 1.7 million Cambodians perished due to disease, starvation, forced labor, and execution. Ninety percent of Khmer court musicians and dancers were dead, 9 judges were left in country, the majority of the nation's teachers (three quarters) died or fled the country, and out of an estimated 550 doctors, only 48 survived. To date, only 3 Khmer Rouge leaders have been successfully tried and convicted of crimes against humanity (in 2010 and 2014, respectively).

25. Quoted in Owen and Kiernan, "Bombs Over Cambodia," 66.

26. Immanuel Kant, "The Critique of Pure Reason," in *Kant's Critique of Aesthetic Judgement*, trans. James Creed Meredith, 112–113 (1781; Oxford: Clarendon Press, 1911).

27. Edmund Burke, *Philosophical Enquiry into the Origins of Our Ideas of the Sublime and Beautiful* (1758; New York: Simon and Brown, 2013), 36–37.

28. See "National Register Information System," *National Register of Historic Places* (National Park Service). http://www.nps.gov/nr/research/. Accessed December 9, 2015.

29. Ibid.

30. Fort Huachuca is also a training site for the Thunderbirds air fleet, which performed signal operations during the invasion of Iraq in 2003.

31. Doug Murray, "Back in the Saddle Again," *The 'Nam* 1, no. 33. Consultant: Larry Hama. (New York: Marvel Comics, August 1989), 1.

32. Ibid., 2.

33. Tay Ninh Province is located in southwestern Viet Nam, along the Viet Nam–Cambodia border.

34. Murray, "Back in the Saddle Again," 3.

35. Ibid.

36. Ibid., 13–15. It should be noted that the depiction of the North Vietnamese "enemy" is not absolutely moderate; at one point, a North Vietnamese soldier suggests to his comrade that "We will deal with these dogs soon enough." However, this negative mention to U.S. troops is singular within the larger narrative of "Back in the Saddle."

37. Ibid., 27.

38. Ibid.

39. Viet Thanh Nguyen, "Remembering War, Dreaming Peace: On Cosmopolitanism, Compassion, and Literature," in *Four Decades On: Vietnam, the United States, and the Legacies of the Second Indochina War*, ed. Scott Laderman and Edwin A. Martini (Durham, N.C.: Duke University Press, 2013), 132.

11

Naturalizing War

The Stories We Tell about the Vietnam War

BRENDA M. BOYLE

Film and prose fictions by Americans about the Vietnam War have been produced for at least the last fifty years, but Westerners have told stories about the country and the people of Viet Nam for much longer. Well before March 1965—when U.S. Marines stormed the shores at Da Nang—stories were told that might have incited the escalation of American involvement in Viet Nam's conflict. For instance, post–World War II U.S. narratives made the threat posed by Viet Minh "reds" to ordinary Vietnamese parallel to "redskins" threatening frontier Americans, thereby casting Vietnamese people as children and females needing rescue.[1] These rescue stories appeared against a backdrop of nineteenth- and early-twentieth-century orientalizing by Western journalists, scholars, missionaries, hunters, and travel writers who cast the Vietnamese as backward and primitive, confirming American belief in racial hierarchies, reinforcing American exceptionalism, and establishing grounds for interventions.[2] American exceptionalism—that the United States is uniquely virtuous—rhetorically underwrites these interventions.

Actor Burt Lancaster said of the challenge in 1978 of producing *Go Tell the Spartans*, one of the earliest Vietnam War combat films, "You can't avoid things, and anyway, history eventually examines everything. I think this is a good time to take a good hard look at what we were doing in Vietnam."[3] This "good, hard look" at exceptionalism and its failure in the Vietnam War exposes its underside, baring a rationale that Americans themselves caused the failure. That is, if the United States is "exceptional" and superior to all other nation-states, then no other nation has the capacity to defeat it; it alone can defeat itself. This paradoxical "friendly fire" discourse dominates the canon of prose and film Vietnam War fiction and relies on an ahistoricity that obscures American involvement in Viet Nam long before Marines came ashore in 1965.[4] We see the power of this discourse in its replication not only in twenty-first-century

Vietnam War novels but also in film and prose narratives about the century's U.S. wars in Iraq and Afghanistan. Just as the pre-1965 rescue stories can be regarded as precipitating the Vietnam War, the U.S. Vietnam War fiction and film canons can be regarded as precipitating subsequent wars. From the twenty-first-century perspective, the most hazardous effect of the dehistoricizing discourse is to naturalize war, to make war seem a force of human nature and therefore inevitable.

American film and prose fiction narratives simultaneously lay the foundations for intervention and trace dominant American national sensibilities. Because those fictional interpretations number in the thousands, cultural critics must be selective in their analyses, thereby forming a canon or dominant discourse about the war. The canon of Vietnam War narratives was established in the late 1970s, the 1980s, and the early 1990s, a period film historian Lawrence H. Suid characterizes as endeavoring to rehabilitate the image of Vietnam War U.S. veterans.[5] These narratives typically focus on individual male, American foot soldiers while asserting collective camaraderie among individuals; depict racial and socioeconomic tensions rarely overcome by this camaraderie; exclude humanizing portrayals of Vietnamese people, whether from the North or South; exclude female characters except as Vietnamese prostitutes, Viet Cong, or American nurses; and conclude that American soldiers were victimized physically, psychologically, morally, or politically. This canon comprises prose fiction such as Michael Herr's *Dispatches* (1977), James Webb's *Fields of Fire* (1978), Bobbie Ann Mason's *In Country* (1985), Larry Heinemann's *Paco's Story* (1986), and Tim O'Brien's *The Things They Carried* (1990). Cinematic fiction includes *Coming Home* (1978) and *The Deer Hunter* (1978), *Apocalypse Now* (1979) and films that appeared in the 1980s: *Platoon* (1986), *Full Metal Jacket* (1987), *Hamburger Hill* (1987), *Casualties of War* (1989), and *Born on the Fourth of July* (1989).[6]

But the narrative rehabilitation Suid cites demands omissions, as does presidential candidate Ronald Reagan's 1980 public initiation of the rehabilitation when he cast the war as a "noble cause."[7] Just as the canon's texts typically omit the war's impact on Vietnamese people and their country, they also omit the historical context of U.S. involvement in Viet Nam, thereby underpinning Americans' common misapprehension of the United States' longstanding engagement in and with Viet Nam. Given Americans' ambivalent relationship with history and subsequent reliance on the fictional canon for their understanding of the war, few now would know that France colonized Viet Nam in the nineteenth century; that Vichy France surrendered Viet Nam to the Japanese during World War II; that the United States supported Viet Minh resistance against the occupying Japanese; that Ho Chi Minh invoked the American Declaration of Independence in his 1945 Proclamation of Independence of the

Democratic Republic of Viet Nam; and that—contrary to its own principles of sovereign independence and reversing its previously supportive position—the United States financially buoyed France's war to recolonize "Indochine" against Viet Minh objectives.

FIGURE 11.1 Cartoon: "What's so funny, monsieur? I'm only trying to find my way." Copyright 1964 by Bill Mauldin. Courtesy of the Bill Mauldin Estate LLC.

The 1964 Bill Mauldin cartoon reproduced here illustrates American ignorance about the French debacle in Viet Nam. Education in the United States, says James Loewen, promotes socialization, not inquiry: "it encourages students not to think about society but merely to trust that it is good. To the degree that American history in particular is celebratory, it offers no way to understand any problem—such as the Vietnam War . . . that has historical roots. Therefore," Loewen concludes, "we might expect that the *more* traditional schooling in history that Americans have, the *less* they will understand Vietnam or any other historically based problem."[8] Absent extra-American historical context but with faith in the exceptionalist truth-telling by American veteran-authors and veteran-filmmakers, these canonical texts lead readers and viewers to imagine American troops were victimized by a uniquely violent, traumatizing, and fragmented conflict engendered primarily not by Cold War concerns or Vietnamese nationalism but by domestic American conflicts if not character. As *Platoon*'s protagonist, played by Charlie Sheen, eulogizes in voiceover at the film's end, "we did not fight the enemy . . . we fought ourselves." In effect, the canonical prose and film fiction casts over readers and spectators a fog of "friendly fire" amnesia, freeing them from reckoning with all of the war's legacies.[9]

This amnesiatic "friendly fire" trope is obvious when we compare the canon to fiction and film of the prewar and war eras. Though, like the canonical texts, these early stories orientalize Viet Nam and the Vietnamese, they do not resort to the "friendly fire" trope of the canonical works nor do they overlook the historically fraught relations between Viet Nam and the West. For instance, two pre-American-war novels—British Graham Greene's *The Quiet American* (1955) and Americans William J. Lederer and Eugene Burdick's *The Ugly American* (1958)—predict an outcome entirely different from the generally ahistorical Vietnam War texts of the canon.[10] Both novels were published in an era bookended by American president Dwight Eisenhower's "domino theory" (1954) and his cautions about the "military-industrial complex" (1961), and in the shadow of the failed American war in Korea (1950–1953). Both are set during France's post–World War II recolonizing conflict with the Viet Minh. Both explicitly problematize longstanding American engagement in Viet Nam.

The objective in this chapter, then, is to explore in these two and other early fictional texts their treatment of one element of history, the French war in Viet Nam, and thus to decipher some effects of the American canon's omissions. After examining briefly a number of early texts, the chapter culminates in a detailed comparison of two, Daniel Ford's 1967 novel, *Incident at Muc Wa* and its canonical 1978 film rendition, and a Burt Lancaster vehicle, *Go Tell the Spartans*.[11] The chapter's discussion does not take Ford's or any of the other early texts as authoritative—"Here's how the war *really* occurred"—nor does it assume history is static, an unalterable story impervious to interpretation.

The discussion does not assume there is One True Source and then only lesser derivatives of that One True Source. It does not assume that all film adaptations should be faithful to their prose fiction sources or vice versa; they are different media entirely. The comparison, however, illustrates the differences between the pre-canon and canon era's narrative discourses and notes the effect of the prevalent discourse.

Comparisons between the two pre-American-war novels already mentioned and their film versions elucidate the "friendly fire" discourse in terms of American character. Graham Greene's novel juxtaposes an aging, cynical British journalist (Fowler) who has spent years in Asia and a young, idealistic, newly arrived American (Pyle) with book-learned notions about American good deeds and on the U.S. government payroll. In trying to effect change, Pyle mucks things up and is killed while, although involved in the American's death, Fowler claims inactive detachment, distinguishing his role as an objective "reporter" from a subjective "correspondent." Although the novel posits both men's stances as troubling, that Pyle suffers a brutal death suggests his confidence in American exceptionalist obligations to influence affairs abroad is misguided if not arrogant. A 1956 *New York Times* review summarizes the novel's argument: "America is a crassly materialistic and 'innocent' nation with no understanding of other peoples. When her representatives intervene in other countries' affairs it causes only suffering. America should leave Asians to work out their own destinies, even when this means the victory of communism."[12] The reviewer surmises American readers will not appreciate Greene's "caricatures" of Americans, a conclusion perhaps explaining the "sanitized" film version of 1958, starring war hero Audie Murphy as Pyle, and the apolitical tone of the post-9/11/2001 version.[13] Says the *New York Times* reviewer of 2002's film, "If [Greene's] 'The Quiet American' unequivocally views American intervention in Vietnam as an arrogant blunder, the movie . . . doesn't convey much strong political passion. Pyle [played by Brendan Fraser] may be buffoonish, but he's not evil."[14] Although Greene's novel implicates faults in American exceptionalist character, the film versions negate this "friendly fire" conclusion. In the cinematic renditions, Americans are not traumatized by inherent wounding or uniquely tragic flaw. Individuals' racialized hubris toward Asians, yes; collective inherent flaw in the American makeup, no. The differences among these texts demonstrate the inconsistency with which questions of inherent flaws differed before the canon.

Lederer and Burdick's bestseller, *The Ugly American*, reaches an indictment less pointed than Greene's novel.[15] Through a series of individual portraits more than plotline, it asserts that acquisitiveness motivates most Americans in Asia circumstantially, not inherently, and they conspire with similarly motivated French colonizers to improve their material circumstances. However, the novel counteroffers a minority of exceptional, more characteristically American people who are instead motivated to help Asian people improve their everyday lives. The eponymous "ugly American" is one of those exceptional people. Homer Atkins, an aging, humble, and wealthy engineer, is "ugly" because he has spent his life laboring physically and consequently has damaged hands: "he was most proud and confident of his ugly strong hands. Atkins knew that he could always make a living with them."[16] The other exceptions to the rule of self-servingly materialist Americans include men (and Atkins's wife, Emma) who, like Atkins, learn the local language, respect the local culture, and follow the leads of ordinary Asians: American ambassador to Sarkhan Gilbert MacWhite, who risks his career by criticizing the official American ventures in Viet Nam; Army major "Tex" Wolchek, American advisor to French forces in Viet Nam who advocates using Maoist tactics; Father Finian, who develops a cadre of Burmese men to persuade Burmese to reject communism; John Colvin, who aims to enhance the local diet by introducing American cattle to Sarkhan; and Air Force colonel Hillandale, who practices the palmistry valued by Asians and ridiculed by American embassy staff. In heroizing these characters, the novel displays a strain of anti-intellectualism, opposing the materialistic, educated elite against the exceptional pragmatists who rely on action and physical labor to help the Asians help themselves.[17]

The 1958 novel is hardly recognizable in the 1962 screen version of *The Ugly American*, described by the *New York Times* as being a "seminar . . . about cold war politics."[18] Instead of the book's series of individual portraits, including ones of the French fighting in Viet Nam, the film focuses on Ambassador MacWhite's realization that the war in Sarkhan is one the United States must fight but about which most Americans will be indifferent. Given the film's 1962 release, by which time the United States had more than fifteen thousand military advisors assigned to Viet Nam, the film's tone necessarily differed from the novel's broader indictment.[19] For the novel's chauvinism of most Americans abroad, the film substitutes American isolationism that will permit a "domino" to fall. American character is not an essential, immutable quality; instead, it is responsive to the period's historical exigencies.

Like prose and film fiction, early 1960s nonfiction also historicized American commitments to Viet Nam, especially in light of the 1946–1954 failed French recolonizing mission and the subsequent and troublesome Ngo Dinh Diem administration of South Vietnam. Although unnoticed by Americans when it was first published in 1961, Bernard Fall's *Street without Joy: The French Debacle in Indochina* "became standard reading for the U.S. officer corps in Vietnam."[20] Fall concludes that the French "debacle" was their refusal to adjust their conventional tactics, and he predicts, in a chapter added to the 1964 edition, a similar U.S. refusal. In 1966 Fall published *Hell in a Very Small Place: The*

Siege of Dien Bien Phu, a history of the 1954 battle that confirmed France's failure. Explaining the necessity of his uncomplimentary profile of French leadership in Viet Nam and presaging what would happen in the American War's canon, Fall writes, "Myths and misinformation that had hardened into 'fact' over the years would not only distort history irremediably but also prevent others [e.g., Americans] who have a more immediate concern with Viet-Nam from understanding present-day events which in many ways are shaped by events at Dien Bien Phu in the spring of 1954."[21]

Similar to Fall, even at the outset of "the Vietnam War" in 1965, U.S. journalist David Halberstam concludes in *The Making of a Quagmire* that hope for Western solutions to Vietnamese differences is slim, given the legacy of the previous decade:

> The American mission in Vietnam started out [in 1954] with the highest hopes and idealism. It failed for a number of reasons: not for lack of its own good intentions, not for lack of long working hours and patience . . . but because the legacy of mistakes was too large, because the United States was unable to face reality in Indochina, and because we responded with clichés to desperately complicated and serious challenges. . . . In writing this book I became more and more haunted by the historical implications of the French Indochina war and the warped legacy it left us. I am certain now that only a miracle could have saved us in 1954; heirs to such uneven odds, we found ourselves caught in a limited, ineffective and almost certainly doomed holding action.[22]

In *Our Vietnam Nightmare* (1965), American journalist Marguerite Higgins also historicizes the conflict, blaming the aftereffects of French colonialism for the American status she finds. In her conclusion, however, Higgins implicates the United States in a similarly orientalizing exceptionalism by authorizing the overthrow of Diem in 1963: "Can we Americans escape the feelings of blood on our hands after grasping the height of moral arrogance implicit in the U.S. decision that led to the overthrow and murder of an *Oriental* ruler because he did not live up to our dubious *Occidental* concepts of how to run an *Oriental* country?"[23]

Finally, scholar Hans Morgenthau also weighed in at this turning point in American engagement, arguing in 1965 for withdrawal. To those in favor of continued and escalating engagement for fear of sullying American prestige, Morgenthau retorts that France's prestige was actually heightened when it "demonstrated the wisdom and courage to liquidate two losing enterprises [Algeria and Viet Nam] on which it had staked its 'honor.' . . . To say, then," Morgenthau concludes, "that we ought not to be in Vietnam but cannot leave because our prestige would suffer is to confound ephemeral fluctuations of public opinion with the lasting foundation of national power and prestige and to think little of American power and of the prestige which reflects that power."[24]

Two nonfiction books published during the American War, in 1972, also contemplate this early period of the war and likewise conclude that the historical context in Viet Nam dooms the U.S. enterprise to failure. In *War Comes to Long An*, Jeffrey Race studies the 1967 "revolutionary movement" in one southern Vietnamese province, Long An, concluding that "despite all the problems within the revolutionary movement . . . the fact remains that by 1965 it had won in Long An, and the [American-allied South Vietnamese] government had lost."[25] Lamenting how little American scholarship there was on Viet Nam when she arrived in 1966, Frances Fitzgerald explains in the preface to *Fire in the Lake* that her greatest influence was a French scholar, Paul Mus. This claim emphasizes once again the French shadow on U.S. doings in Viet Nam, a claim that is reinforced by Fitzgerald's assertion that the United States unfortunately intervened at the chaotic moment of Viet Nam's transition from colonial to postcolonial state.[26]

Few prose fictions were published during the 1965–1973 American War, and even fewer mainstream films were produced. While these rare texts do not engage in lengthy historical exposés, like the prewar texts just discussed but unlike the postwar canonical texts, they make frequent references to the French in Viet Nam (but rarely to American support of the French), but casually enough to suggest that readers would have been familiar with the French war. Departing somewhat from the historically contextualized prewar texts, author Robin Moore insists his story of American Special Forces in Viet Nam during 1964, *The Green Berets* (1965), is universally true as it transcends history, culture, time, geography, or agency.

> *The Green Berets* tells the story of Special Forces fighting Communism in Indo-China in 1964, but it could well have been written about the wearers of the green beret in many other countries in which they find themselves throughout the world. In essence, these stories will be true of the political problems and combat situations Special Forces are facing in 1965, or for that matter 1975, wherever Americans must fight to keep the perimeter of the free world from shrinking further.[27]

Nonetheless, throughout the novel Moore's references to the French experience are frequent but offhand, as though readers would be familiar with a situation that did not require explanation: a unit is "out of that old French camp just in time"; it is better to speak the old occupier's language, French, than the new one's, English; and there are people of mixed French and indigenous heritage still in Viet Nam.[28] The Green Berets' presence in Viet Nam seems inadvertent: they find themselves in Viet Nam only because "Vietnam was divided into two separate states" in 1955 and Diem's "dictatorship" had been overthrown.[29] Despite this relative ahistoricism, the novel does not resort to the "friendly fire" trope evident in the later canon, perhaps because in Moore's tales the Green Berets always win. When the even less historical film version of the novel starring an overweight and aging John Wayne appeared in 1968, however, its sunny representation of the Vietnam War was not well received by critics and became "unintentional high camp" to soldiers at war.[30]

Other U.S. prose fiction published during the war include a novel by William Wilson, *The LBJ Brigade* (1966); a novel by journalist David Halberstam, *One Very Hot Day* (1967); and a collection of short stories by Tom Mayer, *The Weary Falcon* (1971).[31] All three emphasize the historical specificity of American involvement in Viet Nam in light of the preceding French war there. The narrator of Wilson's novel joins Sergeant Sace, "an expert on staying alive" because of his long involvement in Viet Nam, first with the French, then as an American military advisor, and now with the U.S. Army.[32] Corporal Handson, the ubiquitous "college boy" character of Vietnam War narratives, ridicules the American mission, saying, "The French were here for years and they couldn't do a damn thing," and Sace disabuses the narrator of any idealistic motivations for being in Viet Nam: "There ain't no right or wrong out here. Livin is the only thing that counts. We're white men fightin colored men," lessons learned from his long tenure in Viet Nam.[33]

Halberstam's novel, *One Very Hot Day*, contrasts the dissipated war-weariness of an over-aged American captain, Beaupre, against the vigor of Lieutenant Anderson, a young, energetic, Vietnamese-speaking West Pointer. A third character, one who mirrors Beaupre more than Anderson, is Vietnamese over-aged Lieutenant Thuong, a man originally from northern Viet Nam who has spent eight years at war and voices the historical perspective that neither Beaupre nor Anderson have. The story is set before 1965, when American military personnel were in Viet Nam as "advisors" to the fledgling South Vietnamese military, and evidence of the French war persists. Thuong had believed the "myth of the Americans," "that they could change what no one else could," but after having trained six American lieutenants in three years, Thuong sees that "instead of changing Vietnam, they were changing with it, and becoming [fatalistically] part of it."[34] Thuong often compares the French and Americans, thinking that Americans like maps even more than the French and recalling a friend's mimicking French and American officers.[35] Other Vietnamese refer to all black soldiers as "Senegalese," the Africans who fought for the French in Viet Nam.[36] A Vietnamese prisoner disavows belonging to the French nemesis, the Viet Minh, and another old man swears to the American-advised Vietnamese patrol that he has never done anything to help the French, as though they had not yet departed from Viet Nam.[37]

The French specter is equally ubiquitous in many of Tom Mayer's 1971 short stories. In the collection's title story, "The Weary Falcon," the narrator admires a helicopter pilot, Slade, who had said that "you could learn everything you needed to know from studying the French," that "when the Americans first came . . . the roadsides were littered with fire-gutted French vehicles."[38] "A lot of the old pros are smarter than you think at first," says the narrator, "which explained his [Slade's] interest in the French."[39] Slade dies when his helicopter crashes into the French cemetery, an irony he had predicted in an audiotape to his wife: "He said he thought sometimes we did not learn anything and there was nothing he could do. We were making many of the same mistakes the French made." Now, ironizes the narrator, instead of making it home, Slade "was with the French instead."[40] In other of Mayer's stories, signs of the French war litter the country: a bridge was blown up, perhaps by the Viet Cong, "maybe even the Vietminh"; a rusty French land mine is one among many left behind; American soldiers walk through territory once hunted by "Rich Frenchmen . . . before the war[,] on tiger safaris"; and a patrol walks "along the dunes under the French fort."[41]

The differential historicizing between stories told before and during the Vietnam War and those told in the after-war canonical period—and thus the extent to which they deploy the "friendly fire" trope—is especially clear in Daniel Ford's representation of U.S. military advisors in 1964 Viet Nam, *Incident at Muc Wa* (1967), and its 1978 film rendition referred to at this chapter's outset, *Go Tell the Spartans*. Like the other noncanonical prose texts already discussed, Ford's novel integrates frequent references to the French war. From Vietnamese people speaking French, to bombed-out French armored cars serving as landmarks, to the French haunting of the Muc Wa outpost, the French war in Viet Nam influences the U.S. presence there. Clearly, what the American advisors can and cannot do is shaped by what the French did during their war in Viet Nam, and the advisors often chafe against those limits. General Hardnetz takes umbrage at the "Frenchified fatigues" and at the use of a French word—esprit—to describe American morale.[42] Major Barker creates a model of the Muc Wa outpost but deliberately excludes the French headstone: "Every tree was in place, every hooch, everything except that damned French grave, which would have spoiled the garrison's tough, clean lines."[43] The novel's American advisors are deeply embedded in history, and they know it. The film version, however, isolates and minimizes its references so the French, their war, and American participation in France's war are irrelevant to the U.S. mission in Viet Nam; the exceptional Americans are made to seem outside of history. To accomplish this quarantine of the French war preceding the Americans', the film alters the story and character arcs significantly, disclosing the 1978 film's postwar canonical inheritance.

Ford's novel resembles the dark satire of Joseph Heller's World War II novel *Catch-22*, published seven years earlier. In *Incident at Muc Wa*, both American and South Vietnamese officers are ridiculously inept and grasping, with enlisted soldiers paying the price for such careerist ineptitude. The mission is unclear at best and absurd at worst, with standards as moving targets and allies unworthy of the fiduciary and mortal costs to support them. The crux of the novel's story—the "incident"—is that in 1964 underresourced American advisors are commanded to establish a U.S. garrison at Muc Wa, a derelict French outpost that was overrun and destroyed by the Viet Minh near the end of the French war a decade earlier. A single French headstone remains at Muc Wa to haunt the four American advisors and the Montagnard mercenaries building the garrison. Though Viet Cong had not previously been detected in this area, the outpost's reestablishment attracts and is consequently ravaged by a massive Viet Cong force. The Americans are ordered to "exfiltrate," and although no one survives the slaughter, it is downplayed in the Saigon newspaper as an "incident."

Ford's most sympathetic character, Corporal Courcey, is not at all like Heller's Yossarian; Courcey is ugly and a "college man" who volunteers to come to Viet Nam and dies there as an outcome of his humanist faith in nobility and justice in combat. Courcey's liberal education shows when he cites the "Law of the First Night"; predictably, for this era, is influenced by Ernest Hemingway; and, on encountering the French tombstone, silently recalls Simonides' epitaph to the Spartans who died at the 480 BCE Battle of Thermopylae: "Go, stranger. Tell the Spartans that we lie here in obedience to their laws."[44] The novel opens with Courcey's romantic interest, Rebecca Shaw, seeking him out at Fort Bragg only to discover he already is on his way to Viet Nam; as a journalist, she follows him there. She continues to appear throughout the novel. Courcey is assigned to a "Raider" unit in Pleiku, and he arrives there with two other men: 2nd Lt. Ray Hamilton (Courcey's friend from Fort Bragg) and Sergeant Oleonowski, a hardened soldier who has seen combat in Korea and Viet Nam and is waiting in Pleiku for a permanent assignment.

Major Barker, the Raider Group's commander, feels inferior for being short in stature, believing it ruins his prospects for promotion. At forty-three, he is an old major, having served already in World War II and the Korean War, but he only became an officer with a battlefield commission in Korea. He enjoys alcohol and frequently leaves his office for the Officers Club, where he can imbibe freely. Captain Olivetti is Barker's executive officer. Eager to be out of Viet Nam but ambitious, all he wants is enough time in combat to win the Combat Infantryman's Badge, which will ensure his promotion. Although Barker resents being ordered to set up yet another "static defense post," neither he nor Olivetti is tactically astute, with both hoping more for their personal advancement than for U.S. military success in South Vietnam.[45] Both are misogynistic brutes and regard the few females in their combat universe—Vietnamese and American— as "meat" to be used sexually by males.[46]

Barker sends Olivetti with Hamilton, Courcey, Oleonowski, Toffee (a Raider radioman), and Montagnard mercenaries led by Montagnard/French "Cowboy" to establish the Muc Wa outpost. En route to Muc Wa the small unit encounters a refugee family, and Cowboy kills one of its male members on sight; Olivetti condones the indiscriminate killing. The family also includes Butterfly, the sixteen-year-old girl who Oleonowski rapes; when she later is found to be preg- nant, he considers her his wife. Later, foreseeing an overwhelming Viet Cong (VC) attack at Muc Wa, Barker sends a helicopter to extricate only the Americans. As a matter of principle, Courcey refuses to leave behind the Montagnards while Olivetti, Oleonowski, and Butterfly happily evacuate. Courcey survives the VC attack but a lone VC subsequently shoots him near the French headstone. Dying, Courcey laments his idealistic solidarity with all of the Vietnamese—Montagnard and VC—and in the novel's closing lines thinks: "A man should be careful what he chooses to love, what he chooses to fight for. . . . Because life will damned well make the choice stick."[47] The novel is cautionary, a warning that what happened to the French—ending up in a grave in Viet Nam—will happen to the Americans, too. American exceptionalism cannot save Ford's characters from the locomotive of history.

Go Tell the Spartans—with the intervention of the 1965–1973 war, postwar amnesia, and pressure beginning in the late 1970s to explain the war, "to take a good, hard look"—tells an entirely different story. A vehicle for the talents and treasure of actor Burt Lancaster as Major Barker, it employs the "friendly fire" trope, excising the French war nearly entirely, thus surmising that honorable, by-nature exceptional American men should escape history's momentum. If they cannot, exceptionalism suggests, they have only themselves to blame. With the "friendly fire" trope, exceptionalism puts them in a double bind, insisting that only Americans can defeat Americans.

In the film version, Major Barker, not Corporal Courcey, is the sympathetic character, a refocalization that sidelines French war history. Budgetary con- cerns might have prohibited the film's replication of the novel's physical reminders of the French war, but the rewriting of the characters and their plot arcs in lieu of almost any historical specificity is remarkable. Whereas the novel, laden as it is with references to the French, frames them as the Americans' predecessors, the film's references are limited: Major Barker complains that what fated the French was their "static defense outposts"; General Harnitz[48] rails against "Frenchified fatigues" and the use of the French word "esprit"; Courcey discovers a French graveyard at Muc Wa, strewn with 302 wooden crosses and a gateway inscribed in French with Simonides' Thermopylae epitaph;[49] and Barker's Vietnamese counterpart, Colonel Minh, speaks French and lives in gilded (signifying French) decadence. The film's isolation of these instances says more about the Americans than it does the French, insinuating that plain-speaking and self-sacrificing Americans never would conduct their war as indulgently as the French had theirs. To establish this ethos, the film opens with three lines of text to explain why Americans are in Viet Nam:

> In 1954, the French lost their war *to keep* Indo-China colonies and those colonies *became* North and South Vietnam.

> Then the North aided a *rebellion* in the South and the United States *sent in* "Military Advisors" to help South Vietnam fight the *Communists.*

> In 1964, the war in Vietnam was still a little one—confused and *far away.*

These lines—with italics added for emphasis—assign no political culpability to the French recolonizing, to the division of Viet Nam into two political entities, to the United States' obligation to "send in" advisors, to the notion that "Communists" were in the North and they fomented "rebellion" in the South, and that the "far away" war was one being fought and endured not by close-by Vietnamese who lived in Viet Nam but by those "sent in" or, perhaps even more, by those senders in the far distance. These things just happened, according to the canonical-era film, outside of history, ideological motivation, or agents, and the victims of these circumstances are the benevolent and exceptional helpers, the American military advisors. The story prefaced by these lines, then, is about the stalwart Americans alone who are unconfined by historical context, not the mired-in-history French nor the Vietnamese of whichever ideological stripe.

The story's revision is evident mostly in the characters. Whereas novel-Oleonowski departs Muc Wa with his pregnant Montagnard bride, traumatized film-Oleo commits suicide without ever having raped or captured a bride. Novel-Olivetti is a torture/rape/murder-condoning thug when it advantages him; film-Olivetti is a bright-eyed, gum-chewing naïf who never imagines such atrocities. Novel-Barker has low esteem for himself and for others as well as a taste for alcohol; played in the film by sixty-five-year-old Lancaster with a World War II filmography, he is the wise old officer who cares naught for military protocol but deeply for his soldiers and will do anything for them, including going to certain death. Film-Barker brings the helicopter to evacuate the Americans and stays behind with Courcey and the Montagnards as the VC are about to attack; he is killed and stripped naked after the assault. Played by Craig Wasson, who also played a hippie/draftee in 1978's *Boys of Company C,* film-Courcey is not ugly but has a boyish, sweet face and a World War II film naiveté that has him offering chocolate to the refugee family. Film-Courcey differs most from novel-Courcey in that he does not die at the film's conclusion. Instead, after film-Courcey spots the dead Barker, he stumbles into the cross-strewn French cemetery and sees the VC who has haunted him throughout the story prepare to shoot him but then collapse. Courcey says, "I'm goin' home, Charlie . . . if they'll let me," staggers away, and the film credits roll.

Why is this difference between earlier narratives and canonical ones meaningful? In *Friendly Fire: American Images of the Vietnam War*, Katherine Kinney alleges that the friendly fire story of Americans combating one another is "virtually the only story that has been told by Americans about the Vietnam War."[50] This is true of the canon but not of the fictions produced before the canonical era. While the canon's narrative homogeneity is troubling, more important is that the effect of its ahistorical decontextualization of the U.S. intervention in Viet Nam confines readers and spectators almost exclusively to emotional responses. American characters feel intensely their victimized state, affective conditions with which spectators and readers cannot argue. Audiences cannot reasonably contest or critically examine pathos-driven characters; the sole relationship for audiences to have with the canon's characters and their actions is emotional. Even when the canon's American characters are psychologically complex or atrocious, audiences blindered from the historical context are led to view them primarily as victims—of violence, trauma, U.S. politicians and military superiors—and to empathize with their plight. It is not our fault, these characters whimper. We have only done what we were told, they insist. You would do the same thing in this situation, they accuse. Support us, remember us, honor us, they plead. We gave our lives to support your freedoms, insinuate the dead. How can audience members challenge such pathetic appeals? How can emotions be disputed as incorrect or inauthentic? Thus, the battle for the meaning of the Vietnam War as narrated in the canon's prose and film fictions is less about Viet Nam and the Vietnamese than it is about the emotional states of American characters and audience members. This situation is a closed loop: characters emote, audience members feel and in the process are taught that feeling about war is the most authentic reaction, and then audience members expect war narratives to be about feeling.

Furthermore, the canon's ahistorical "friendly fire" discourse is not limited to those texts produced in the canonical era, having become an orthodoxy evident in twenty-first-century Vietnam War films and novels, in narratives about the U.S. wars in Iraq and Afghanistan, and in the documentary *In Country*, discussed in this volume's introduction. Post-9/11 Vietnam War films such as *We Were Soldiers* (2002) and *Rescue Dawn* (2006) focus exclusively on the exceptional individual U.S. military man, and Ben Stiller's 2008 *Tropic Thunder* satirizes such a focus. Films are not alone in this, however, since Vietnam War novels published in the U.S. global war on terror era also use a version of the "friendly fire" trope, what has been termed elsewhere as the "Support the Troops Syndrome."[51] This refers to how Americans have been exhorted—in the press, by governmental representatives, and, not least, by bumper stickers—during the Iraq and Afghanistan wars to resist holding individual "troops" responsible for war, an outcome of the allegedly poor treatment experienced by military personnel returning from Vietnam.[52] Reflecting the "friendly fire" ethos, the syndrome's logic demands that we must simultaneously mourn U.S. warriors as victims of war, not as complicit, and laud them as noble and heroic, not self-serving.[53] Consequently, the Vietnam War novels of Denis Johnson, *Tree of Smoke* (2007); Karl Marlantes, *Matterhorn* (2010); and Tatjana Soli, *The Lotus Eaters* (2010), conclude that although the war might have been a disaster for Americans individually and as a nation, the uplifting outcomes for the American characters are redemptive, making the war worthwhile. The amnesia of the canon era persists so audiences think that while the Vietnam War broke Americans, they healed more strongly.

Similarly, like the Vietnam War canon, narratives emerging from the wars in Iraq and Afghanistan focus as much or more on the woundedness of individual U.S. military personnel than on the historical exigencies of why the United States is at war in those countries. In the August 2015 book review essay "First-Person Shooters: What's Missing in Contemporary War Fiction," Sam Sacks notes both the appearance of elements common to the Vietnam War fiction canon and the absence of any historical explanations for the current wars. "All pain may be the same," Sacks remarks, "but all wars are not, and in the search for reconciliation [between the few military personnel who fight all the wars and the many civilians who do not] that distinction has gone missing." Moreover, "Redemption seems to rely on a shared incomprehension of what these wars were about."[54] Although Sacks ascribes the replication of these elements to the dominance of creative writing programs since the mid-twentieth century, and the "anxious metafictional meditation" and "fetishization of authenticity" to the programs' mantra that writers construct stories from their own experiences, the cause for this dominance is less important than its effects.[55]

So what that the canonical Vietnam War texts induce pathos? So what that the canon's dominant discourse prevails in recently produced Vietnam War films and novels? So what that this discourse also appears in the narratives of the United States' most recent wars? Certainly, that texts are homogenous and audience responses are circumscribed is disturbing. More disquieting, however, is that exclusively emotional responses naturalize war. Where wars are fought, against whom, and why are immaterial in the canon; wars are not an outcome of particular circumstances, and evil is not subject to interpretation. Evil exists, people who recognize evil are good, and good people combat evil.

The omission of historical context in the American canon naturalizes the Vietnam War so that war happens because of human nature, not human conditions. This thinking leads spectators—and citizens—to conclude that it is fruitless to try to avoid war because it is natural and inevitable, a mode of thinking that may also have led the United States into its wars in Iraq and Afghanistan. That, finally, is the greatest hazard of excising history from war narratives: we go to war because we think it is in our nature to do so and, consequently, there is no alternative to the warring one.

NOTES

1. Scott Laderman, "Hollywood's Vietnam, 1929–1964: Scripting Intervention, Spotlighting Injustice," *Pacific Historical Review* 78, no. 4 (November 2009): 578–607.

2. Mark Philip Bradley, *Imagining Vietnam and America: The Making of Postcolonial Vietnam, 1919–1950* (Chapel Hill: University of North Carolina Press, 2000).

3. Lawrence H. Suid, *Guts & Glory: The Making of the American Military Image in Film* (Lexington: University Press of Kentucky, 2002), 350.

4. For "friendly fire," see Katherine Kinney, *Friendly Fire: American Images of the Vietnam War* (New York: Oxford University Press, 2000). For "exceptionalism," see William V. Spanos, *American Exceptionalism in the Age of Globalization: The Specter of Vietnam* (Albany: State University of New York Press, 2008); Donald E. Pease, *The New American Exceptionalism* (Minneapolis: University of Minnesota Press, 2009); and Christian G. Appy, *American Reckoning: The Vietnam War and Our National Identity* (New York: Penguin Random House, 2015).

5. Suid, *Guts & Glory*.

6. See Brenda M. Boyle, ed., *The Vietnam War* (London: Bloomsbury Press, 2014), for analyses of the prose canonical works.

7. Ronald Reagan, "Peace: Restoring the Margin of Safety," speech presented at Veterans of Foreign Wars Convention, Chicago, Illinois, August 18, 1980, accessed May 27, 2014. http://www.reagan.utexas.edu/archives/reference/8.18.80.html.

8. James W. Loewen, *The Lies My Teacher Told Me: Everything Your American History Textbook Got Wrong* (New York: Simon & Schuster, 2007), 351. Emphasis in original.

9. In the foreword to Jeremy M. Devine's *Vietnam at 24 Frames A Second* (Austin: University of Texas Press, 1999), Thomas Schatz confirms the Vietnam War films' ahistoricity and subsequent representation of the United States being "at war not with a common enemy but with itself" (viii).

10. William J. Lederer and Eugene Burdick, *The Ugly American* (New York: Norton, 1958); and Graham Greene, The Quiet American (London: Heinemann, 1955).

11. Daniel Ford, *Incident at Muc Wa* (New York: Doubleday, 1967); and *Go Tell the Spartans*, dir. Ted Post, Mar Vista, 1978.

12. Robert Gorham Davis, "The Quiet American," *New York Times*, March 11, 1956, accessed May 27, 2014, http://www.nytimes.com/1956/03/11/books/greene56-quiet.html?_r=0.

13. Devine, *Vietnam*, 8–12. In *The Vietnam Lobby: The American Friends of Vietnam, 1955–1975* (Chapel Hill: University of North Carolina Press, 1997), Joseph G. Morgan

points out that the 1958 film version favored the controversial prime minister of
South Vietnam, Ngo Dinh Diem. "The AFV also used a movie premiere to put Diem's
government in a favorable light. On January 22, 1958, it sponsored the Washington
screening of *The Quiet American*, a film version of Graham Greene's novel. The book
bitterly condemned the American intervention in Vietnam, but movie producer
Joseph Mankiewicz instead offered a ringing affirmation of America's involvement by
portraying the protagonist as a dedicated idealist instead of the dangerous and igno-
rant meddler in the novel. . . . [The AFV hosts] regarded it [the film] as 'an unqualified
success.' Graham Greene took a far different view of the affair. 'Far was it from my
mind, when I wrote 'The Quiet American,' that the book would become the source of
profit to one of the most corrupt governments in Southeast Asia" (52–53).

14. Stephen Holden, "A Jaded Affair in a Vietnam Already at War," *New York Times*,
    November 22, 2002, accessed May 29, 2014, http://www.nytimes.com/movie/review?
    res=9A06EFDE1539F931A15752C1A9649C8B63.

15. The novel was on the *New York Times* bestseller list for seventy-six weeks and sold
    5 million copies. Michael Meyer, "Still 'Ugly' After All These Years," *New York Times*,
    July 12, 2009, accessed May 27, 2014, http://www.nytimes.com/2009/07/12/books/
    review/Meyer-t.html?pagewanted=all.

16. Lederer and Burdick, *The Ugly American*, 206.

17. John Hellmann, *American Myth and the Legacy of Vietnam* (New York: Columbia
    University Press, 1986), 3–38. For a contemporaneous discussion of American
    anti-intellectualism, see Richard Hofstadter, *Anti-intellectualism in American Life*
    (New York: Alfred A. Knopf, 1963).

18. Bosley Crowther, "'The Ugly American': Marlon Brando Stars as the U.S. Diplomat,"
    New York Times, April 12, 1963, accessed May 29, 2014, http://www.nytimes.com/movie/
    review?res=9403E7DD103CE63ABC4A52DFB2668388679EDE.

19. David L. Anderson, *The Columbia Guide to the Vietnam War* (New York: Columbia
    University Press, 2002), 286.

20. Bernard B. Fall, *Street without Joy*, Stackpole Military History Series (Mechanicsburg,
    Penn.: Stackpole Books, 2005), 3.

21. Bernard B. Fall, *Hell in a Very Small Place: The Siege of Dien Bien Phu* (Cambridge, Mass.:
    Da Capo Press, 2002), x.

22. David Halberstam, *The Making of A Quagmire* (New York: Random House, 1965),
    320–321.

23. Marguerite Higgins, *Our Vietnam Nightmare* (New York: Harper & Row, 1965), 296.
    Emphasis in original.

24. Hans J. Morgenthau, *Vietnam and the United States* (Washington, D.C.: Public Affairs
    Press, 1965), 11.

25. Jeffrey Race, *War Comes to Long An* (Berkeley: University of California Press, 1972), xv.

26. Frances Fitzgerald, *Fire in the Lake: The Vietnamese and the Americans in Vietnam*
    (New York: Random House, 1972), 7.

27. Robin Moore, *The Green Berets* (New York: Crown Publishers, 1965), 13.

28. Ibid., 25, 141, 201.

29. Ibid., 11.

30. Devine, *Vietnam*, 45.

31. William Wilson, *The LBJ Brigade* (Los Angeles: Apocalypse, 1966); David Halberstam, *One Very Hot Day* (Boston: Houghton Mifflin, 1967); and Tom Mayer, *The Weary Falcon* (Boston: Houghton Mifflin, 1971).

32. Wilson, *The LBJ Brigade*, 11.

33. Ibid., 15, 57.

34. Halberstam, *One Very Hot Day*, 44–48.

35. Ibid., 127, 178.

36. Ibid., 105.

37. Ibid., 122.

38. Mayer, *The Weary Falcon*, 9.

39. Ibid., 28.

40. Ibid., 51.

41. Ibid., 62, 66, 69, 120.

42. Ford, *Incident at Muc Wa*, 88.

43. Ibid., 87–88.

44. Ibid., 50, 55.

45. Ibid., 11.

46. Ibid., 51.

47. Ibid., 178.

48. His name was General Hardnetz—Hard Nuts—in Ford's novel.

49. In the film, Courcey translates the French for Hamilton: "Stranger, when you find us lying here, go tell the Spartans we obeyed their orders." This conveys bitterness by the Spartans who died toward the Spartans who issued the orders. The novel's line instead suggests resignation to the lawful situation: "Tell the Spartans we lie here in obedience to their laws." See "Hooah! We . . . Are . . . Sparta," in Kirk Combe and Brenda Boyle, *Masculinity and Monstrosity in Contemporary Hollywood Films* (New York: Palgrave Macmillan, 2013), 73–120.

50. Kinney, *Friendly*, 4.

51. Brenda M. Boyle, "American Totem Society in the Twenty-first Century: Denis Johnson's *Tree of Smoke*, Karl Marlantes' *Matterhorn*, and Tatjana Soli's *The Lotus Eaters*," in Boyle, *The Vietnam War*, 185–213.

52. See Jerry Lembcke, *The Spitting Image: Myth, Memory, and the Legacy of Vietnam* (New York: New York University Press, 1998); and Thomas D. Beamish, Harvey Molotch, and Richard Flacks, "Who Supports the Troops? Vietnam, the Gulf War, and the Making of Collective Memory," *Social Problems* 42, no. 3 (August 1995): 344–360.

53. See Andrew Bacevich, "I Lost My Son to a War I Oppose. We Were Both Doing Our Duty," *Washington Post*, May 27, 2007.

54. Sam Sacks, "First-Person Shooters: What's Missing in Contemporary War Fiction," *Harper's Magazine*, August 2015, 84.

55. Ibid., 86.

APPENDIX A: ARCHIVES

The Socialist Republic of Viet Nam

Diplomatic Academy of Viet Nam, Hanoi

Film Institute, Hanoi

Institute of History (one of many in the Vietnam Academy of Social Sciences), Hanoi

Institute for Military History, Hanoi

Ministry of Foreign Affairs, Hanoi

National Center for the Social Sciences and Humanities of Vietnam, Hanoi

Viet Nam National Archives III, Hanoi

France

Archives du Ministère des affaires étrangères diplomatiques, Paris

Bibliothèque nationale de France, Paris

Dépôt des archives d'Outre-Mer, Aix-en-Provence

Service historique de l'Armée de Terre, Vincennes

United States

Library of Congress, Washington, D.C.

National Archives and Records Administration, Washington, D.C., and College Park, Maryland

National Personnel Records Center, St. Louis, Missouri

National Security Archives, Washington, D.C.

Presidential Libraries:

    Harry S. Truman Library, Independence, Missouri

    Dwight D. Eisenhower Library, Abilene, Kansas

    John Fitzgerald Kennedy Library, Boston, Massachusetts

    Lyndon Baines Johnson Library and Museum, Austin, Texas

    Richard Nixon Library, Yorba Linda, California

    Gerald R. Ford Library, Ann Arbor, Michigan

Vietnam Archive at Texas Tech University, Lubbock, Texas

Other Countries

Australia: Australian National Archives, Canberra

Canada: Library and Archives Canada, Ottawa

Germany: Bundesarchiv Deutschland, Koblenz

Hungary: Hungarian National Archives, Budapest

Korea: National Library of Korea, Seoul

People's Republic of China: Archives of the Ministry of Foreign Affairs (Beijing); State Archives Administration, Beijing

United Kingdom: National Archives of the United Kingdom, Twickenham

Libraries with Pertinent Special Collections

National Library of Australia, Canberra

State Library of South Australia, Adelaide

Syracuse University, Syracuse, New York, USA

University of Arizona, Tucson, Arizona, USA

University of Massachusetts, Amherst, Massachusetts, USA

University of Melbourne, Melbourne, Australia

Yale University, New Haven, Connecticut, USA

APPENDIX B: PUBLICATIONS SINCE 2000

American Military/War

Adams, Jon Robert. *Male Armor: The Soldier-Hero in Contemporary American Culture.* Charlottesville: University of Virginia Press, 2008.

Cuordileone, K. A. *Manhood and American Political Culture in the Cold War.* New York: Routledge, 2005.

Dean, Robert D. *Imperial Brotherhood: Gender and the Making of Cold War Foreign Policy.* Amherst: University of Massachusetts Press, 2001.

Dudziak, Mary L. *War Time: An Idea, Its History, Its Consequences.* New York: Oxford University Press, 2012.

Eberwein, Robert. *Armed Forces: Masculinity and Sexuality in the American War Film.* New Brunswick, N.J.: Rutgers University Press, 2007.

Huebner, Andrew J. *The Warrior Image: Soldiers in American Culture from the Second World War to the Vietnam Era.* Chapel Hill: University of North Carolina Press, 2008.

Mann, Bonnie. *Sovereign Masculinity: Gender Lessons from the War on Terror.* New York: Oxford University Press, 2014.

Mieszkowski, Jan. *Watching War.* Stanford, Calif.: Stanford University Press, 2012.

Mundey, Lisa M. *American Militarism and Anti-Militarism in Popular Media, 1945–1970.* Jefferson, N.C.: McFarland, 2012.

Paget, Karen M. *Patriotic Betrayal: The Inside Story of the CIA's Secret Campaign to Enroll American Students in the Crusade Against Communism.* New Haven, Conn.: Yale University Press, 2015.

Phillips, Kimberley L. *WAR! What Is It Good For? Black Freedom Struggles and the U.S. Military from World War II to Iraq.* Chapel Hill: University of North Carolina Press, 2012.

Savage, Kirk. *Monument Wars: Washington, D.C., the National Mall, and the Transformation of the Memorial Landscape.* Berkeley: University of California Press, 2009.

Savelsberg, Joachim J., and Ryan D. King. *American Memories: Atrocities and the Law.* New York: Russell Sage, 2011.

American Vietnam War/Culture

Appy, Christian. *American Reckoning: The Vietnam War and Our National Identity.* New York: Penguin Random House, 2015.

Boyle, Brenda M. *Masculinity in Vietnam War Narratives: A Critical Study of Fiction, Films and Nonfiction Writings.* Jefferson, N.C.: McFarland, 2009.

———, ed. *The Vietnam War.* Topics in Contemporary North American Literature. London: Bloomsbury Press, 2014.

Combe, Kirk C., and Brenda M. Boyle. *Masculinity and Monstrosity in Contemporary Hollywood Films*. New York: Palgrave Macmillan, 2013.

Hawkins, Ty. *Reading Vietnam amid the War on Terror*. New York: Palgrave Macmillan, 2012.

Ryan, Maureen. *The Other Side of Grief: The Home Front and the Aftermath in American Narratives of the Vietnam War*. Amherst: University of Massachusetts Press, 2008.

Spanos, William V. *American Exceptionalism in the Age of Globalization: The Specter of Vietnam*. Albany: State University of New York Press, 2008.

Vernon, Alex, and Catherine Calloway, eds. *Approaches to Teaching the Works of Tim O'Brien*. New York: Modern Language Association of America, 2010.

Weaver, Gina Marie. *Ideologies of Forgetting: Rape in the Vietnam War*. Albany: State University of New York Press, 2010.

American Vietnam War/History

Appy, Christian G. *Patriots: The Vietnam War Remembered from All Sides*. New York: Viking, 2003.

Bradley, Mark Philip, and Marilyn B. Young, eds. *Making Sense of the Vietnam Wars: Local, National, and Transnational Perspectives*. New York: Oxford University Press, 2008.

Chapman, Jessica. *Cauldron of Resistance: Ngo Dinh Diem, the United States, and 1950s Southern Vietnam*. Ithaca, N.Y.: Cornell University Press, 2013.

Laderman, Scott, and Edwin A. Martini, eds. *Four Decades On: Vietnam, the United States, and the Legacies of the Second Indochina War*. Durham, N.C.: Duke University Press, 2013.

Lair, Meredith H. *Armed with Abundance: Consumerism and Soldiering in the Vietnam War*. Chapel Hill: University of North Carolina Press, 2011.

Lawrence, Mark Atwood. *Assuming the Burden: Europe and the American Commitment to War in Vietnam*. Berkeley: University of California Press, 2007.

Logevall, Fredrik. *Choosing War: The Lost Chance for Peace and the Escalation of War in Vietnam*. Berkeley: University of California Press, 2001.

———. *Embers of War: The Fall of an Empire and the Making of America's Vietnam*. New York: Random House, 2014.

Lucks, Daniel S. *Selma to Saigon: The Civil Rights Movement and the Vietnam War*. Lexington: University Press of Kentucky, 2014.

Martini, Edwin A. *Agent Orange: History, Science, and the Politics of Uncertainty*. Amherst: University of Massachusetts Press, 2012.

Milam, Ron. *Not a Gentleman's War: An Inside View of Junior Officers in the Vietnam War*. Chapel Hill: University of North Carolina Press, 2009.

Miller, Edward. *Misalliance: Ngo Dinh Diem, the United States, and the Fate of South Vietnam*. Cambridge, Mass.: Harvard University Press, 2013.

Moyar, Mark. *Triumph Forsaken: The Vietnam War, 1954–1965*. Cambridge: Cambridge University Press, 2006.

Phillips, Rufus. *Why Vietnam Matters: An Eyewitness Account of Lessons Not Learned*. Annapolis, Md.: Naval Institute Press, 2008.

Schandler, Herbert Y. *America in Vietnam: The War That Couldn't Be Won*. Lanham, Md.: Rowman & Littlefield, 2009.

Schulzinger, Robert D. *A Time for Peace: The Legacy of the Vietnam War*. New York: Oxford University Press, 2006.

Statler, Kathryn C. *Replacing France: The Origins of American Intervention in Vietnam.* Lexington: University Press of Kentucky, 2007.

Stur, Heather Marie. *Beyond Combat: Women and Gender in the Vietnam War Era.* New York: Cambridge University Press, 2011.

Tonneson, Stein. *Vietnam 1946: How the War Began.* Berkeley: University of California Press, 2010.

Turse, Nick. *Kill Anything That Moves: The Real American War in Vietnam.* New York: Henry Holt, 2013.

Wiest, Andrew, ed. *Rolling Thunder in a Gentle Land: The Vietnam War Revisited.* Oxford: Osprey Publishing, 2006.

Wiest, Andrew, and Michael J. Doidge, eds. *Triumph Revisited: Historians Battle for the Vietnam War.* New York: Routledge, 2010.

American Vietnam War/Memory

Barden, Thomas E., ed. *Steinbeck in Vietnam: Dispatches from the War.* Charlottesville: University of Virginia Press, 2012.

Bleakney, Julia. *Revisiting Vietnam: Memoirs, Memorials, Museums.* New York: Routledge, 2006.

Hagopian, Patrick. *The Vietnam War in American Memory: Veterans, Memorials, and the Politics of Healing.* Amherst: University of Massachusetts Press, 2009.

Kieran, David. *Forever Vietnam: How a Divisive War Changed American Public Memory.* Amherst: University of Massachusetts Press, 2014.

Laderman, Scott. *Tours of Vietnam: War, Travel Guides, and Memory.* Durham, N.C.: Duke University Press, 2009.

Prados, John, ed. *In Country: Remembering the Vietnam War.* Lanham, Md.: Rowman & Littlefield, 2011.

Wiest, Andrew. *Vietnam: A View from the Front Lines.* Oxford: Osprey Publishing, 2013.

American Postwar Relations

Martini, Edwin. *Invisible Enemies: The American War on Vietnam, 1975–2000.* Amherst: University of Massachusetts Press, 2007.

Stern, Lewis M. *Defense Relations between the United States and Vietnam: The Process of Normalization, 1977–2003.* Jefferson, N.C.: McFarland, 2005.

Australia

Doyle, Jeff, Jeffrey Grey, and Peter Pierce. *Australia's Vietnam War.* College Station: Texas A&M Press, 2002.

Vietnamese Americans

Chong, Sylvia Shin Huey. *The Oriental Obscene: Violence and Racial Fantasies in the Vietnam Era.* Durham, N.C.: Duke University Press, 2012.

Espiritu, Yến Lê. *Body Counts: The Vietnam War and Militarized Refugees.* Berkeley: University of California Press, 2014.

Janette, Michele, ed. *My Viet: Vietnamese American Literature in English, 1962–Present.* Honolulu: University of Hawai'i Press, 2011.

Lam, Quang Thi. *The Twenty-Five Year Century: A South Vietnamese General Remembers the Indochina War to the Fall of Saigon.* Denton: University of North Texas Press, 2001.

Lieu, Nhi T. *The American Dream in Vietnamese.* Minneapolis: University of Minnesota Press, 2011.

Nguyen, Mimi Thi. *The Gift of Freedom: War, Debt, and Other Refugee Passages.* Durham, N.C.: Duke University Press, 2012.

Pelaud, Isabelle Thuy. *This Is All I Choose to Tell: History and Hybridity in Vietnamese American Literature.* Philadelphia: Temple University Press, 2011.

Viet Nam/Southeast Asia

Asselin, Pierre. *A Bitter Peace: Washington, Hanoi, and the Making of the Paris Agreement.* Chapel Hill: University of North Carolina Press, 2003.

———. *Hanoi's Road to the Vietnam War, 1954–1965.* Berkeley: University of California Press, 2013.

Britto, Karl Ashoka. *Disorientation: France, Vietnam, and the Ambivalence of Interculturality.* Hong Kong: Hong Kong University Press, 2004.

Day, Tony, and Maya H. T. Liem, eds. *Cultures at War: The Cold War and Cultural Expression in Southeast Asia.* Ithaca, N.Y.: Cornell Southeast Asia Program Publications, 2010.

Duong, Lan P. *Treacherous Subjects: Gender, Culture, and Trans-Vietnamese Feminism.* Philadelphia: Temple University Press, 2012.

Jennings, Eric T. *Imperial Heights: Dalat and the Making and Undoing of French Indochina.* Berkeley: University of California Press, 2012.

Journal of Vietnamese Studies. University of California Press, 2012– .

Keith, Charles. *Catholic Vietnam: A Church from Empire to Nation.* Berkeley: University of California Press, 2012.

Kwon, Heonik. *After the Massacre: Commemoration and Consolation in Ha My and My Lai.* Berkeley: University of California Press, 2006.

———. *Ghosts of War in Vietnam.* Cambridge: Cambridge University Press, 2013.

———. *The Other Cold War.* New York: Columbia University Press, 2010.

Marr, David. *Vietnam: State, War, and Revolution (1945–1946).* Berkeley: University of California Press, 2013.

McHale, Shawn. *Print and Power: Confucianism, Communism, and Buddhism in the Making of Modern Vietnam.* Honolulu: University of Hawai'i Press, 2003.

Nguyen Cong Luan. *Nationalist in the Viet Nam Wars: Memoirs of a Victim Turned Soldier.* Bloomington: Indiana University Press, 2012.

Nguyen, Lien-Hang T. *Hanoi's War: An International History of the War for Peace in Vietnam.* Chapel Hill: University of North Carolina Press, 2012.

Pholsena, Vatthana, and Oliver Tappe, eds. *Interactions with a Violent Past: Reading Post Conflict Landscapes in Cambodia, Laos, and Vietnam.* Singapore: National University of Singapore Press, 2013.

Quinn-Judge, Sophie. *Ho Chi Minh: The Missing Years.* Berkeley: University of California Press, 2003.

Schlund-Vials, Cathy. *War, Genocide, and Justice: Cambodian American Memory Work.* Minneapolis: University of Minnesota Press, 2012.

Schwenkel, Christina. *The American War in Contemporary Vietnam: Transnational Remembrance and Representation.* Bloomington: Indiana University Press, 2009.

Wilcox, Wynn, ed. *Vietnam and the West: New Approaches.* Ithaca, N.Y.: Cornell Southeast Asia Program Publications, 2010.

Zhai, Qiang. *China and the Vietnam Wars, 1950–1975.* Chapel Hill: University of North Carolina Press, 2000.

Zinoman, Peter. *Vietnamese Colonial Republican: The Political Vision of Vu Trong Phung.* Berkeley: University of California Press, 2013.

NOTES ON CONTRIBUTORS

BRENDA M. BOYLE is an associate professor of English at Denison University, Granville, Ohio. She is the editor of and contributor to *The Vietnam War* (2014); coauthor of *Masculinity and Monstrosity in Contemporary Hollywood Films* (2013); and author of *Masculinity in Vietnam War Narratives: A Critical Study of Fiction, Films and Nonfiction Writing* (2009).

LAN DUONG is an associate professor of media and cultural studies at the University of California–Riverside. She is the author of *Treacherous Subjects: Gender, Culture, and Trans-Vietnamese Feminism* (2012); coeditor of *Troubling Borders: An Anthology of Art and Literature by Southeast Asian Women in the Diaspora* (2014); and author of numerous articles appearing in journals such as *Inter-Asia Cultural Studies*, the *Journal of Asian American Studies, Amerasia, Asian Cinema, Discourse, Velvet Light Trap*, and the anthologies *Transnational Feminism in Film* (2011) and *Southeast Asian Cinema* (2012).

YẾN LÊ ESPIRITU is a professor of ethnic studies at the University of California–San Diego. She is the author of *Body Counts: The Vietnam War and Militarized Refuge(es)* (2014); *Asian American Women and Men: Labor, Laws, and Love*, second edition (2008); *Home Bound: Filipino American Lives across Cultures, Communities, and Countries* (2003); and many edited collections, journal articles, and book chapters dealing with immigration and refugees studies.

DIANE NIBLACK FOX taught Vietnamese history and anthropology at the College of the Holy Cross, Worcester, Massachusetts. She is the author of articles, essays, and a dissertation on Agent Orange: "One Significant Ghost—Agent Orange: Narratives of Trauma, Survival, and Responsibility." She is also the former coordinator of the Agent Orange Educational Project and Resource Center of the War Legacies Project.

HEONIK KWON is a senior research fellow in social science and professor of social anthropology at the University of Cambridge, Great Britain. He is the author of *North Korea: Beyond Charismatic Politics* (2012), *The Other Cold War* (2010), and *Ghosts of War in Vietnam* (2008).

LEONIE JONES holds the position of lecturer in film and cinema studies at the University of Southern Queensland, Australia. She is the writer and director of three feature military documentaries and a feature film. Her research focuses on Australian veteran memory and war commemoration.

JEEHYUN LIM is an assistant professor of English at Denison University, Granville, Ohio. She is the author of the forthcoming monograph, *Bilingual Brokers: Race, Capital, and the Cultural Politics of Bilingualism.* Her essays on U.S. ethnic literature and Asian American studies have appeared in journals including *Modern Fiction Studies, Journal of Transnational American_Studies,* and *Multi-Ethnic Literatures of the United States.*

ROBERT MASON is a lecturer of migration and security studies at Griffith University, Brisbane, Australia. He is the author of a number of works relating to Latino/a populations in Australia and the Asia-Pacific. He is also the editor of several collections, and many journal articles and book chapters dealing with migration and refugees.

VIET THANH NGUYEN is an associate professor of English and American studies and ethnicity at the University of Southern California, Los Angeles. He is the author of *The Sympathizer: A Novel* (2015); *Race and Resistance: Literature and Politics in Asian America* (2002); editor of various collections of essays; and author of many journal articles and book chapters concerning war and memory, race and ethnicity, especially regarding Viet Nam and Vietnamese in the United States.

VINH NGUYEN is an assistant professor of diaspora literature at Renison University College, the University of Waterloo, Canada. He is the author of "Refugee Gratitude: Narrating 'Success' and Intersubjectivity in Kim Thuy's *Ru*" (2014) and two forthcoming essays: "Me-Search, Hauntings, and Critical Distance" (2015) in *Life Writing* and "Documenting Vietnamese Refugees: Ann Hui's Boat People" (2016) in *Migration by Boat.*

CATHY J. SCHLUND-VIALS is an associate professor of English and Asian American studies at the University of Connecticut in the United States. She is the author of *War, Genocide, and Justice: Cambodian American Memory Work* (2012) and *Modeling Citizenship: Jewish and Asian American Writing* (2011). Additionally, she has published numerous articles and book chapters and has essay collections forthcoming and in progress.

QUAN TUE TRAN is a PhD candidate in American studies at Yale University, New Haven, Connecticut. She has been the Vice Provost for Diversity Pre-doctoral Fellow at the University of Connecticut-Storrs (2013–2014); instructor in the Feminist, Gender, Sexuality Studies program at Wesleyan University (fall 2015); and currently is a lecturer in the Ethnicity, Race, and Migration program at Yale University (2015–2016). Tran is the author of one journal article, "Remembering the Boat People Exodus: A Tale of Two Memorials" (2012) and is the coeditor of *Routes of Engagement: Viet Nam and Diasporas,* which is in progress.

INDEX